POSTCARD HISTORY SERIES

Henderson

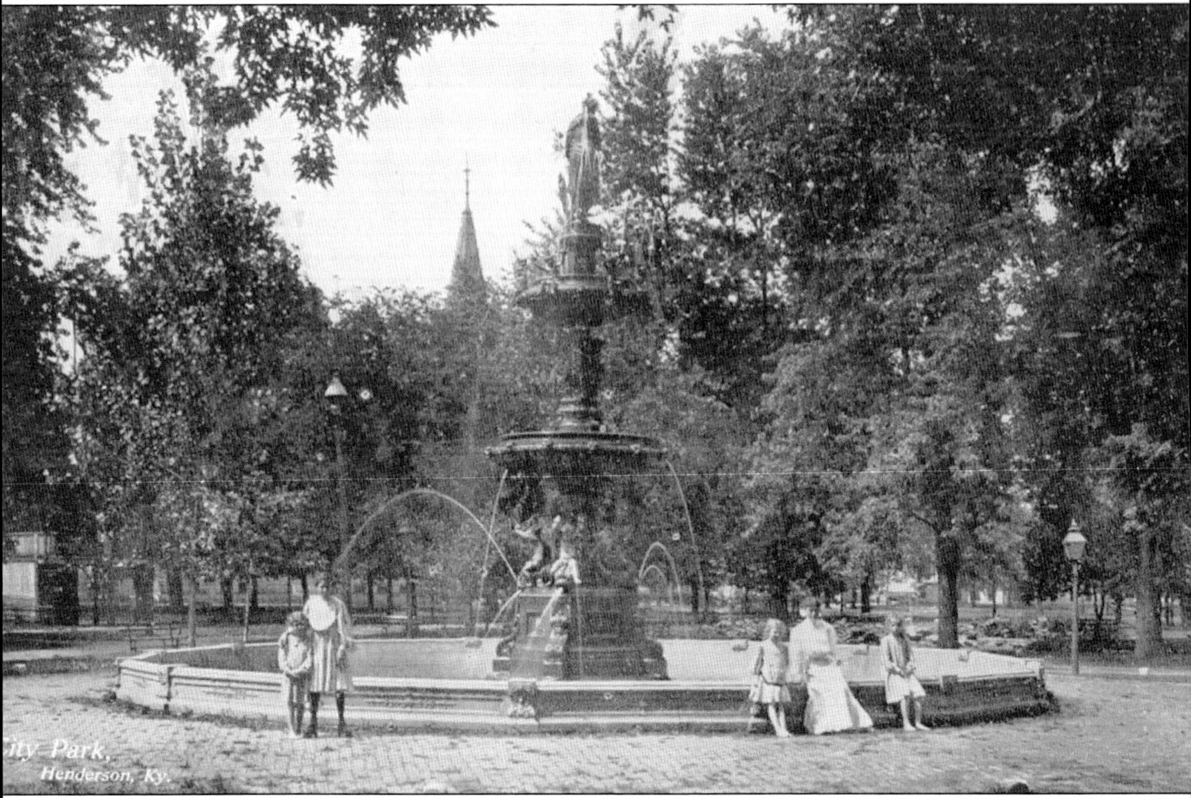

ON THE FRONT COVER: The City Park Fountain, referred to in earlier days as the "Lady in the Park," first graced Central Park in 1892. After its near destruction by vandals in 1962, the intricate French-built fountain and its pool were dismantled. Today a replica of the fountain sits on the original site.

ON THE BACK COVER: Large lettered postcards with three-dimensional effects were popular during the mid-20th century. This one, published by Curt Teich and Company (the largest postcard printer of the day), includes nine Henderson scenes in its lettering: (in order) the H shows the Audubon Park Museum; the E shows the Audubon Park Tea House; the N shows the post office; the D shows Atkinson Park Drive; the E shows the Henderson County Courthouse; the R shows Dade Park; the S shows a Presbyterian church; the O shows the American Legion Hall; and the N shows the Soaper Hotel. In the lower left corner is the 1932 automobile bridge across the Ohio River.

POSTCARD HISTORY SERIES

Henderson

Susan Sommers Thurman

ARCADIA
PUBLISHING

ISBN 978-0-7385-5355-9

Published by Arcadia Publishing
Charleston, South Carolina

Printed in the United States of America

Library of Congress Control Number: 2007942108

For all general information contact Arcadia Publishing at:
Telephone 843-853-2070
Fax 843-853-0044
E-mail sales@arcadiapublishing.com
For customer service and orders:
Toll-Free 1-888-313-2665

Visit us on the Internet at www.arcadiapublishing.com

This book is dedicated to all those who have made Henderson the impressive and unique place it is and especially to my favorite Hendersonian, my husband, Mike Thurman

Acknowledgments

In compiling the images and information for this book, I have been overwhelmed with kindness, generosity, knowledge, and patience from everyone I have approached. I am deeply grateful to these following people for being such a help in getting this book ready for print: Pam Austin, Rachel Baar, Marcus Baltzell, Frank Boyett, Gail Bushrod, Sharon Chancellor, Amber Clark, Rebecca Emerson, Allison Fowler, Paula Fowler, Bill Gary, Carol Gatlin, Linda Hallmark, Claude Hays, Gail King, Lou Mahon, Steve Martin, Mary Edith Pritchett, Linda Sinnett, April Spore, Niki Stallings, Keith Stallins, Tony Strawn, Terry and Nancy Todd, Pam Vincent, Nancy Voyles, Don Wathen, Donna White, and my husband, Mike Thurman. Unless otherwise noted, all images are courtesy of the author's collection.

Contents

Introduction 6

1. Getting Around 9
2. Leisure Time 19
3. Readin', 'Ritin', and 'Rithmetic 45
4. Working Hard 51
5. Praying Hard 67
6. Just Visiting 77
7. Flooding and Freezing 87
8. Strolling Around 93
9. A Mixed Bag 123

INTRODUCTION

Native Americans had long traveled the rich lands that now comprise Henderson and Henderson County, Kentucky, but due to a series of events, settlement by others did not begin until the 1790s. In a 1764 meeting with explorer Daniel Boone, North Carolinian Richard Henderson first heard of the wealth of what was then known as the western lands. Ten years later, Henderson formed a land company formally titled the Richard Henderson Company but more commonly called the Transylvania Company.

In 1775, after negotiations with the Cherokees, the Transylvania Company bought land in what is now Kentucky; that same year, the company sent delegate James Hogg to the Continental Congress to ask permission for this land to become the 14th colony and to be named Transylvania. Virginia blocked that move, and in 1776, Virginia created Kentucky County out of what had been Fincastle County. The Virginia legislature acknowledged the expense the Transylvania Company had incurred in its dealings with the Cherokees, and it compensated the company with the land that later came to be called Henderson County.

Richard Henderson died in 1785 having never visited the town or the county that would be named in his honor. It would be another 12 years before agents from his company came to the area. In the early 1790s, a few families had settled in the area that Native Americans and boatmen called "Red Banks," so named because of the red cliffs seen from the Ohio River. Traveling in a pirogue in March 1797, the Transylvania Company's agent Samuel Hopkins, surveyor Thomas Allin, and lawyer Henry Purviance arrived in the Red Banks area and, using the geography of the river, formally laid out the town in just one week. In order to thwart the spread of fires in the wooden structures that they hoped would soon populate the town, Hopkins insisted that the streets be at least 100 feet wide—foresight in the 1700s that led to the broad boulevards that characterize Henderson today. Another feature of the original design was the large area that was designated to be a municipal park. This downtown area, now called Central Park, is said to be the oldest municipal park west of the Alleghenies.

After they surveyed the town, Hopkins, Allin, and Purviance mapped the rest of the county—a far more difficult task because of spring floodwaters and continuing rain. When the task was finally completed, the company began advertising lots in the town of "Henderson, commonly known by the name of Red Banks." The advertisements boasted that the town's "high situation . . . beautiful manner in which it is laid out . . . fertility of the soil . . . navigation of the Ohio, make it very advantageous to those who may choose to reside there." Purchasers of lots in town faced strict requirements: they had to build a framed, sawed, or hewed log house at least 16-feet square; the house was required to have a dirt, stone, or brick chimney and a plank floor; and the buyers or their representatives had to live on the lot for at least a year after the purchase.

Hopkins's advertisements proved to be a successful inducement for settlers. By 1800, the town's population was 205, and the county's population was 1,468. In the early years of settlement, immigrants arrived almost exclusively by river—first by flatboat and later by steamboat. Their journeys were not without extraordinary peril, with pirates often robbing the boats and even murdering some of the crews.

Despite the dangers of travel and settling, by 1810, the county's population had almost quadrupled. That same year, John James Audubon, the man who would later become Henderson's most famous citizen, traveled downriver to Henderson from Louisville. During his 1810–1819 stay in Henderson, Audubon engaged in a number of business ventures: he owned or was a partner in a general store, a steamboat, and a saw and gristmill. In addition, he bought and sold various plots of land around town (one eastern section of Henderson where he lived for awhile is still referred to as the Audubon section). While at times Audubon enjoyed success in Henderson, he encountered two problems that eventually led to his financial ruin. First, his final local enterprise, the saw and gristmill garnered little business. Also, instead of tending to his various businesses, Audubon far preferred roaming the woods, searching for wildlife to sketch. Audubon left Henderson destitute, but his legacy remains in the two parks that honor him, Audubon Mill Park and Audubon State Park, as well as a number of businesses and organizations that bear his name.

During the 1800s, the population of Henderson and Henderson County continued to rise. The Ohio River highway aided the influx of newcomers, particularly after the advent of steamboat travel. By 1811, Hendersonians had learned of this new mode of transportation, and on December 16, 1811, they eagerly gathered at the riverfront to await the passing of the *New Orleans*, the first steamboat on the lower Ohio River. Ironically, when the steamboat was entering the waters of Henderson County, a horrific earthquake began. (This earthquake—perhaps the most powerful in U.S. history—was so strong that it changed the course of the Ohio River between Henderson and the area that was to become Evansville, Indiana. Before the earthquake, the land that is currently north of the twin bridges on U.S. 41 was south of the Ohio River, which was located approximately where Water Works Road is today.) Just prior to the dual arrival of the steamboat and the earthquake, Hendersonians had gazed in awe at the Great Comet of 1811, which featured an unusual double tail and was visible to the naked eye for more than eight months. Because of these three unusual occurrences—the arrival of the steamboat, the enormous earthquake, and the great comet—the year 1811 came to be known by locals as *annus mirabilis*, the year of wonders.

In addition, medical problems challenged early settlers, including the cholera epidemic that first arrived in 1832. Once cholera appeared, Henderson wells were contaminated, but—oddly enough—people who drank from the river were generally spared the ravages of the disease. Commerce in town was suspended in hopes of allaying the onslaught, but the disease felled many that year (reportedly, 10 percent of the population) and when it returned the next year. Again in 1848 and in 1850, cholera appeared in the area and caused great concern. Later, in 1879, fears about yellow fever initiated a local panic; Henderson was under a strict quarantine in July of that year to prevent the spread of the disease, and no steamboat coming from south of Paducah could land within five miles of Henderson without permission.

Another unsettling saga in Henderson's history was the institution of slavery, which had been a part of Henderson's life at least since the late 1790s. In 1800, slaves comprised 27 percent of the county's population. Henderson's wealthy tobacco producers and businessmen were the primary owners and renters of slaves. On New Year's Day, the northeast corner of First and Main Streets was the site of the annual renting or selling of slaves. Henderson's location on the Ohio River—the dividing line between slavery and freedom—might have led to a great deal of Underground Railroad activity, but except for a few isolated stories, history has not revealed this to be the case.

Once the Civil War began, Henderson became a border county in a border state. Families were divided in their loyalties and their service. Steamboats, which had come to dominate river travel, could wreak havoc by flying a Union or Confederate flag—even on the boats that were sailing on pleasure excursions.

After the Civil War, steamboats eventually surrendered their transportation power to the iron horse. Henderson's initial interest in the railroad began in 1837 when the Henderson and Nashville Railroad was first incorporated, but nothing substantial came of that transaction. After the Civil War, the newly formed Evansville, Henderson, and Nashville Railroad connected local tracks to those installed in the southern Kentucky city of Guthrie. This connection opened train traffic between Nashville and Henderson. Northbound trains, however, were at a disadvantage when they arrived in Henderson. Since no bridge across the Ohio River had been built, passengers and freight had to be ferried across the river in order to proceed. All of this changed in 1885 with the completion of a railroad bridge that ran down Fourth Street and then across the Ohio River. An engineering marvel for its time, the bridge with its 15 stone piers boasted the largest trestle span in the world.

Shortly after the completion of the railroad bridge, the city of Henderson launched yet another transportation system—trolley cars, or "street railways," as they were called. Powered by mules the first five years of their existence, the trolleys changed to electrical power in 1894, and the trolleys chugged through various parts of town at speeds up to 12 miles per hour. The company that ran the trolley system lasted until 1923; at that time, financial troubles and the rising ownership of the horseless carriage led to the demise of the trolley system in Henderson.

The popularity of the automobile changed the landscape of Henderson. A ferry service had long been located at Henderson's riverbank; when cars began to dominate the scene, they lined up near the Third Street wharf for the ferry to take them to the Indiana side. In addition to that service, from 1912 to 1928, Henderson was a terminus for the only interurban—a combination streetcar-ferry system—that ran on the Ohio River. In normal weather, cars and passengers made the trip from Henderson to Evansville in just 45 minutes.

Bridge construction in the early 1930s forced the end of trans-Ohio ferry service. In 1932, an automobile bridge opened on Highway 41, and ferry service ceased. In the same year, the 1885 railroad bridge was replaced by another built just downriver from the original. Elsewhere in the county, an automobile bridge opened across the Green River in 1931 just upstream from an existing railroad bridge.

Changes in transportation—as well as those in buildings, businesses, parks, and other areas of Henderson and Henderson County—are the focus of this book. The earliest postcard featured in the book is postmarked 1878, but most date from the 1890s to the mid-20th century. Through the postcards and the text, readers can discover parts of Henderson that no longer exist and can appreciate changes that have taken place during the past century.

One

Getting Around

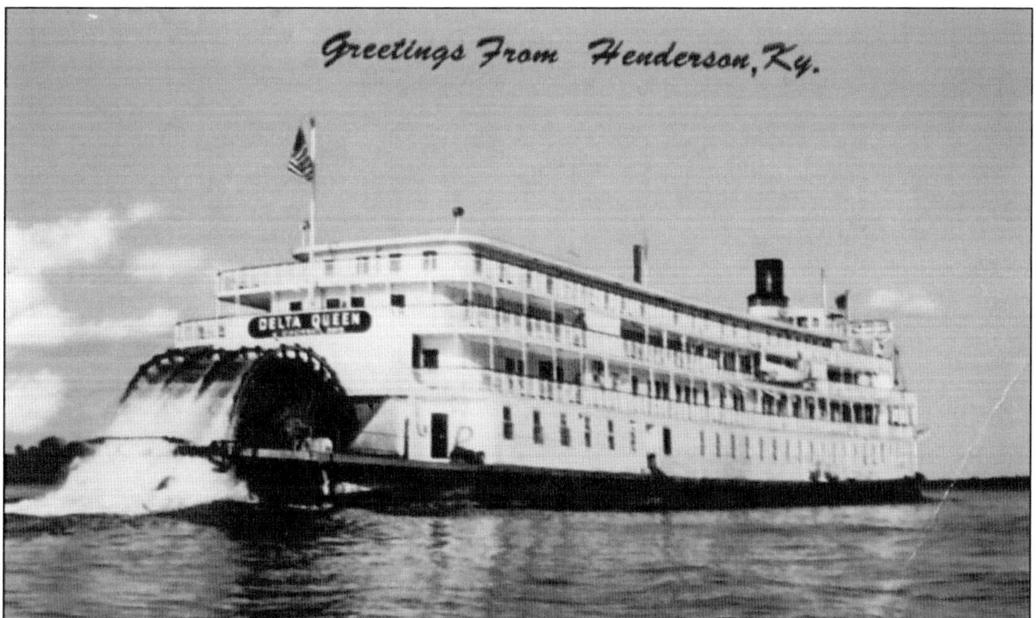

Steamboats such as the *Delta Queen*, built in 1927, have been a part of the Ohio River's landscape for almost 200 years. In 1811, Hendersonians saw their first steamboat (which arrived, coincidentally, at the same time a huge earthquake rocked the area). Six years later, Hendersonian David Prentiss built the first Kentucky steamboat, the *Pike*. Later that year, Samuel Bowen and John James Audubon built a steamboat in Henderson, but it sank after being taken to New Orleans.

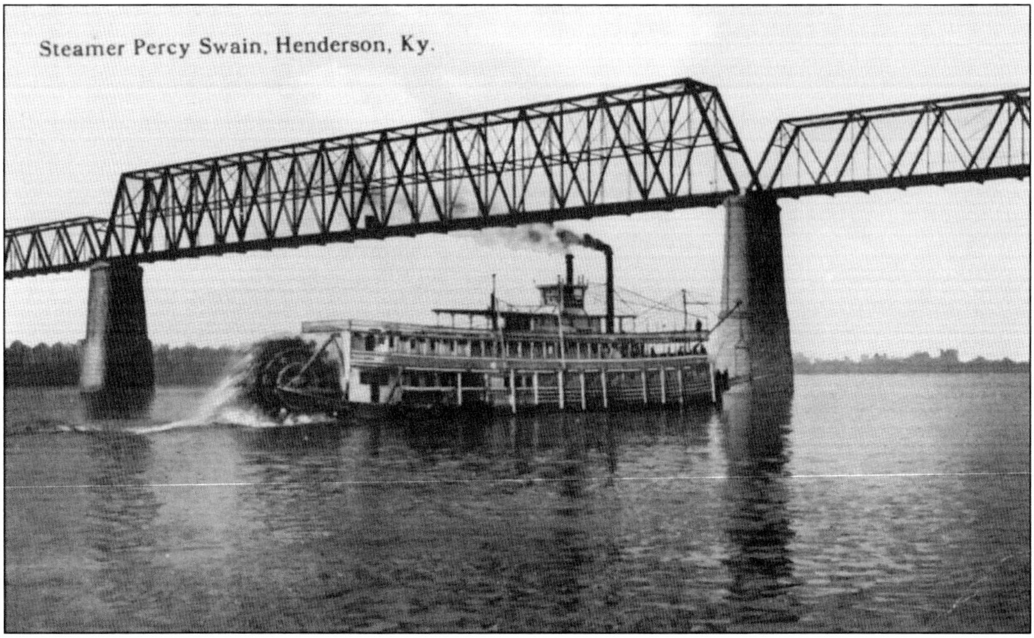

Nearly two centuries have passed since steamboats began plying the Ohio River's waters, and countless vessels like the popular stern-wheeler *Percy Swain*, built in Minnesota in 1910, have brought passengers and cargo to Henderson's shores. Here the *Percy Swain* passes under the Henderson railroad bridge in the early 1900s. She was later lost in Louisiana in 1922.

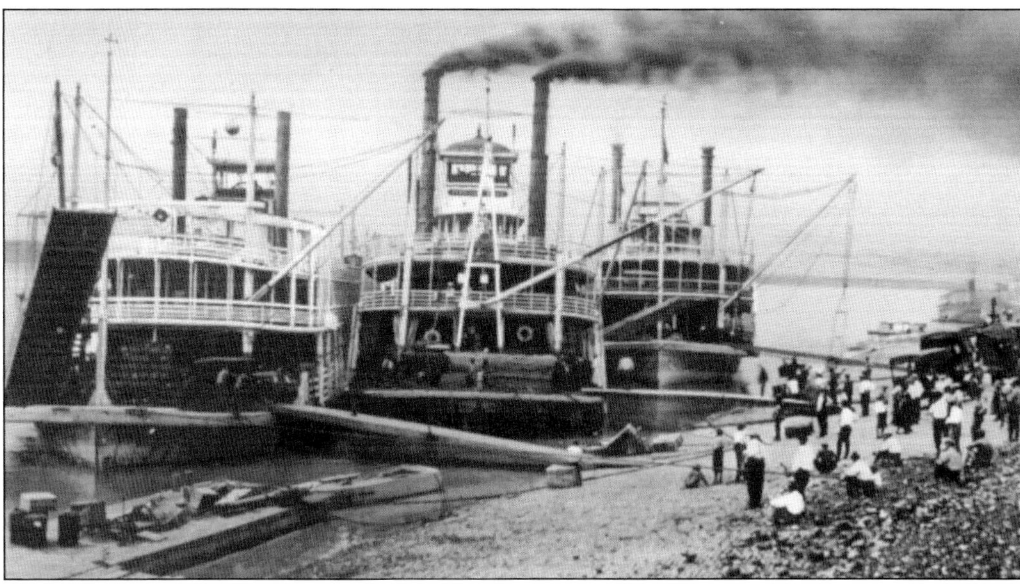

The Henderson wharf was a busy place for many years. Pictured here are the *Piasa* (left), named for a legendary bird of the Illinois Indians; the *Tennessee Bell* (middle); and the *Cape Girardeau* (right), which was built in Jeffersonville, Indiana, in 1923 and sold in 1935. She appears in this card as the excursion boat *Gordon C. Greene*. The *Cape Girardeau/Gordon C. Greene* appeared in such movies as *Gone with the Wind* and *The Kentuckian*.

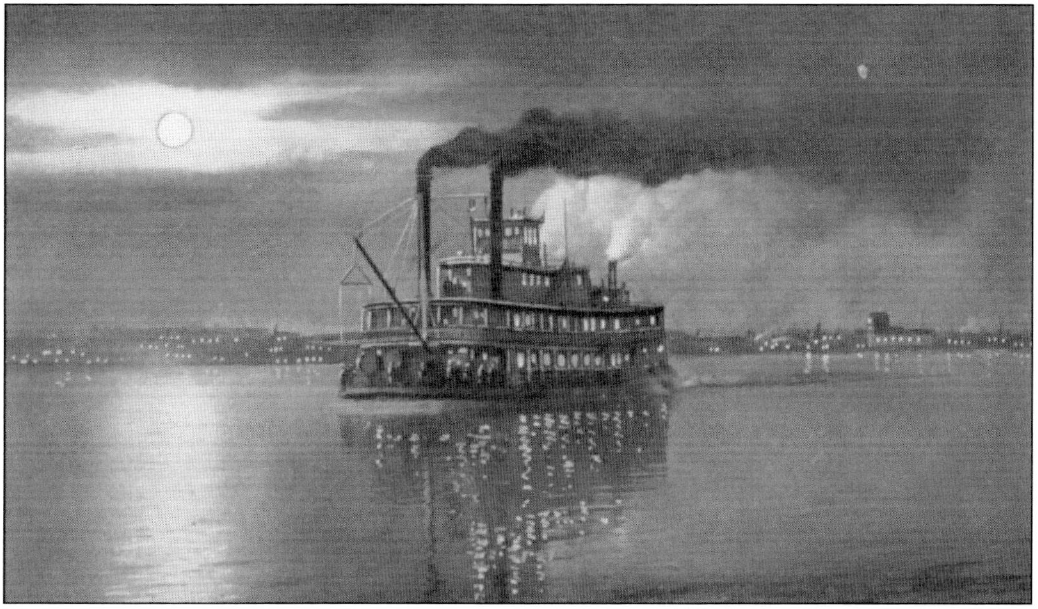

In the early 1800s, steamboats modernized river transportation. They lowered the labor and cash costs of transportation and allowed people and cargo to travel with relative ease both upstream and downstream. Boats signaled their arrival at the wharf by sounding bells (during the first part of the 19th century) or steam whistles (during the latter part of that century). (Courtesy of Henderson County Public Library.)

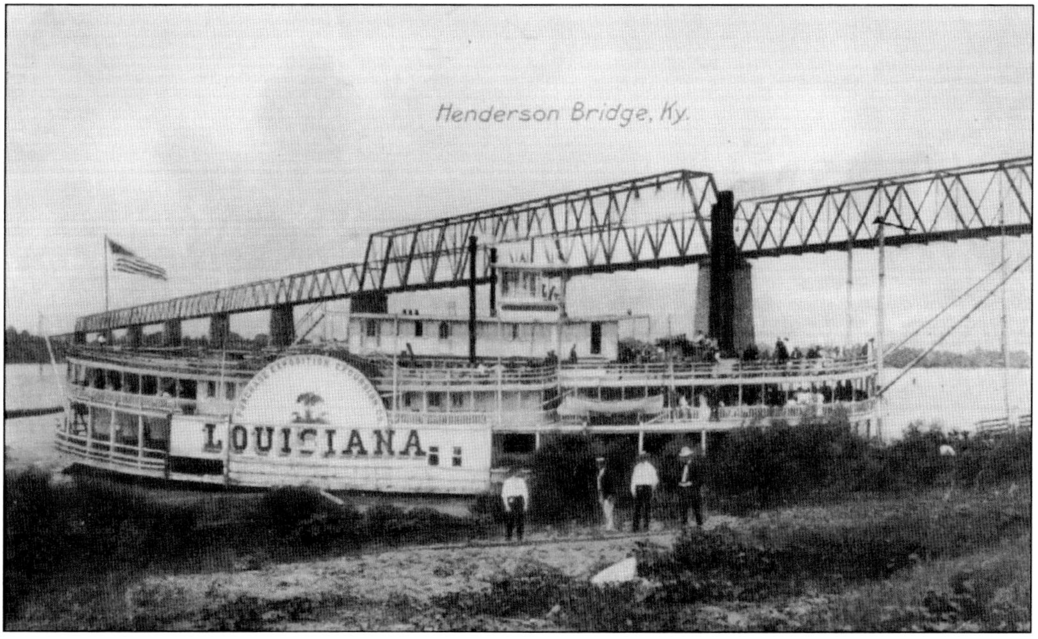

The side-wheeler *Louisiana*, seen here at the foot of the Henderson shore, was built in Jeffersonville, Indiana, in 1880 and was originally the U.S. lighthouse tender *Joseph Henry*. At a sale around 1903, she came into private hands and then ran excursions, including trips during the 1904 St. Louis World's Fair. In 1909, she was renamed the *Pattona* and plied various waters while running excursions from Memphis. (Courtesy of Claud Hays.)

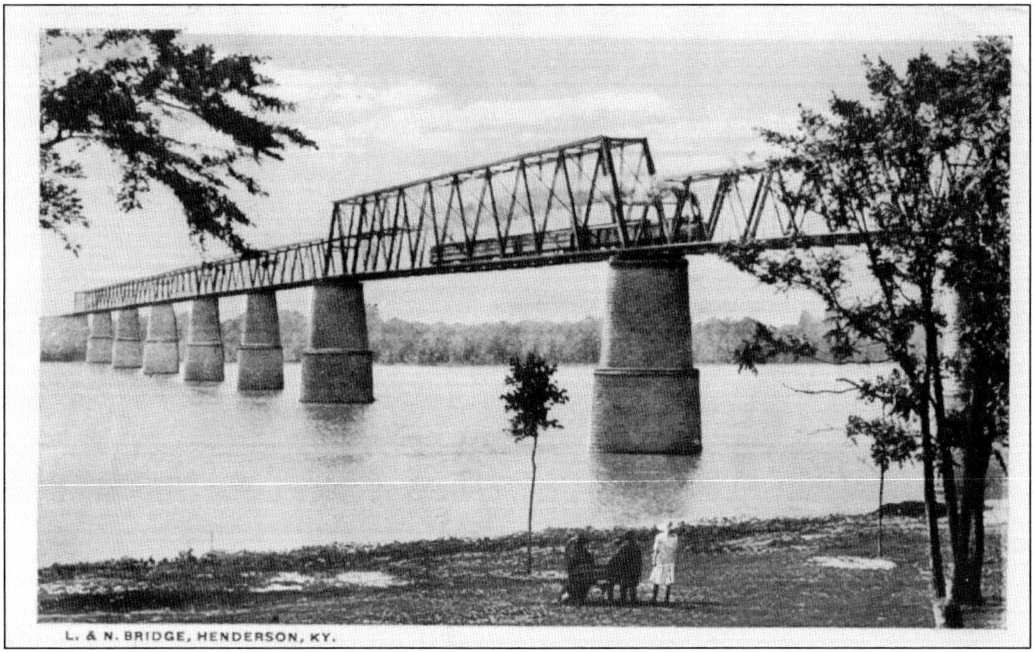

Prior to a railroad bridge being built in Henderson, freight cars had to be transported by ferry across the river. This, of course, was costly, and the desire for a railroad bridge connecting Henderson with the North mounted. In 1872, the Henderson Bridge Company was incorporated; however, surveys for bridge construction did not begin for some time.

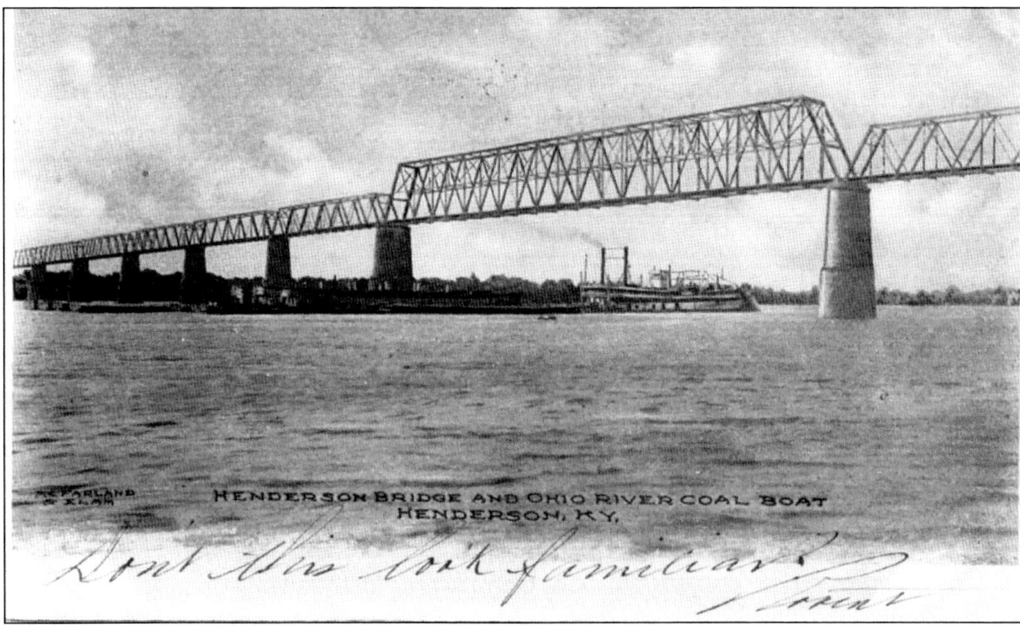

In 1882, preliminary surveys for a railroad bridge were begun to determine necessary distances and courses, as well as the rapidity of the river's current. Also that year, Hendersonian T. M. Jenkins was hired to make borings for the bridge's foundation. The next year, the Louisville company O'Conner and McDonald was contracted to do the masonry work and to build the caissons, but that contract was rescinded the next year.

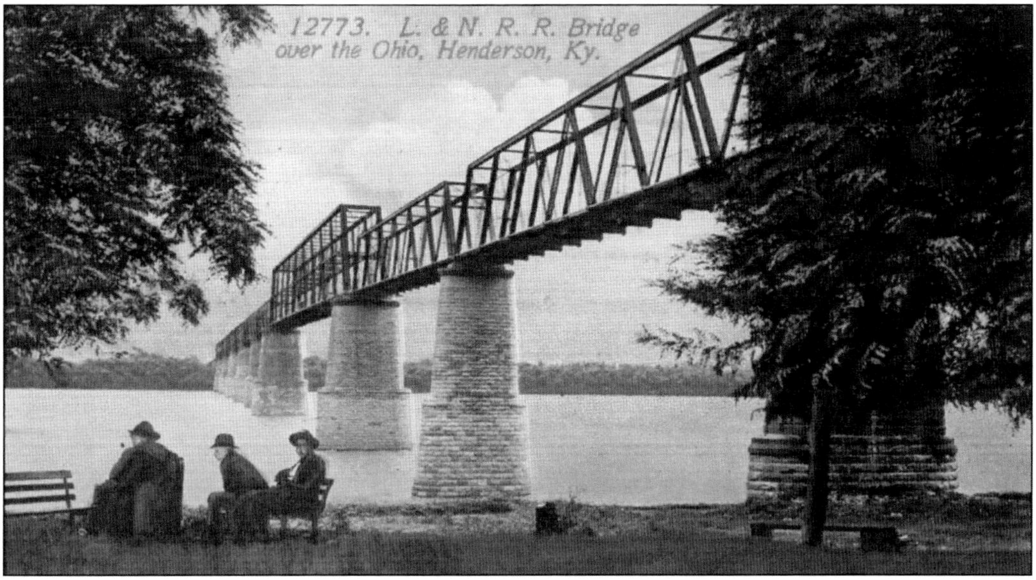

George W. G. Ferris (later famous for the Ferris wheel), the resident engineer for the Louisville Bridge and Iron Company, came to Henderson to oversee the sinking and concreting of the pneumatic caissons under the railroad bridge. After finding that job too taxing, he resigned the position but remained with the company and was given charge of the construction of the superstructure of the bridge. (Courtesy of Terry and Nancy Todd.)

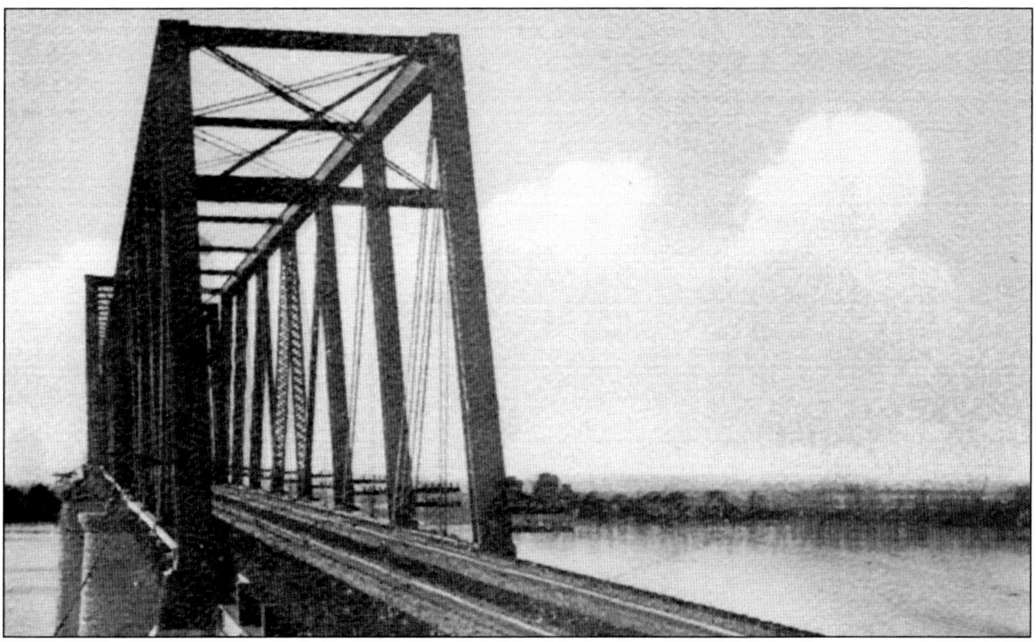

The $2 million iron-and-steel bridge, made with Bedford, Indiana, stone, was an engineering marvel. It was 3,686 feet long and had 15 stone piers, with nine resting on wooden caissons sunk to a bedrock foundation and then filled with concrete. The 525-foot channel span was reported to be longer than any other iron or steel span in the world. When the bridge opened on July 13, 1885, Henderson hosted huge celebrations that lasted for several days. (Courtesy of Terry and Nancy Todd.)

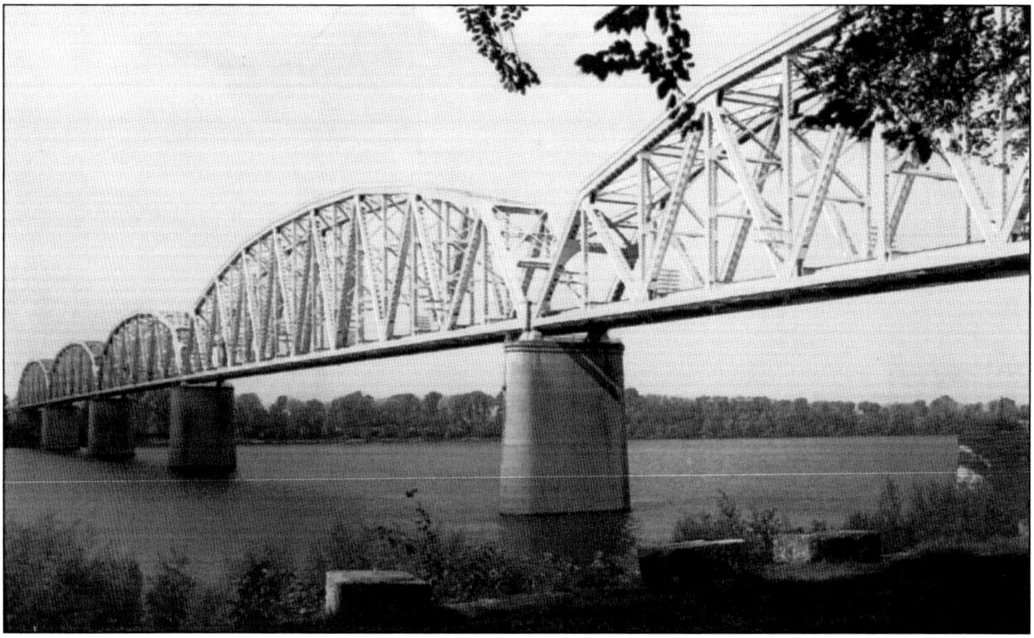

A new railroad bridge between Henderson and Vanderburgh County in Indiana was built just upriver from the original bridge. Constructed at a cost of about $4 million, the bridge is 12,123 feet long and stands 100 feet above the bridge deck. When this bridge was dedicated on December 31, 1932, both the old and new bridges hosted trains passing over them. (Courtesy of Terry and Nancy Todd.)

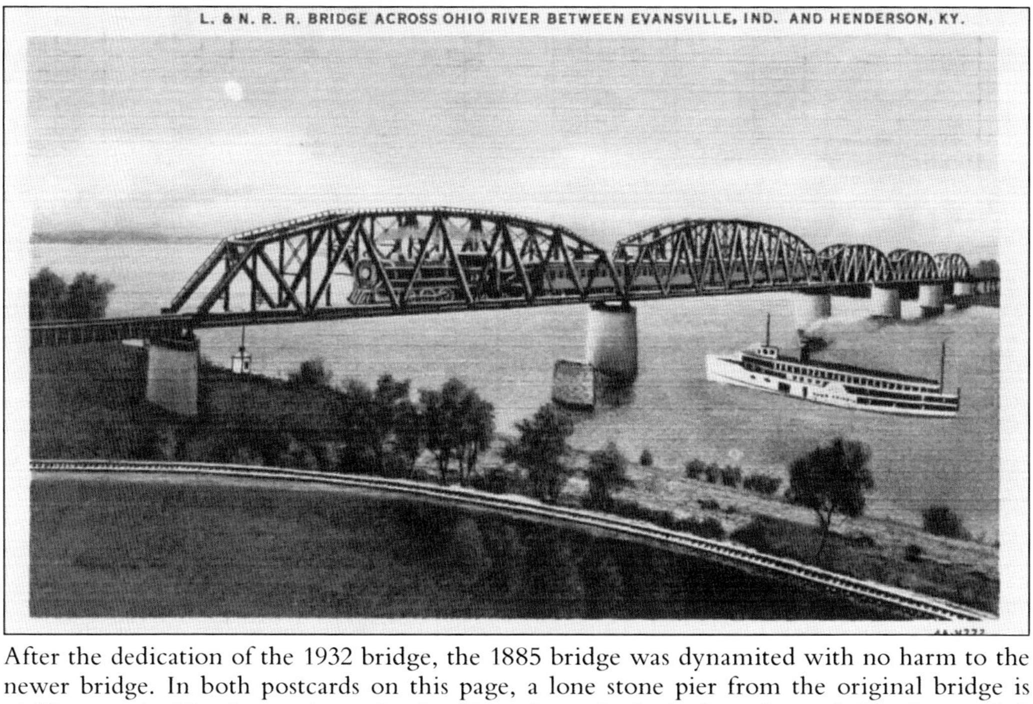

After the dedication of the 1932 bridge, the 1885 bridge was dynamited with no harm to the newer bridge. In both postcards on this page, a lone stone pier from the original bridge is visible near the Henderson shore. A wharf boat formerly docked nearby, and this pier was left in the water to protect it from damage by winter's ice floes.

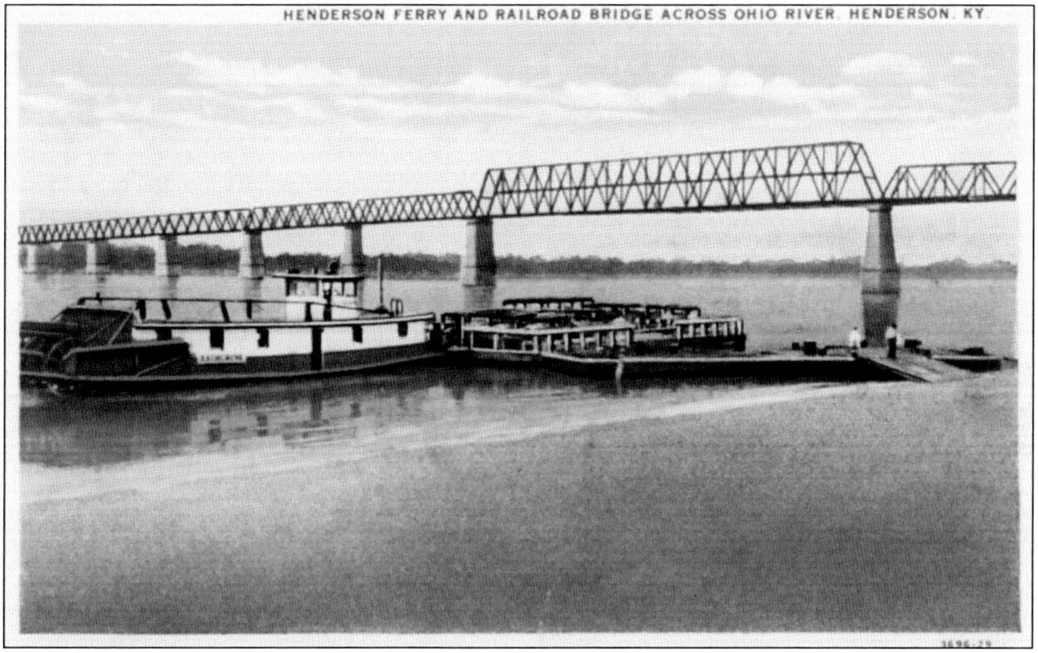

Ferry service began in Henderson soon after the town was settled. Gen. Samuel Hopkins established the county's first public ferry near his plantation at the mouth of the Green River. In 1802, Jonathan Anthony established the town's first ferry, and he continued the service for 33 years before turning the business over to his son.

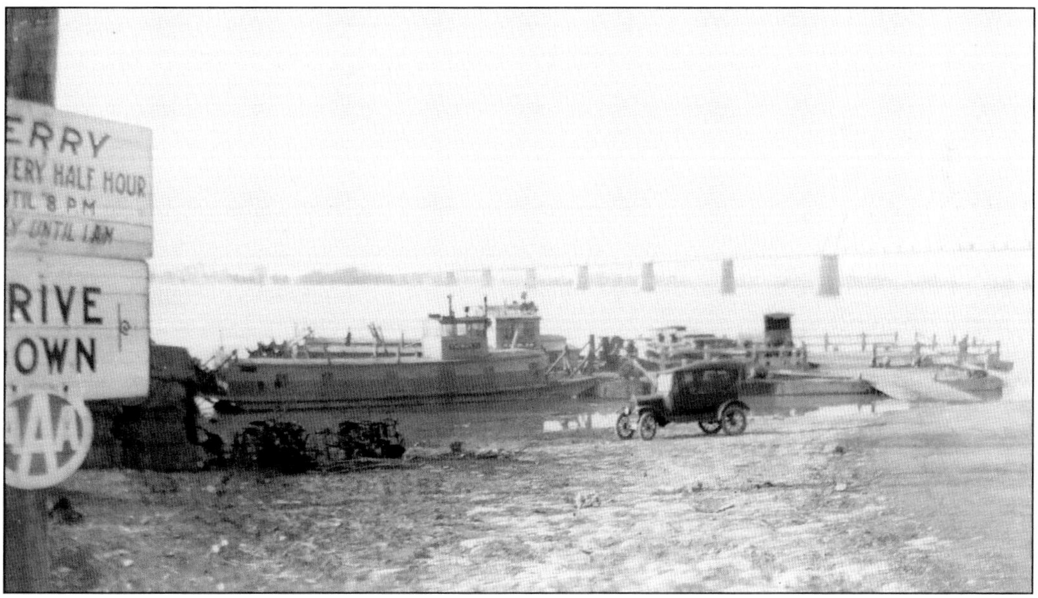

Ferries from downtown Henderson travelled from the wharf at the foot of Third Street directly across the river to the Indiana shore. In the mid-1800s, crude ferries propelled by oars gave way to steam-powered ferries. The *Katherine*, probably the ferry featured in both postcards on this page, ran every half hour during the week and later on the weekends. In 1936, a few years after the automobile bridge opened, ferry service was discontinued. (Courtesy of Henderson County Public Library.)

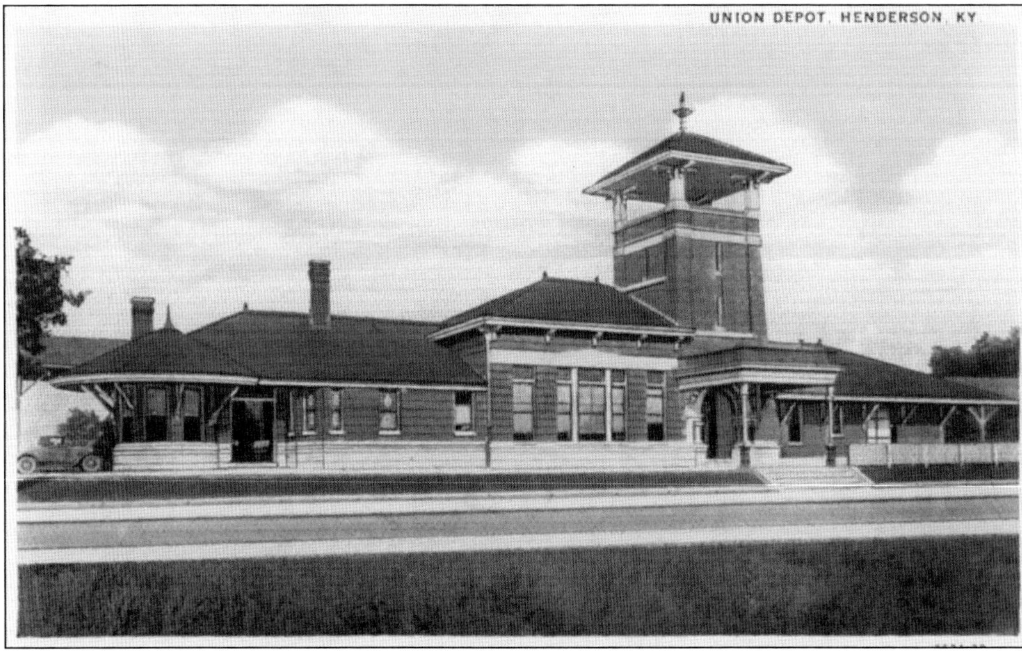

Four stations were erected in the years after the railroad came to Henderson. The last—and the longest enduring—one was Union Station, built by Bailey and Koerner for $25,000; it opened on July 1, 1902, at Fourth and Clark Streets. The seven-room redbrick building featured a stately cupola, arched entrances, impressive oak seats, and marble floors.

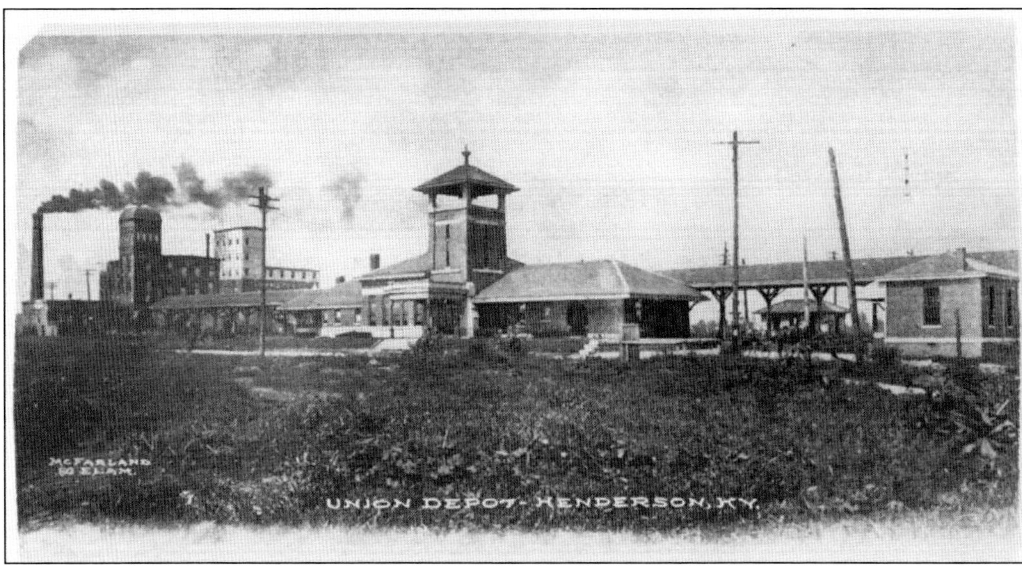

Over the years, the station played host to thousands of arrivals and departures. Visiting dignitaries, including William Jennings Bryan, Harry Truman, and Dwight D. Eisenhower, were greeted by large crowds of local residents during stops at the station. The last passenger train stopped here in 1971. On the left in this scene is the A. Waller and Company elevator and mills, incorporated in 1901. The elevator had a storage capacity of 200,000 bushels, and the mills produced Momaja flour.

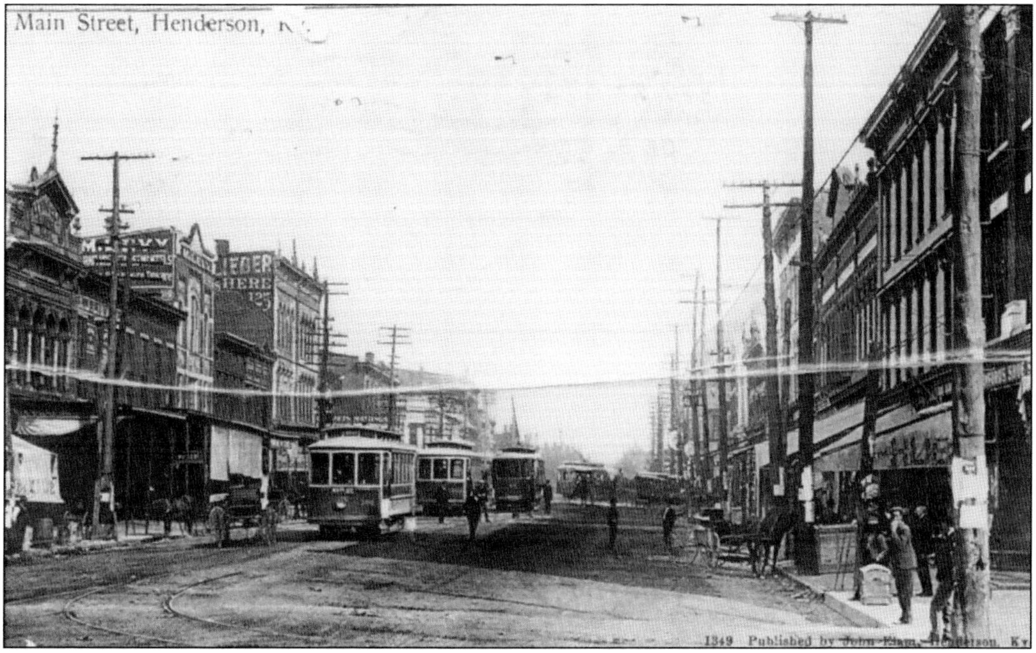

Tracks for Henderson's trolleys (the first in the lower Ohio Valley) were laid in 1887, and service continued until 1923. The trolleys were initially powered by mules, but modernization soon came in the form of electric motor cars that were regulated at a maximum speed of 12 miles per hour. In this pre-1908 postcard showing Main Street, the Kentucky Bakery is on the near left. In the mid-1920s, this building housed the Winstead Hotel. It was renovated in the early 21st century.

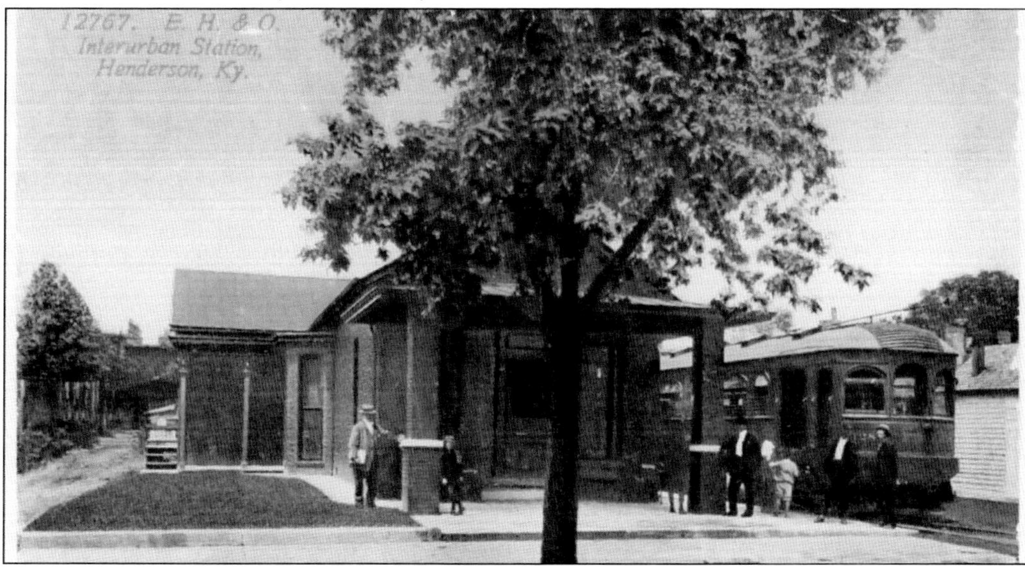

The Henderson-Evansville line was one of the few interurban operations in North America. The combination streetcar-ferry began service on July 28, 1912, and continued until 1928 when the service was replaced by buses. Under ideal conditions, the trip between the two cities took 45 minutes, with 12 minutes on the river. The Henderson Interurban station in this postcard was located at 225 North Elm Street.

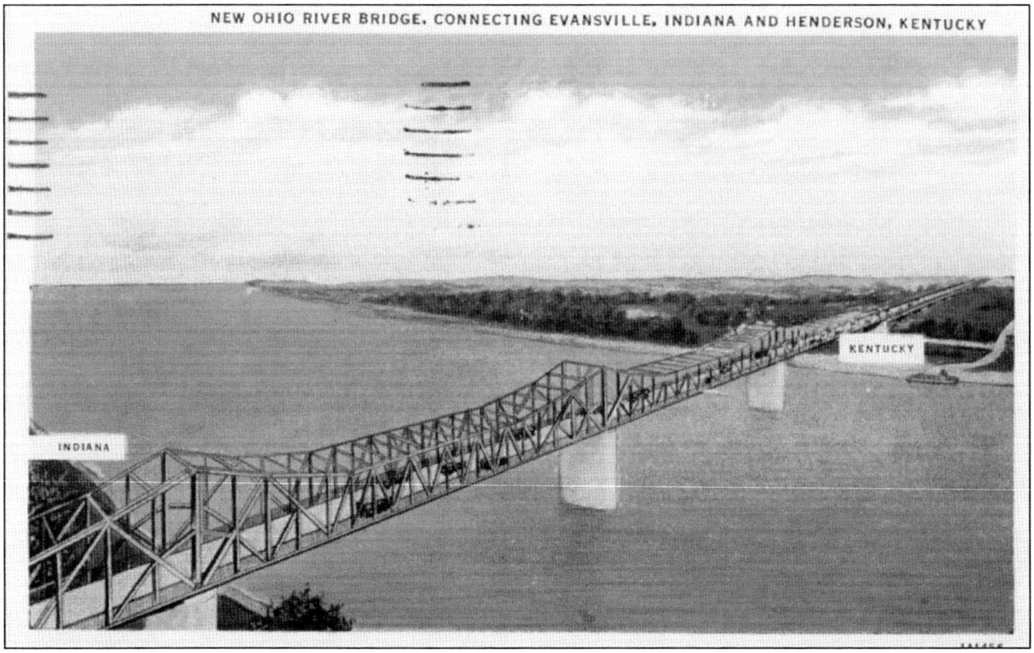

With great hoopla, the Audubon Memorial Bridge opened on July 4, 1932. Initially a toll bridge, the toll ended in 1941. A new bridge, constructed in 1969, is now used for southbound traffic. This postcard mistakenly labels the north (left) side of the river as "Indiana." Because the 1811 earthquake changed the course of the Ohio, the Indiana border is situated about a mile past the bridge.

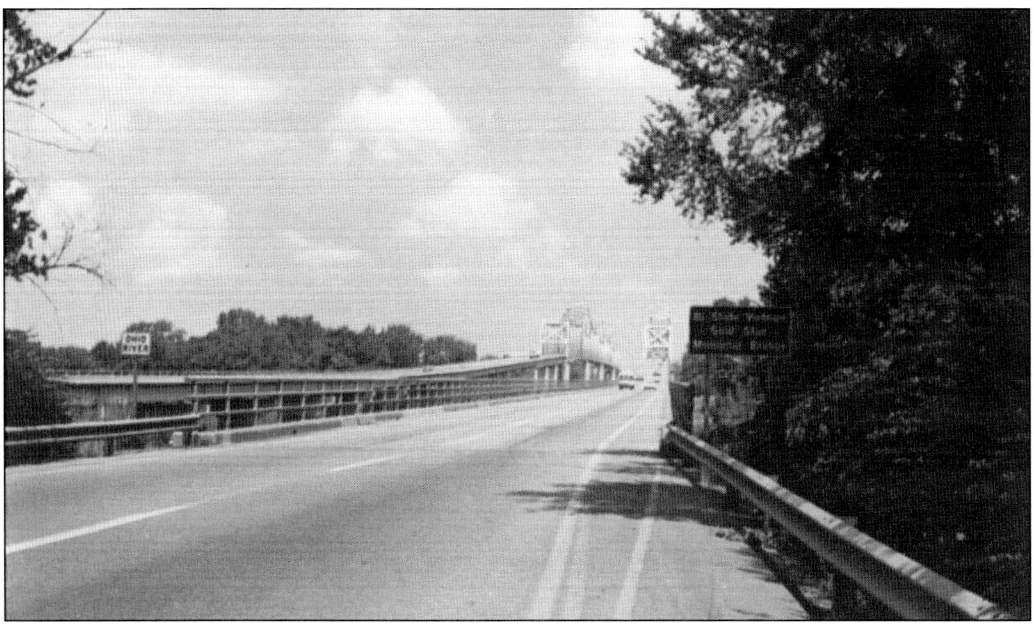

This steel-frame cantilever bridge with its 720-foot span opened in 1969 as the twin automobile bridge crossing the Ohio River on Highway 41 between Henderson and Evansville. This bridge currently accommodates two lanes of northbound traffic. At present, the twin bridges carry around 40,000 vehicles per day.

Two

Leisure Time

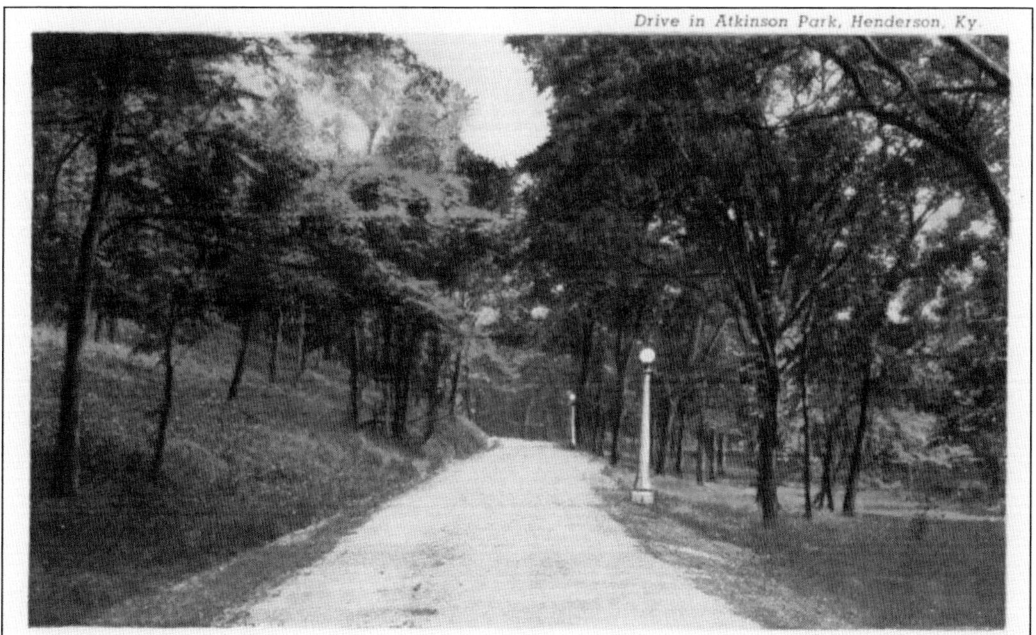

Henderson's Atkinson Park, a mile north of the downtown area, is nestled on a tall bluff, with the Ohio River on the west and North Elm Street on the east. On June 29, 1895, former mayor John C. Atkinson honored his father by giving the city half interest in 74 acres of land that at that time lay just outside the city limits and that joined a section called Reservoir Park, where the waterworks was then located. The land had been purchased from heirs of A. B. Barret for $100 an acre.

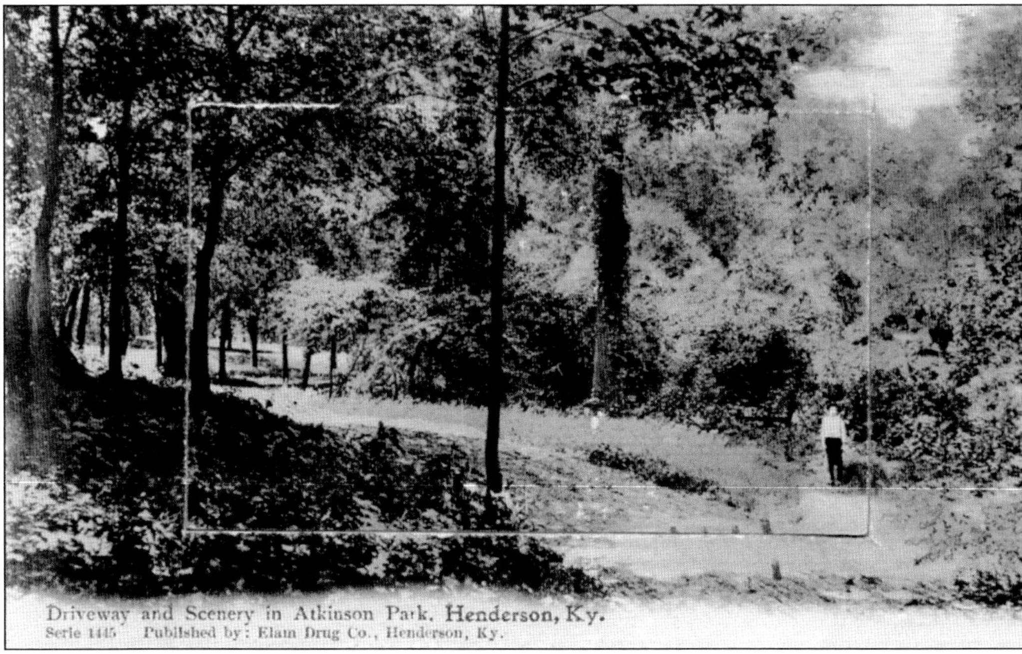

After John C. Atkinson's untimely death at age 42, local citizens began thinking about a fitting tribute for him. At that time, some encouraged the idea of a swimming pool, but others felt that would be "of questionable taste;" in the end, $1,000 was raised to erect the twin stone pillars that mark the original entrance to the park. Ironically, the pillars stand beside the swimming pool that was finally built in 1937.

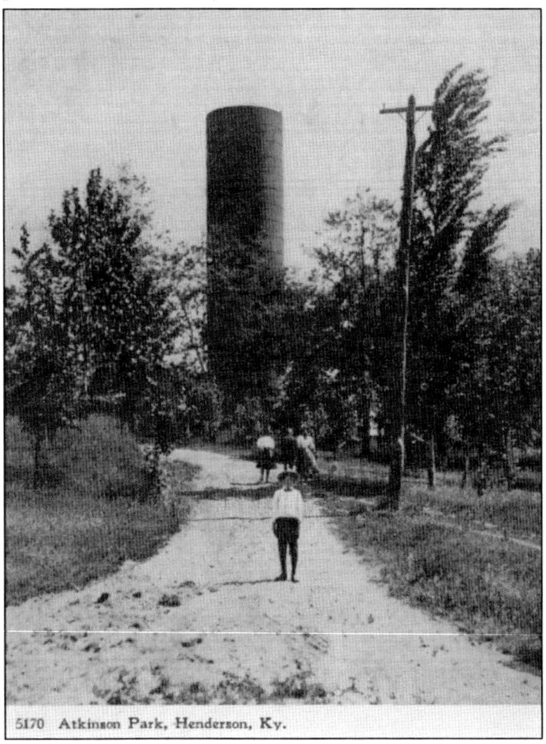

Shortly after acquiring the land donated by John C. Atkinson, the city appropriated funds to clear the area's woods and to erect several buildings, including a dance pavilion, a residence for the park keeper, and barbecue pits. Visible in the rear of this picture is the tower of the city's waterworks. (Courtesy of Pam Austin.)

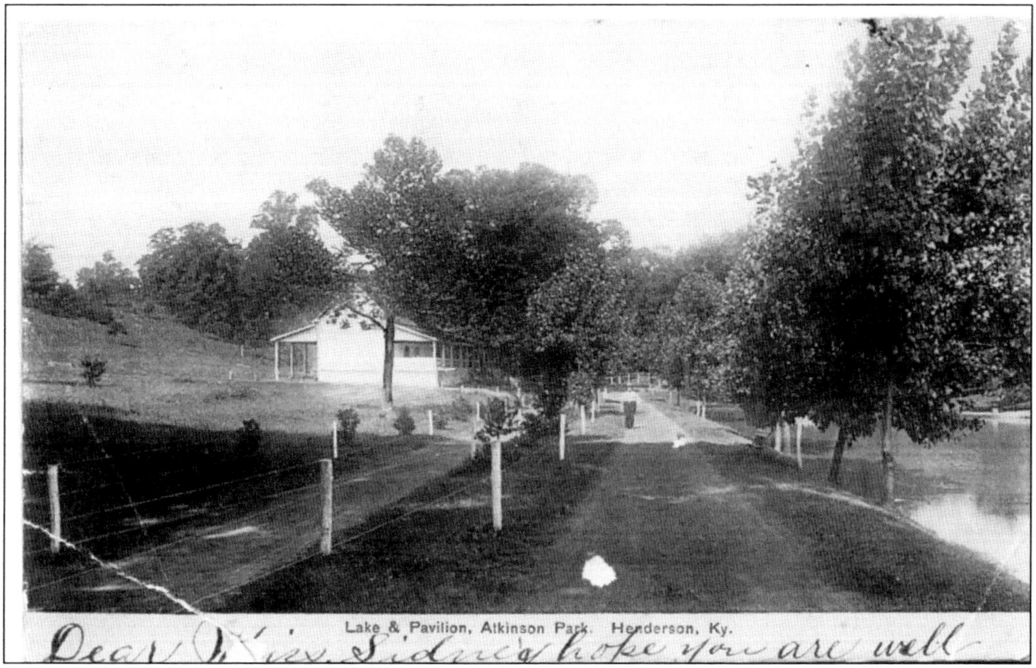

From its beginning, Atkinson Park was the scene of many social functions, including dances in the original pavilion (the building on the left of the driveway and seen as a close-up in the postcard below) and picnics along Tompson Lake, a man-made lake located where the swimming pool now sits.

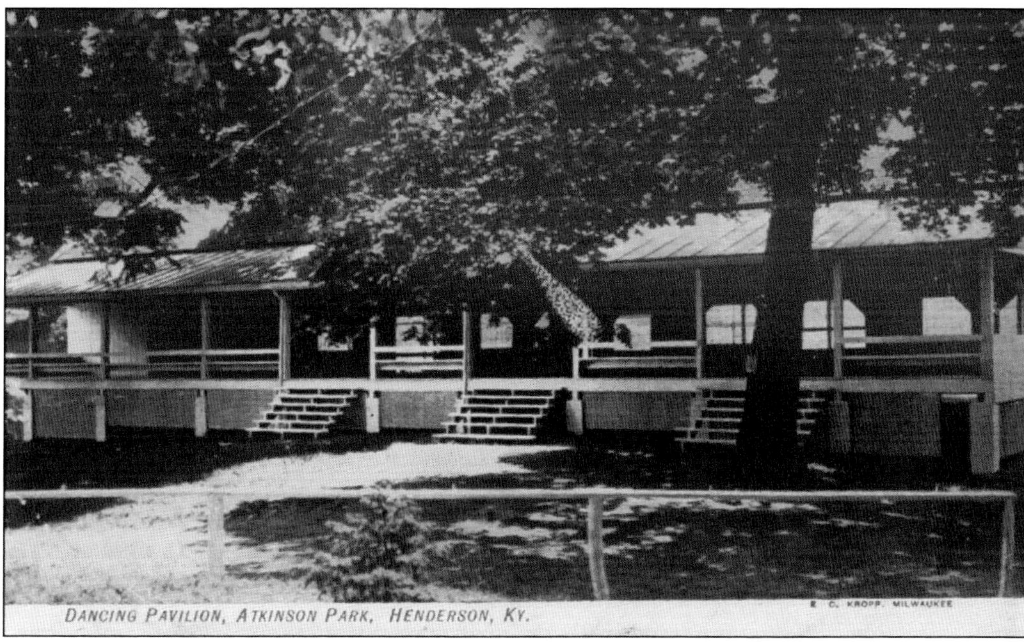

This postcard, postmarked 1907, shows the original dance pavilion where many get-togethers took place during the early days of Atkinson Park. The pavilion sat on the south side of the road that wound through the park, close to its entrance. In 1935, the Works Progress Administration (WPA) built another pavilion, but it was eventually destroyed by fire on November 10, 1967.

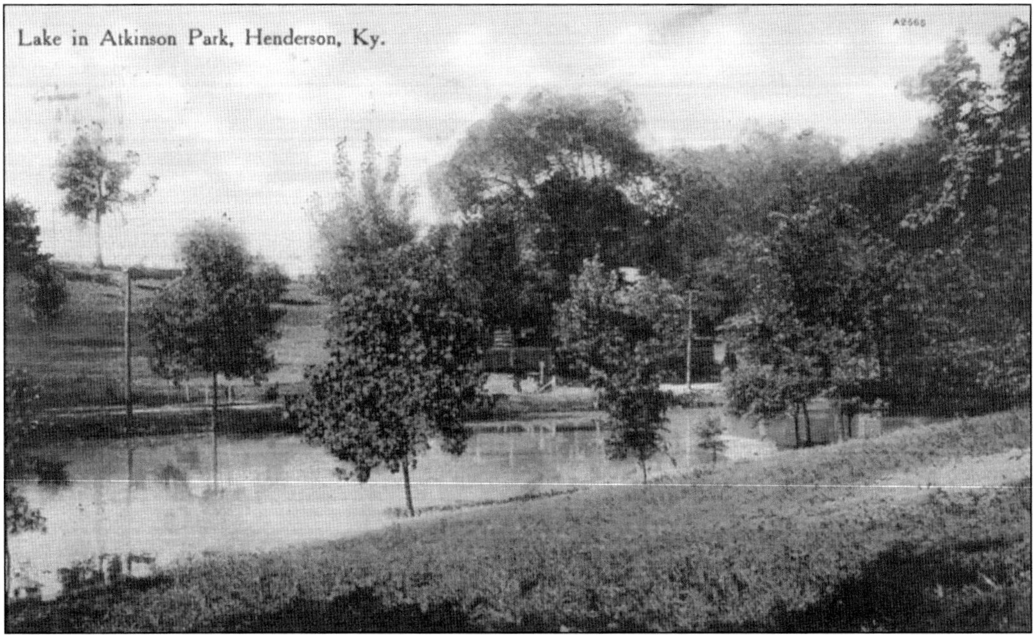

Atkinson Park was home to Tompson Lake (seen in this postcard), golf links, and a tennis court. It was also the site of more unusual activities, such as the 1923 Labor Day greased-pole contest. The local boy who was first to reach the top of the pole could grab the $5 prize. That same year, the Atkinson Park bear escaped and was eventually caught near Eighth Street. That bear and its later companion were sold during the Depression.

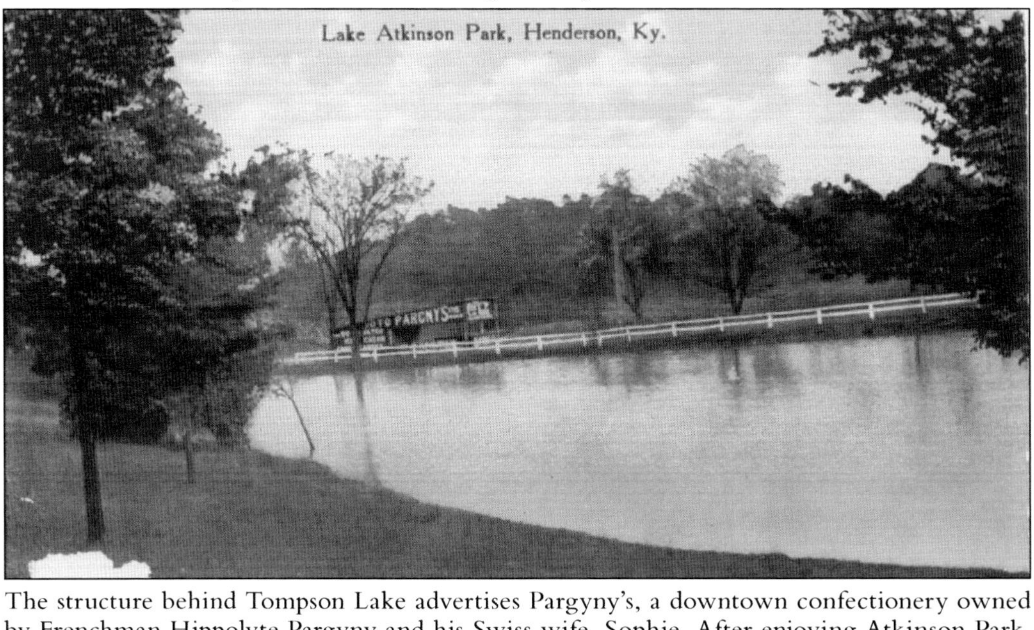

The structure behind Tompson Lake advertises Pargyny's, a downtown confectionery owned by Frenchman Hippolyte Pargyny and his Swiss wife, Sophie. After enjoying Atkinson Park, locals could stroll downtown to Pargyny's, located in the 1873 building at 116 North Main Street. Entering the store with its Napoleonic prints on the walls, customers faced a dilemma: should they turn left to the soda fountain, go right to the confectionery department, or walk to the rear for lunch and ice cream?

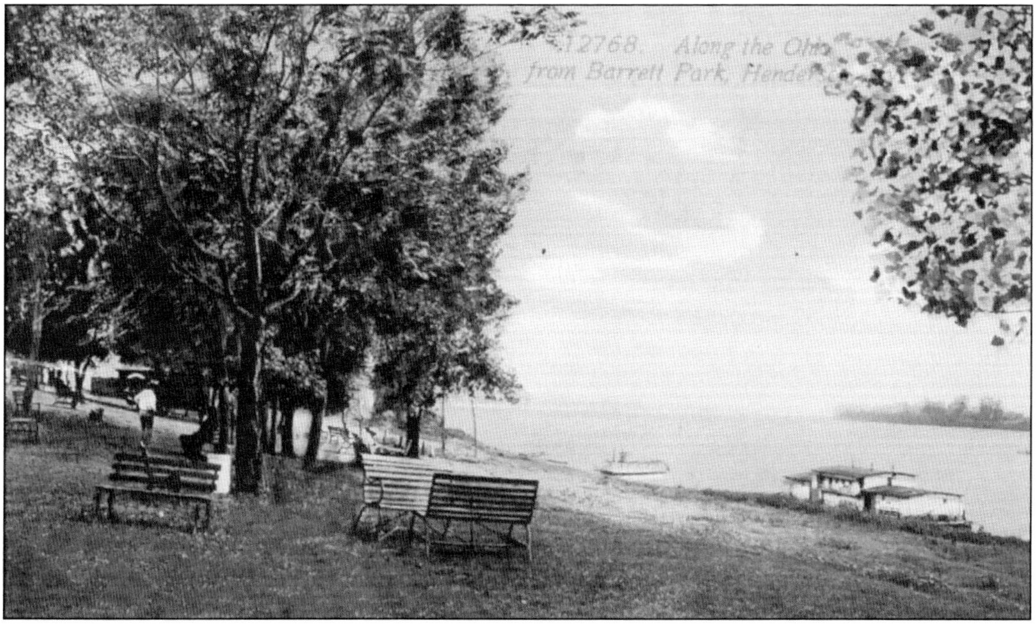

Working with the ladies' literary society, the New Century Club, and the Civic Improvement Society, Hendersonian Lucy Barret persuaded city officials to establish a park on the newly graded riverfront between Third and Fourth Streets—land that had previously been an old dumping ground—and to allot $300 a year for improvement of all of the city-owned riverfront. On August 28, 1903, with music provided by the popular Huhlien's Band, the park was dedicated.

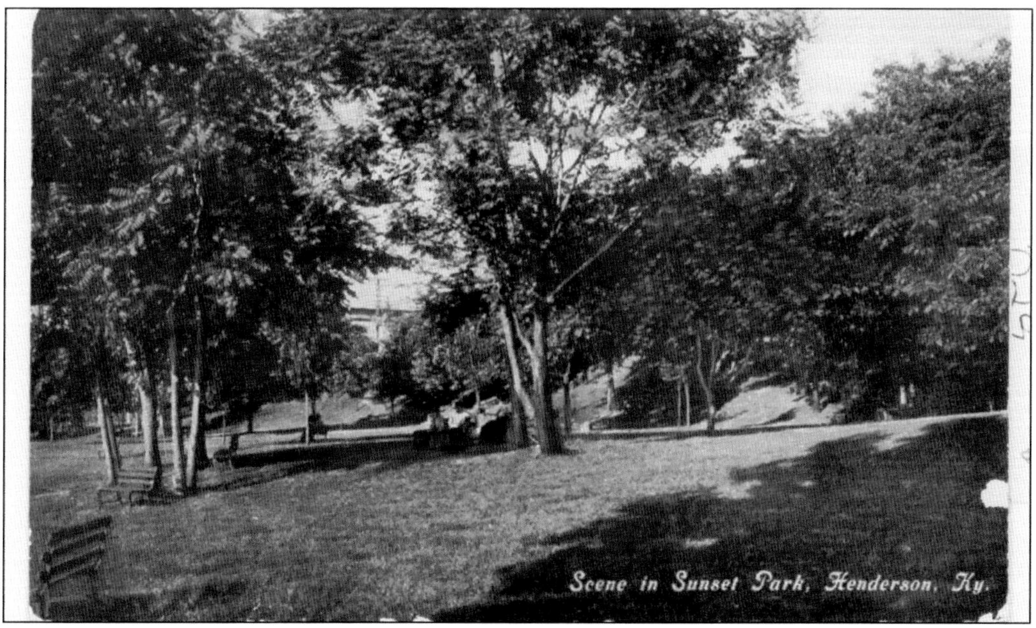

Many local citizens took part in these festivities during the dedication at Barret Park, paying 15¢ for homemade ice cream and cake, with the proceeds earmarked for improvement of the park. In honor of Lucy Barret's efforts, Henderson's Judge Givens named the park "Lucy Barret Park," although in later years the park is commonly referred to as "Sunset Park."

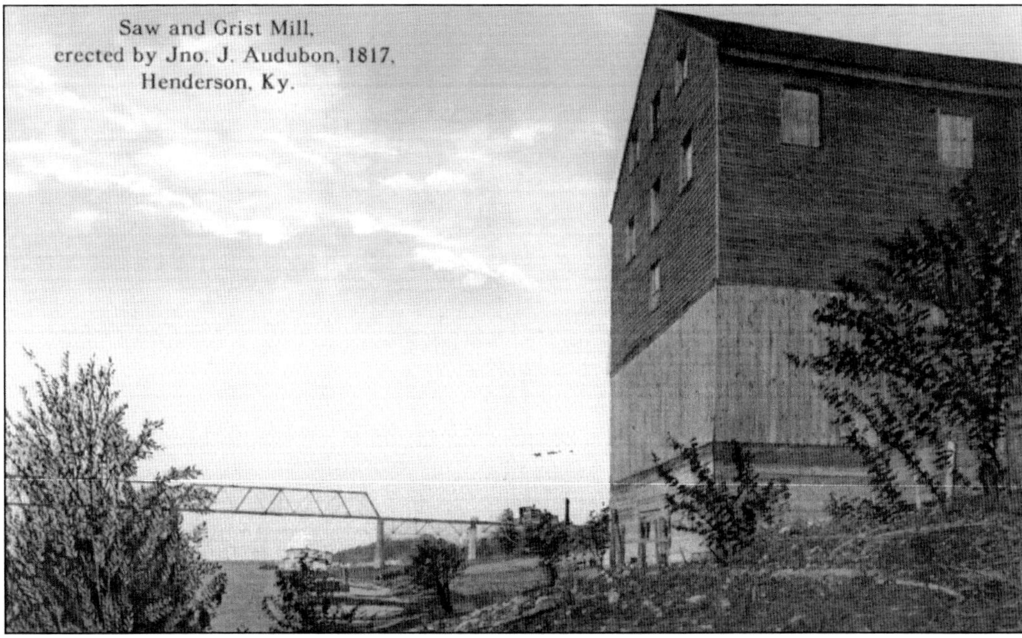

John James Audubon's 1810–1819 stay in Henderson came to an end with the failure of the saw and gristmill he and others built on the riverbank beside what is now the Second Street boat ramp. The four-story building opened for business in 1817, but machinery problems, coupled with the sparse population of the area, led to little business. (Courtesy of Henderson County Public Library.)

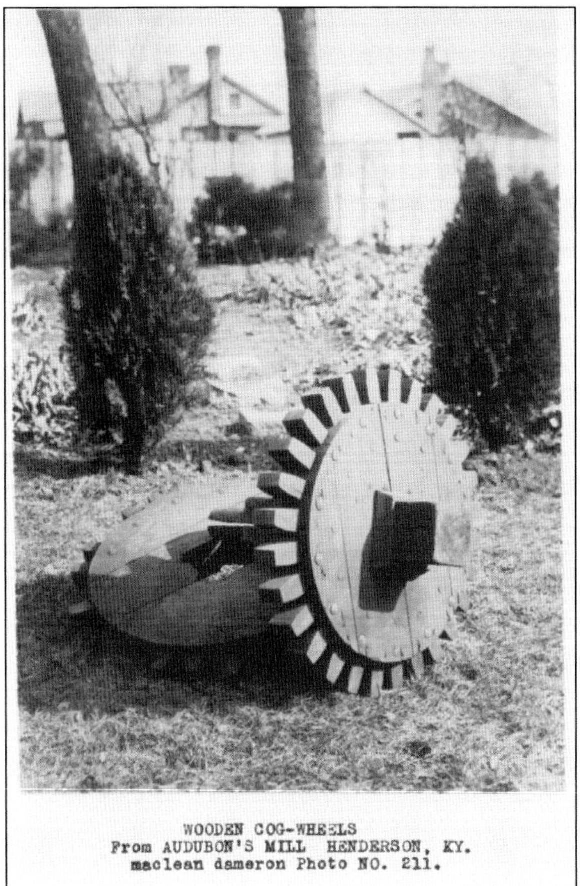

After John James Audubon's departure, later Hendersonians expanded the mill and used the structure as tobacco factories. George Atkinson thrilled Hendersonians in 1832 when he arranged for locals to ride a miniature train engine inside the mill. The building was consumed by fire on March 18, 1913. All that remained were its wooden cogwheels, which are now embedded in stone and sit on the site where the mill stood. (Courtesy of Martin Studio, Maclean Dameron Collection.)

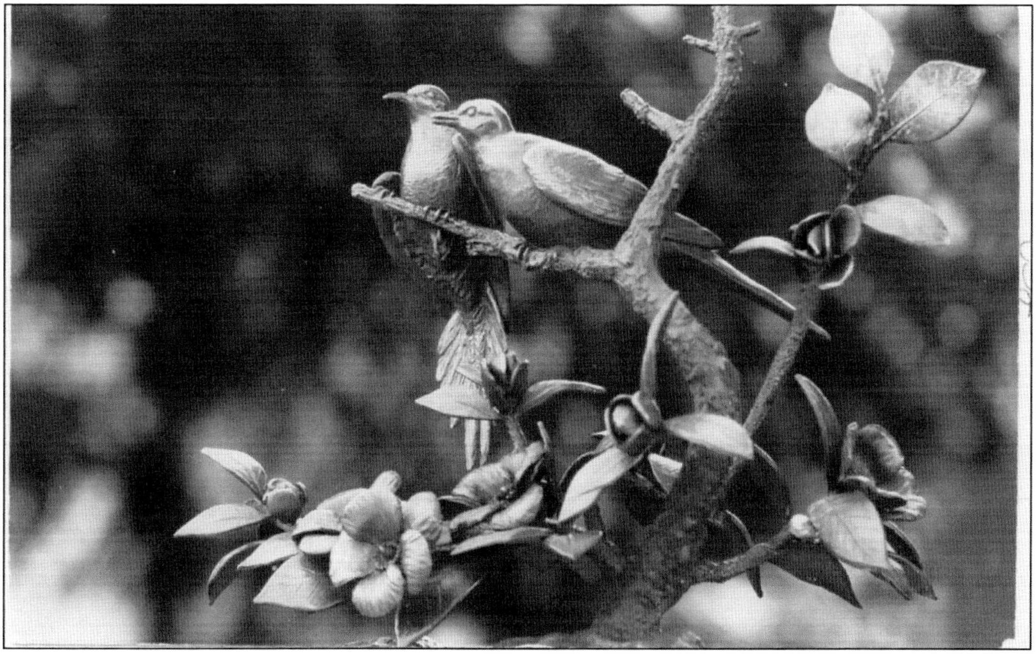

In 2002, sculptor Raymond Graf began to create a series of sculptures based on many of John James Audubon's paintings. The sculptures now decorate downtown Henderson. *Mourning Doves*, the ninth sculpture in the series, sits in front of the First United Methodist Church and was dedicated in memory of John Stanley Hoffman. (Courtesy of Steve Martin, Martin Studio.)

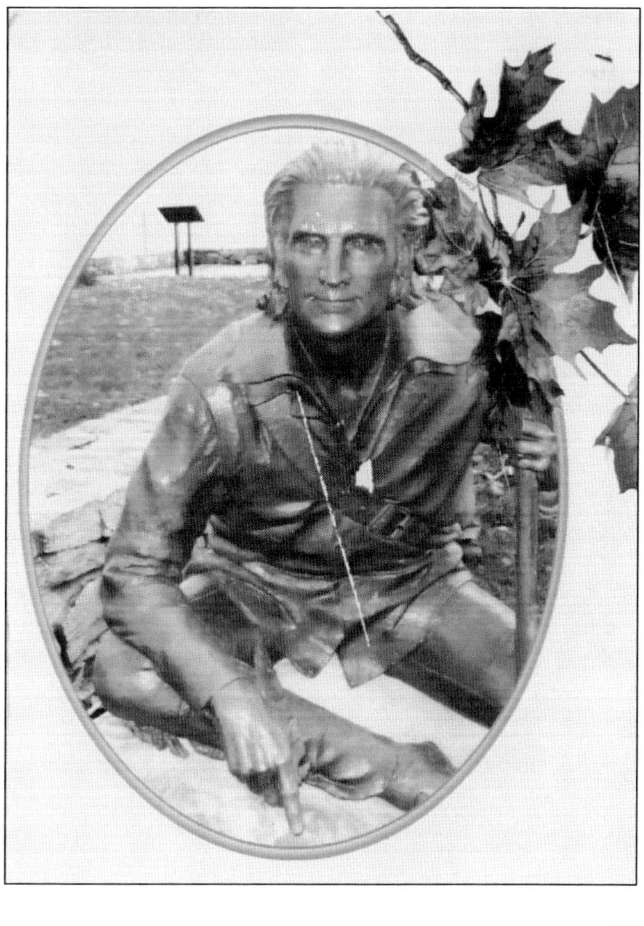

In 2007, Raymond Graff's life-sized sculpture of John James Audubon was erected in Audubon Mill Park, beside the site where the mill stood. Dressed in the type of clothing he would have worn in Henderson and with his rifle in hand, Audubon is looking at a pelican that sits about 10 feet away. Henderson County native Don Ball and his wife, Mira, funded the artwork. (Courtesy of Lou Mahon.)

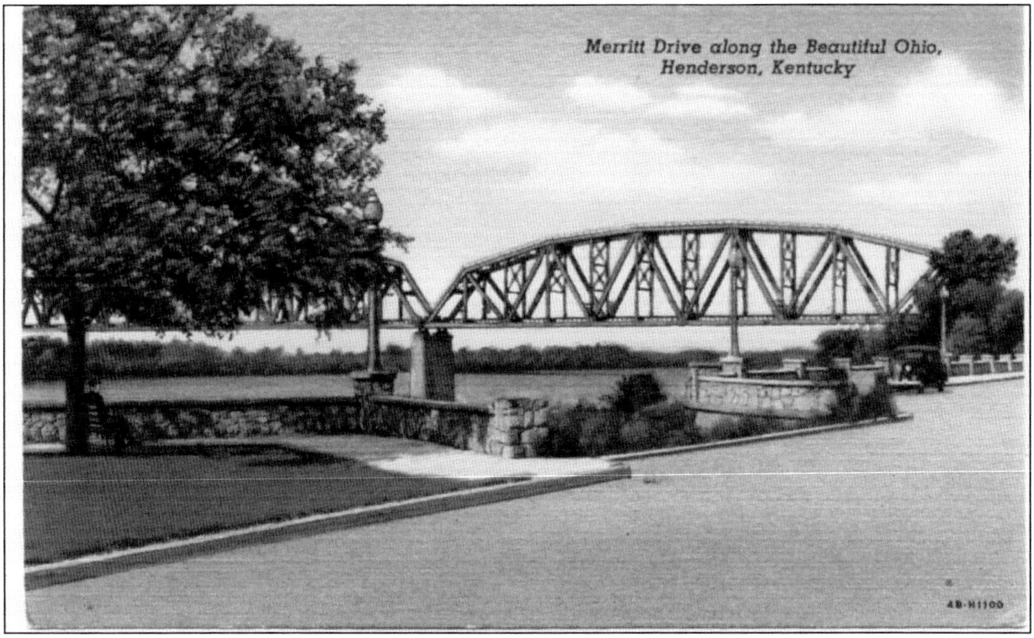

This postcard depicts Merritt Drive (more commonly called Water Street) looking north. In the background, a train is chugging across the 1932 railroad bridge, and in the center of the card is the entrance to the Second Street boat ramp. On the extreme left is the end of the 1932 gateway to Audubon Mill Park.

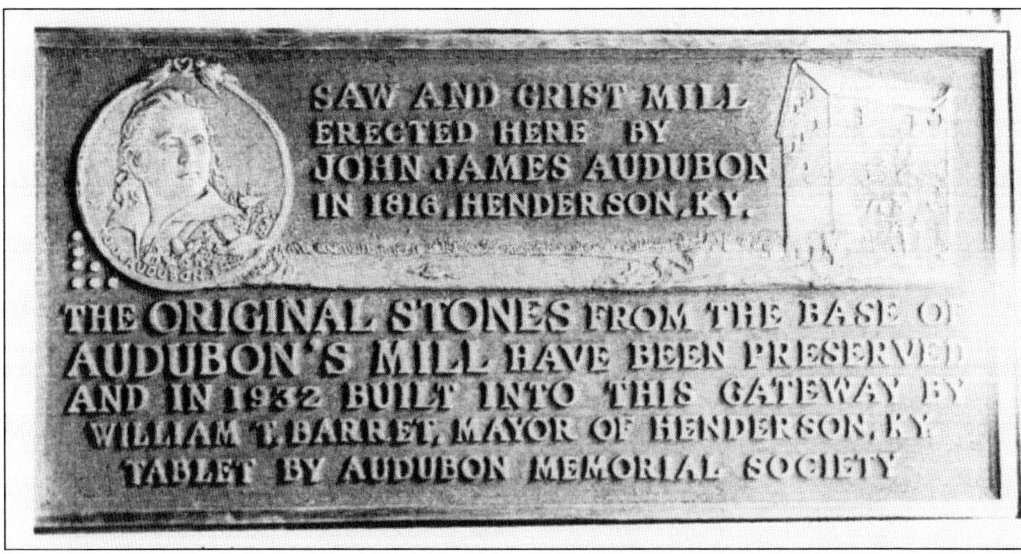

In 1932, this sign was embedded in the gateway to Audubon Mill Park, erected diagonally on the southwest corner of Water and Second Streets. To honor John James Audubon, stones from the base of his failed mill, which had burned in 1913, were used in the gateway. When other renovations were completed in the early part of the 21st century, the stone gateway was moved to the middle of the park, facing Water Street.

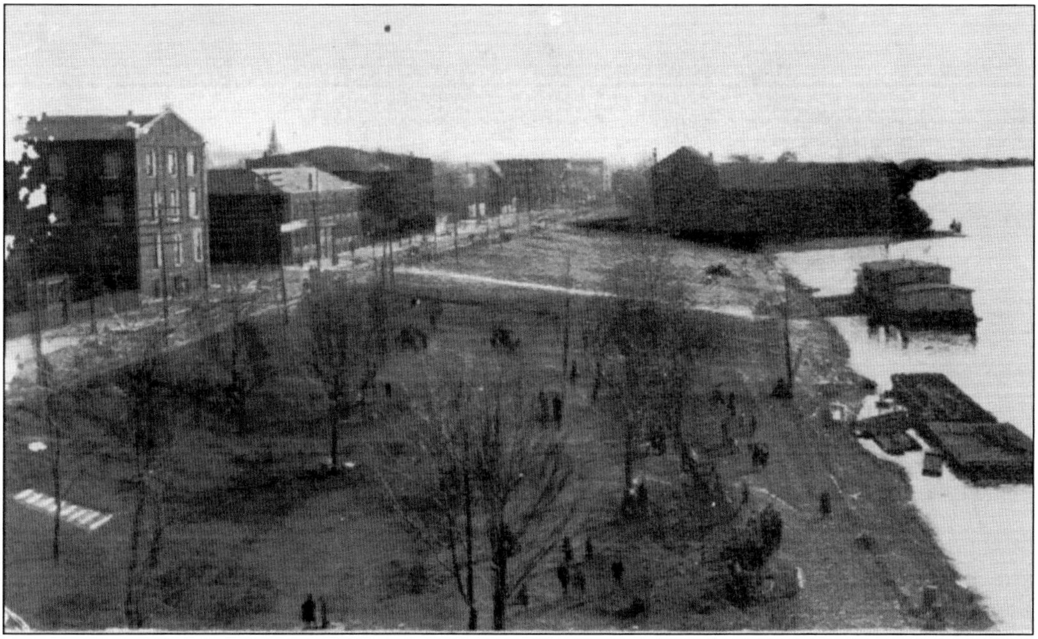

This postcard, postmarked 1910, shows the area between Water Street and the Ohio River that was, at that time, called Riverside Park. The building that had housed John James Audubon's mill (by then the Clark and Clark Tobacco Stemmery) is on the right in the background behind the boats and wharf on the river. Situated along Water Street are many other tobacco businesses.

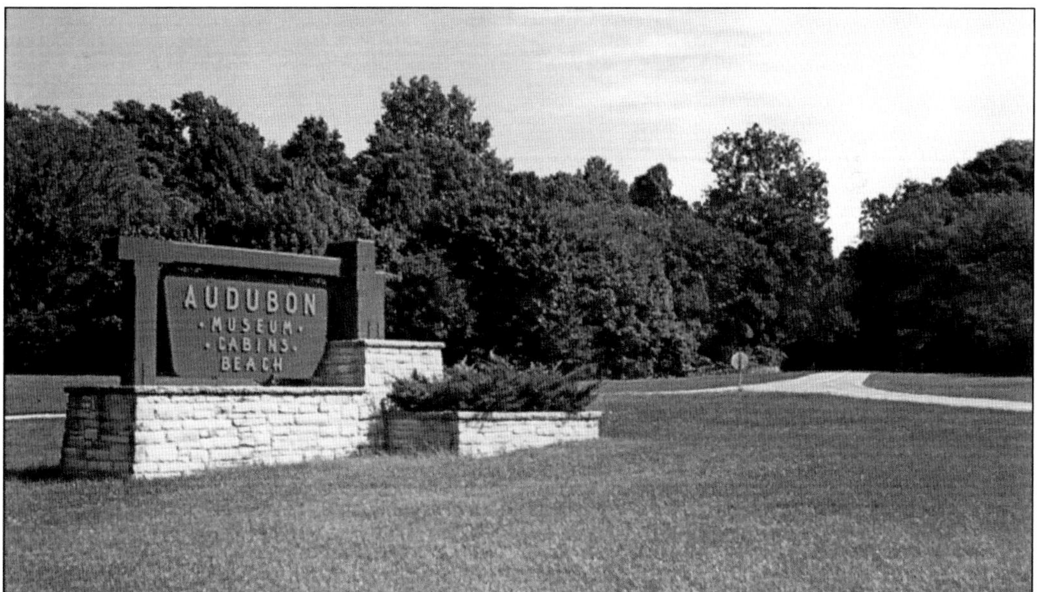

Much tribute for the establishment of Audubon State Park on U.S. 41 North near the Ohio River goes to local historian and librarian Susan Towles. In 1932, Towles and others convinced the Kentucky senate to appropriate $100,000 for construction of the museum. Land for the park was acquired two years later. During a four-year time period, the Civilian Conservation Corps (CCC) and the WPA developed the land into the now-famous Audubon State Park.

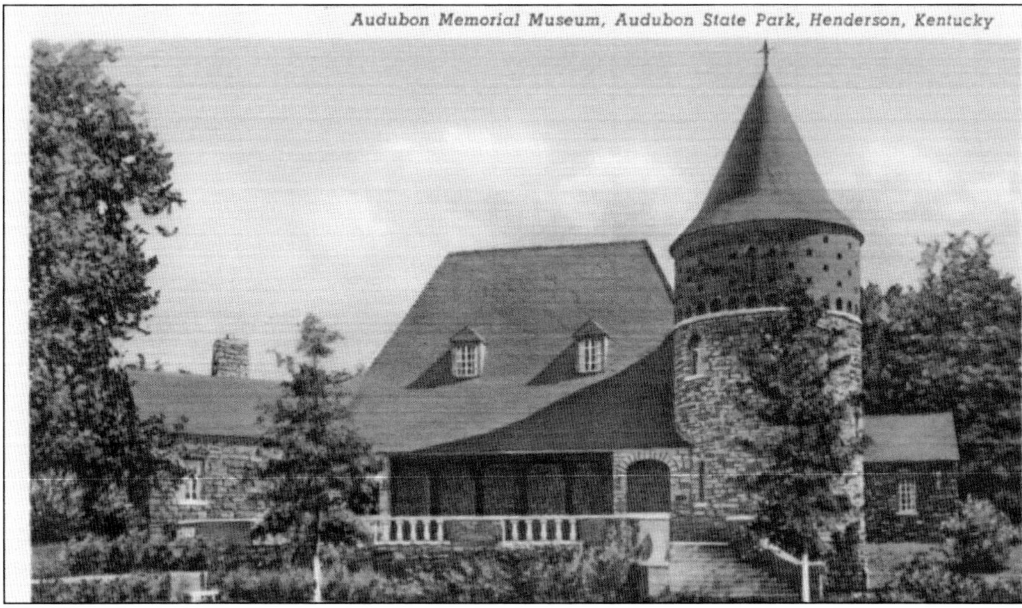

The showcase of the park is its John James Audubon Museum, designed by Bernard S. Alves in the French Norman style to pay homage to Audubon's heritage. At its opening on July 16, 1938, the museum contained 121 Audubon prints, five original Audubon paintings, and a collection of valuable manuscripts donated by Audubon's descendants. The pride of the museum was the $250,000 eclectic collection loaned by Alice Tyler, the widow of Audubon's great-grandson Leonard Sandford Tyler.

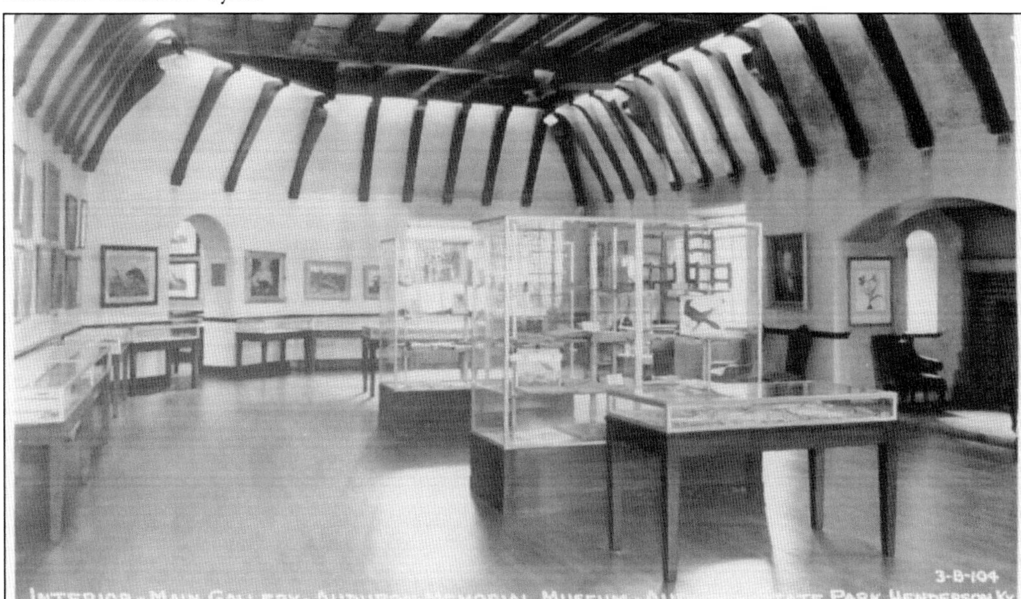

In addition to original John James Audubon paintings and those of his two sons, the museum also features manuscripts of Audubon's notes and writings; many of his letters; examples of the hair jewelry he created; table silver bought for his wife, Lucy; a jeweled cross presented to him by the czar of Russia; a number of volumes from his personal library; and a great deal more Audubon memorabilia.

American artist Henry Inman (1801–1846), famed for his genre, landscape, and portrait paintings, met with John James Audubon in Philadelphia in the late summer of 1832, and it was there that he painted Audubon's portrait. This copy by German American painter Nicola Marschall (1829–1917) hangs in the Audubon Museum.

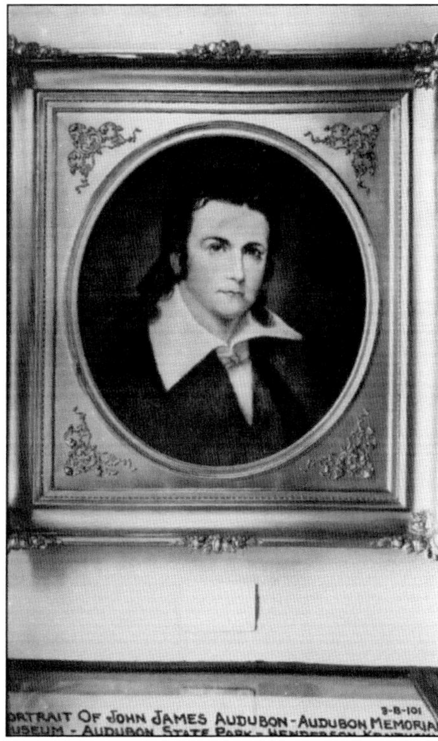

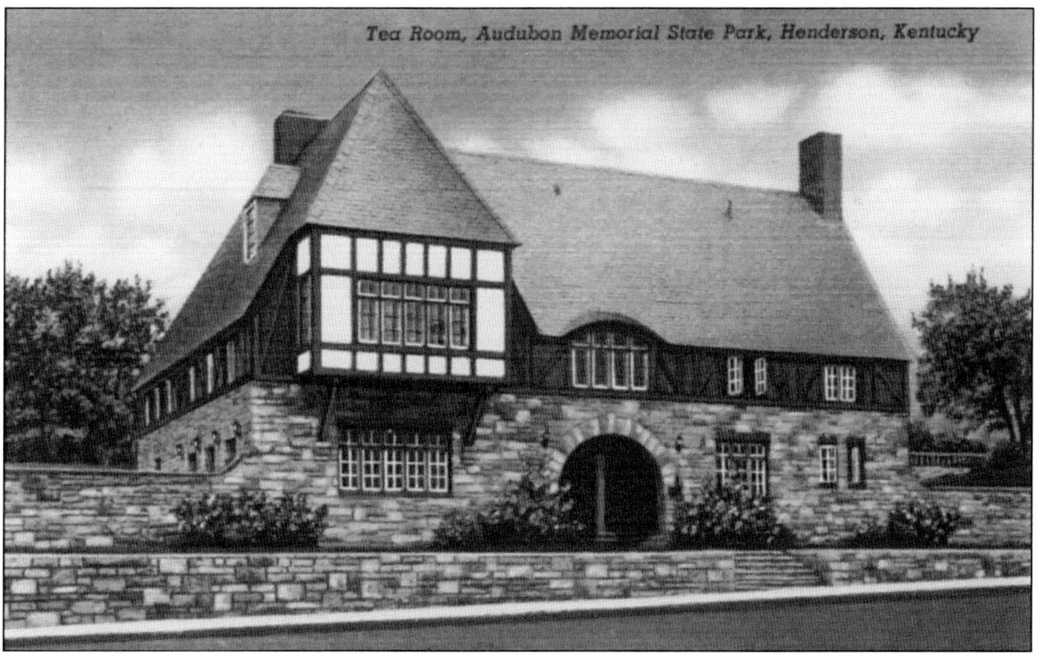

The English cottage–style Tea House was completed in June 1940. Until the beginning of World War II, the Tea House was a restaurant that served three meals each day. Prices for breakfast began at 25¢, lunch at 60¢, cold plates at 35¢, and dinner at $1. Lela Hubbard Smith was the manager. In later years, the Tea House has served as a display area for non–Audubon Henderson history, a nature center, and offices for park administrators.

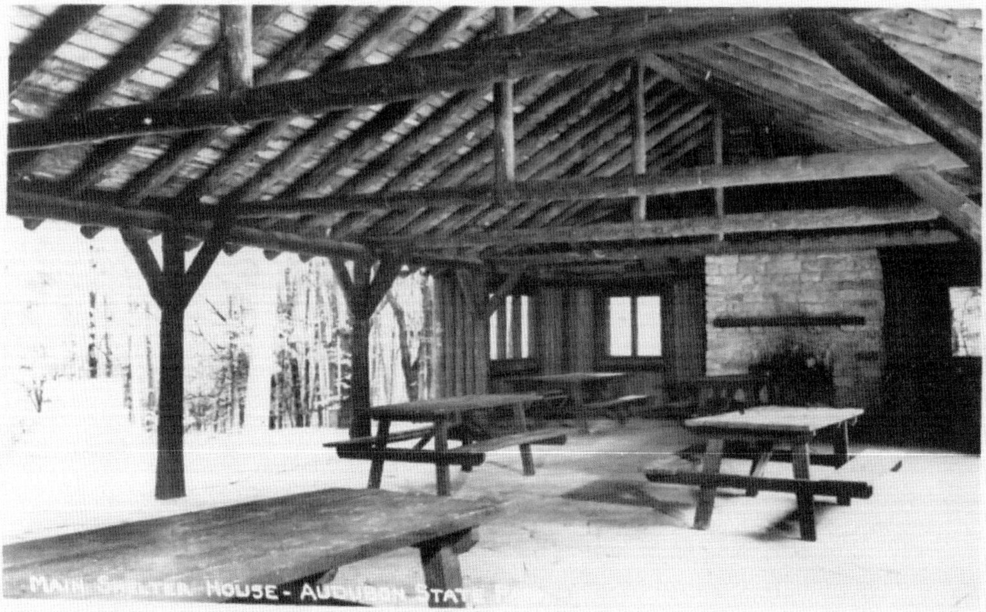

Some of the first work begun by members of the CCC was the construction of a number of shelter houses and picnic areas close to the main roads and parking areas. Additional shelters were built in more remote areas along the park's seven walking trails.

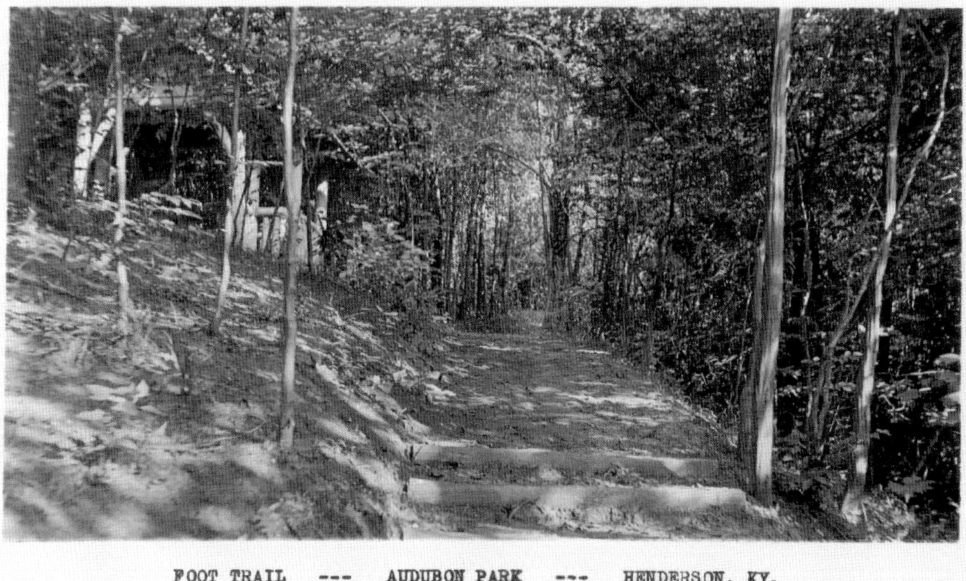

Audubon Park's seven-foot trails were designed to give visitors the greatest advantages in viewing the many varieties of songbirds. Six trails named for birds (the Cardinal, Bluebird, Oriole, Mockingbird, Robin, and Bobwhite Trails) took hikers through various parts of the park, and the seventh—Lakeside Trail—circled the 22-acre lake now called Audubon Lake. (Courtesy of Henderson County Public Library and Martin Studio, Maclean Dameron Collection.)

Visitors hiking along the Bluebird Trail, one of the park's original foot trails, left the picnic and parking area and then walked to the observation tower where they were rewarded with a 20-mile panoramic vista of the Ohio Valley. If they continued on Bluebird Trail, hikers wound around the upper part of Wildlife Lake and then back to the shelter and parking area. (Courtesy of Henderson County Public Library and Martin Studio, Maclean Dameron Collection.)

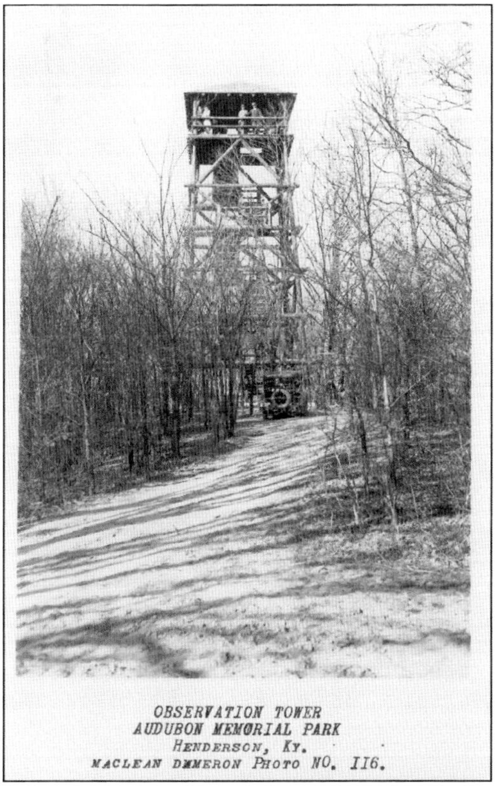

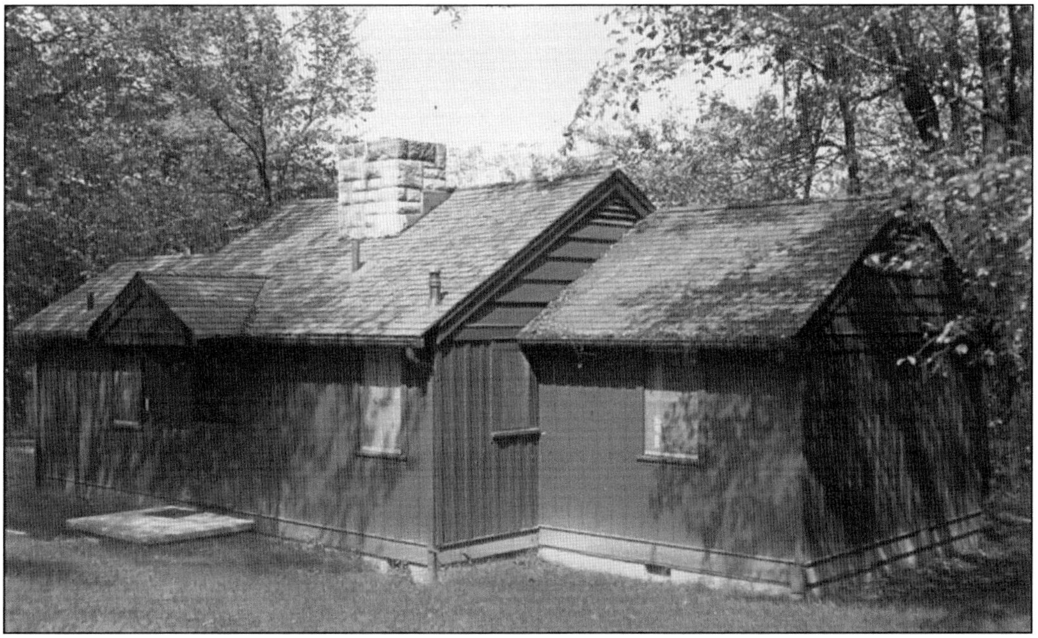

Twenty-six cabins, ranging in size from three to five rooms and complete with kitchen and bath facilities, were initially envisioned to be built around Scenic Lake (later named Audubon Lake). Those plans fell short; today the park features five one-bedroom cabins and one two-bedroom cabin. All sit along Audubon Lake and are near the golf course.

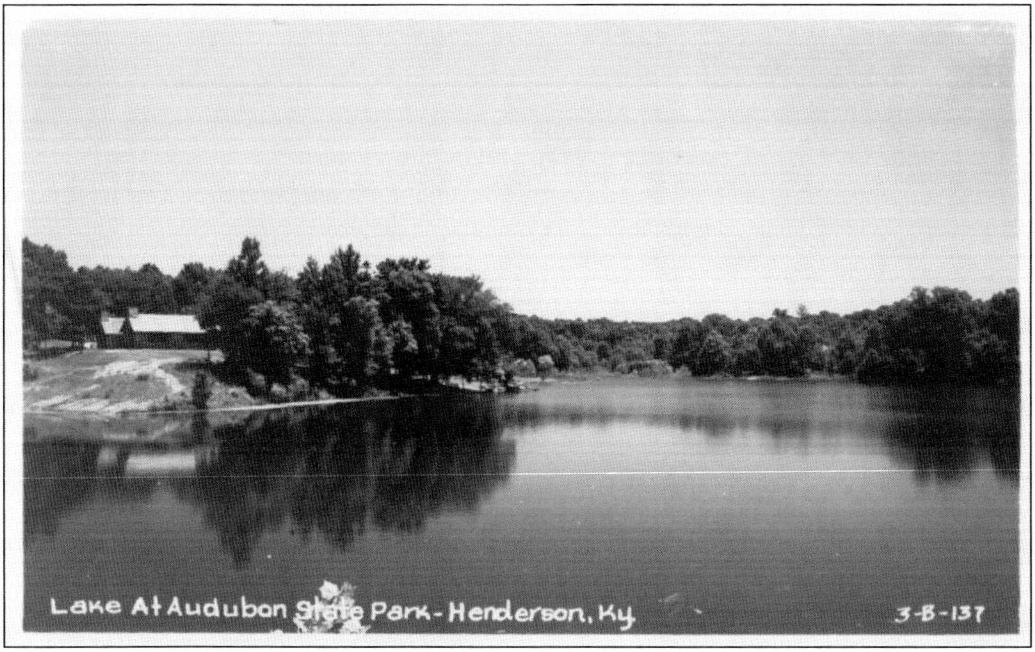

Audubon Park is home to two lakes, Wilderness Lake (accessible only by foot) and Audubon Lake (originally named Scenic Lake). When the park opened in 1938, this lake was used solely for fishing and boating. In 1954, a swimming beach was added, but water-quality problems later forced the beach to close. (Courtesy of Henderson County Public Library and Martin Studio, Maclean Dameron Collection.)

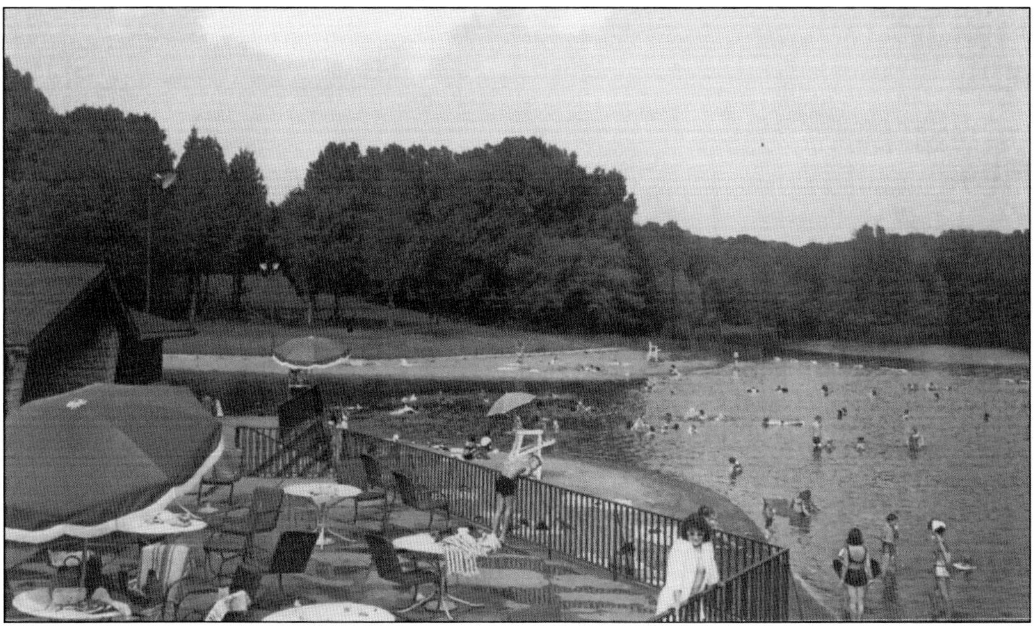

Initial dreams for Audubon Park included a swimming pool, but that dream was never realized. However, construction of a swimming beach, bathhouses, a parking lot, and docks for Audubon Lake, which had been used as a fishing lake since the park's opening, began in 1953, and the $100,000 facilities were opened to the public the following year.

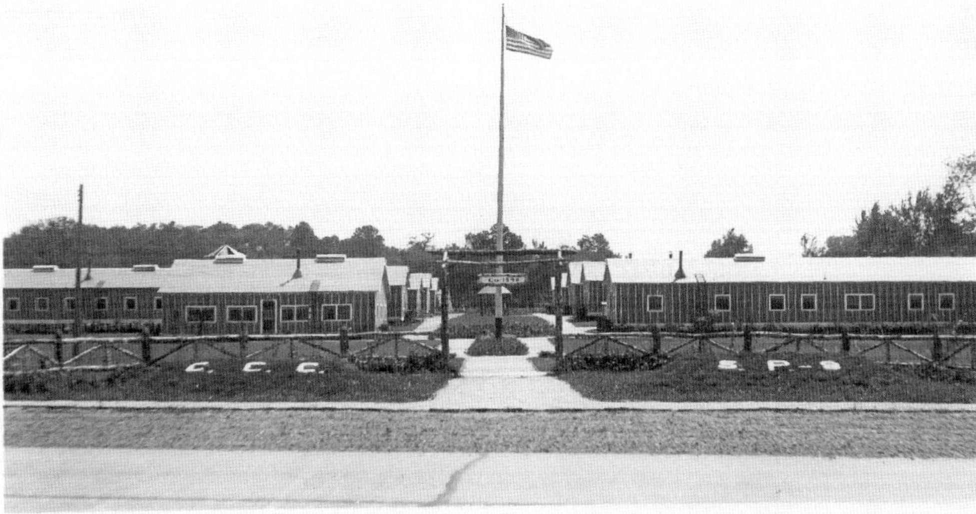

GENERAL VIEW of CAMP CROMWELL --- HENDERSON, KY.
Photo by maclean dameron Henderson, Ky. NO. 104.

In March 1933, Pres. Franklin D. Roosevelt established the CCC to provide work relief for young men. At its peak, the CCC maintained 2,635 work camps, all structured in a military fashion; 561 camps were associated with national, state, and local parks. The Henderson CCC camp (Company No. 1540) was located at the corner of Highway 41 and Watson Lane. (Courtesy of Henderson County Public Library and Martin Studio, Maclean Dameron Collection.)

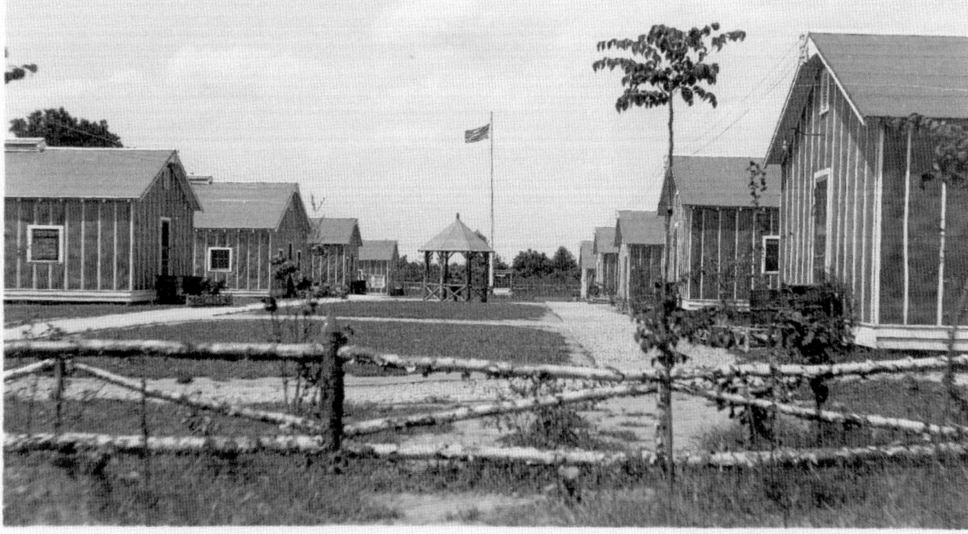

COMPANY STREET --- CAMP CROMWELL --- HENDERSON, KY.
Photo by maclean dameron Henderson, Ky. NO. 107.

When they entered the CCC, 70 percent of corps members were malnourished; on average, members gained more than 11 pounds in their first three months of service. For their 40-hour workweek, corps members were paid $30 a month with the proviso that $25 of that be sent home to their family. (Courtesy of Henderson County Public Library and Martin Studio, Maclean Dameron Collection.)

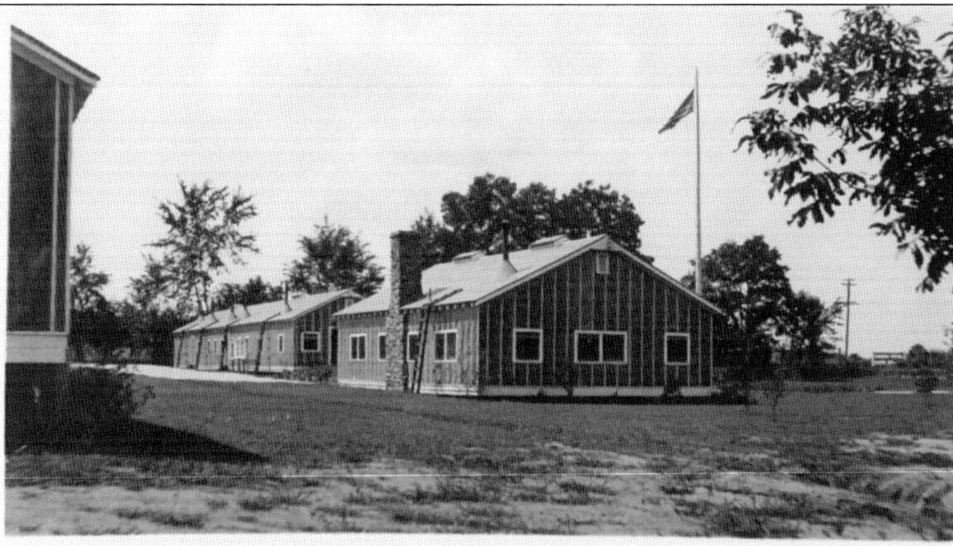

OFFICER'S QUARTERS and ADMINISTRATION BUILDING CAMP CROMWELL
Photo by maclean dameron Henderson, Ky. NO. 103.

The Henderson CCC camp, unofficially named Camp Cromwell to honor Kentucky state parks director Emma Cromwell, opened in late 1934 with around 200 West Virginia corpsmen. They were later joined by local enrollees. During their four years working at Audubon State Park, the men drained swamps; built a lake, trails, shelters, and camping areas; and constructed the tea house and museum. (Courtesy Martin Studio, Maclean Dameron Collection.)

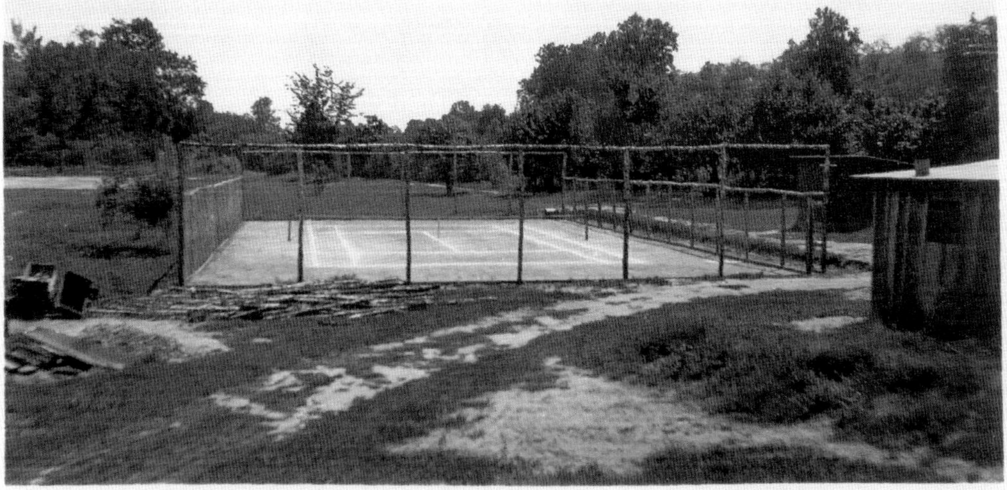

TENNIS COURT --- CAMP CROMWELL --- HENDERSON, KY.
Photo by maclean dameron Henderson, Ky. NO. 105.

When the first enrollees arrived at Camp Cromwell, they lived in pitched tents and, having no showers, resorted to bathing in the Ohio River. Eventually, they built barracks, other buildings, and sporting facilities that included baseball and softball diamonds, croquet and tennis courts, and a boxing ring and amphitheater. Local teams competed as the Camp Cromwell Cardinals. (Courtesy of Henderson County Public Library and Martin Studio, Maclean Dameron Collection.)

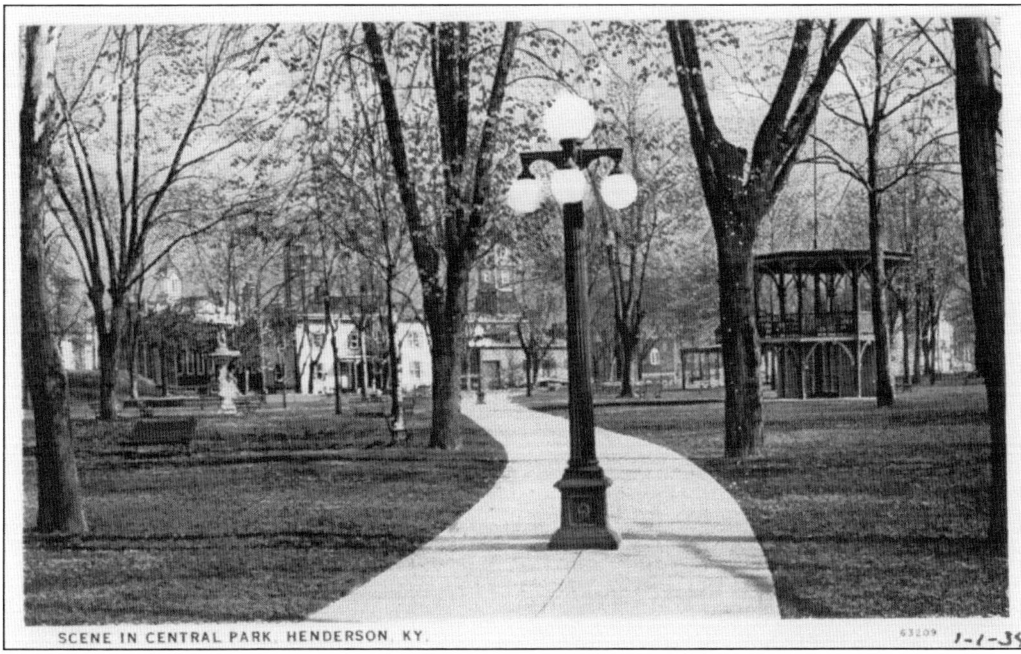

Henderson's Central Park (originally called Transylvania Park and later known as City Park) is thought to be the first municipal park west of the Allegheny Mountains. Although originally covering a much larger area, Central Park is now bounded by Washington, First, Main, and Elm Streets. In the background on the left of this postcard is the former residence of the county jailer; on the right is the old bandstand.

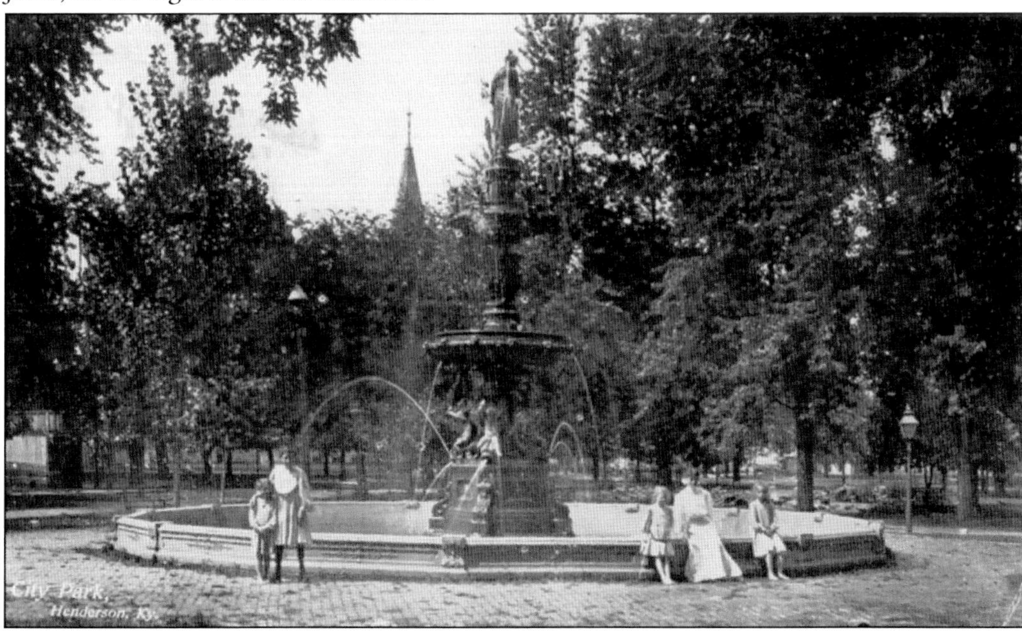

The idea for the "Lady in the Park," the grand fountain that is the showcase of Central Park, was conceived by city clerk J. B. Johnston in the mid-1880s. Concept designs were brought from New York by James E. Rankin Sr., and in the mid-1890s, the French-built fountain and its pool were installed in the middle of the northern edge of the park.

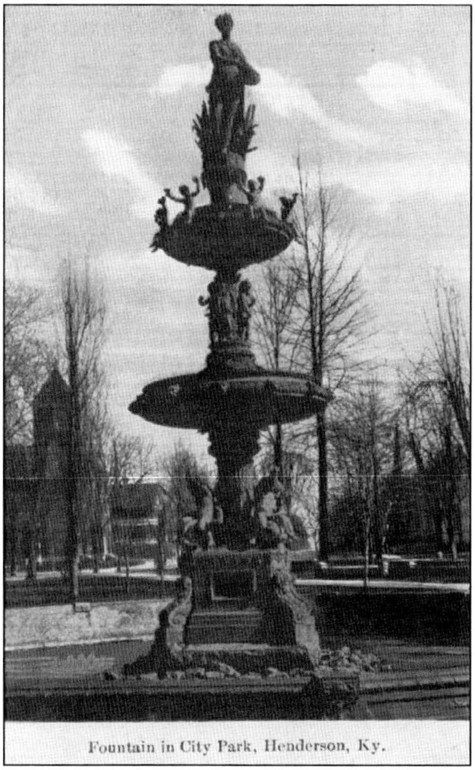

The three-tiered fountain stood nearly 30 feet tall. It was adorned with cherubs and sat in a large pool that sometimes contained fish. Surrounding the pool was an ornamental iron wall that is thought to have been sold during World War II. On the left in the background of this postcard is the First Baptist Church across Elm Street from Central Park.

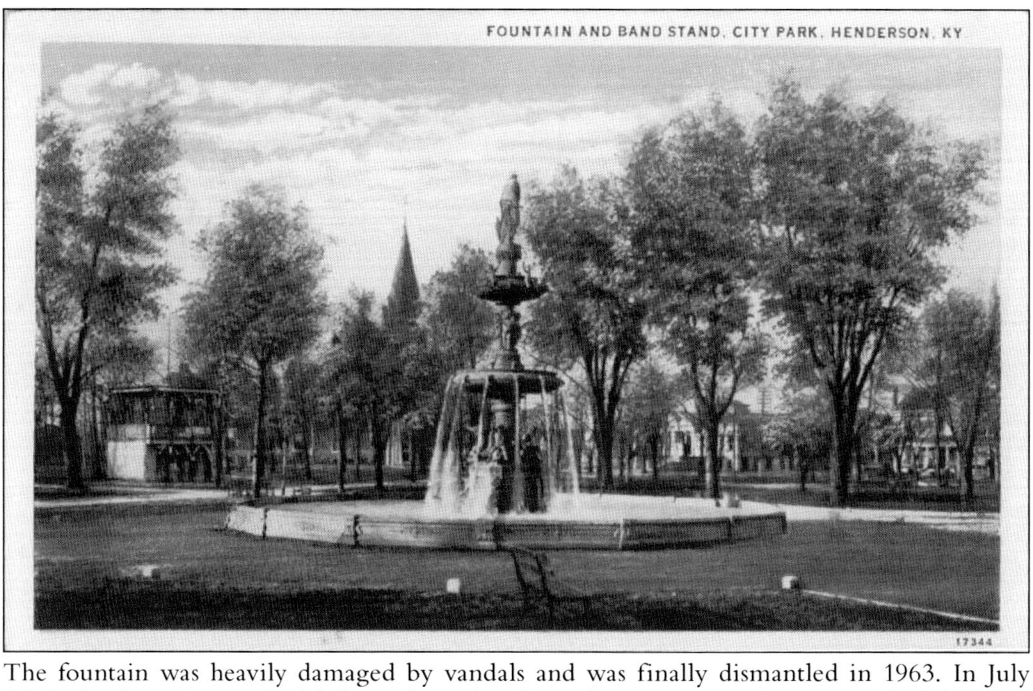

The fountain was heavily damaged by vandals and was finally dismantled in 1963. In July 2003, the fountain was faithfully replicated and stands on its original site. On the left in the background of this postcard is the bandstand, and behind the trees is the First Presbyterian Church. In the background on the right is the Henderson County Public Library.

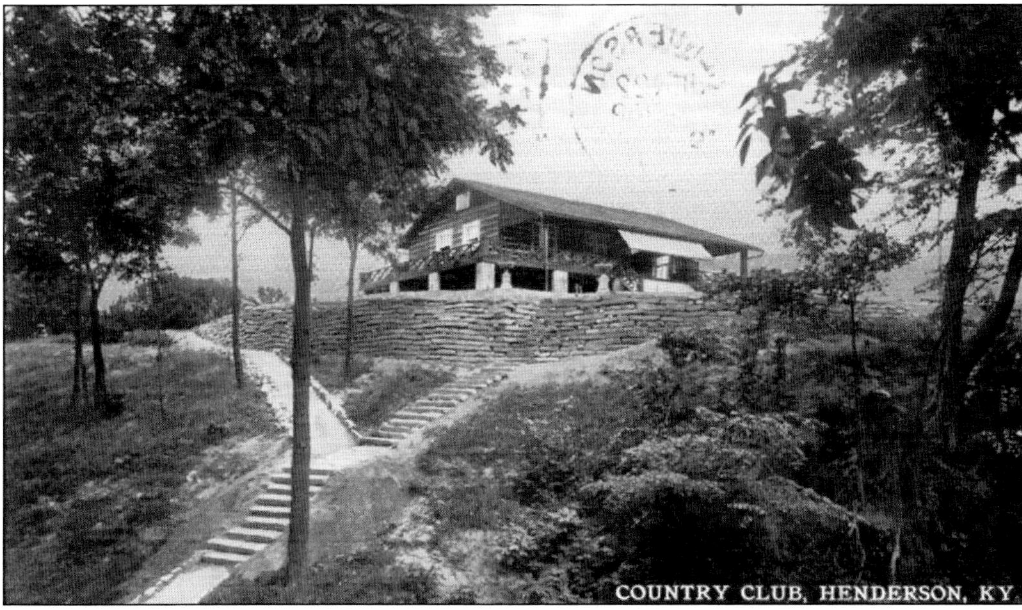

Around 1910, this 10-room log structure was built for about $7,000 on a knoll on North Elm Street across from Atkinson Park. The Henderson Country Club was often visited on Saturday afternoons when many women arrived by trolley to enjoy cakes and sandwiches. Members used the golf course at Atkinson Park, but they had their own tennis court and swimming pool. The structure burned in 1923.

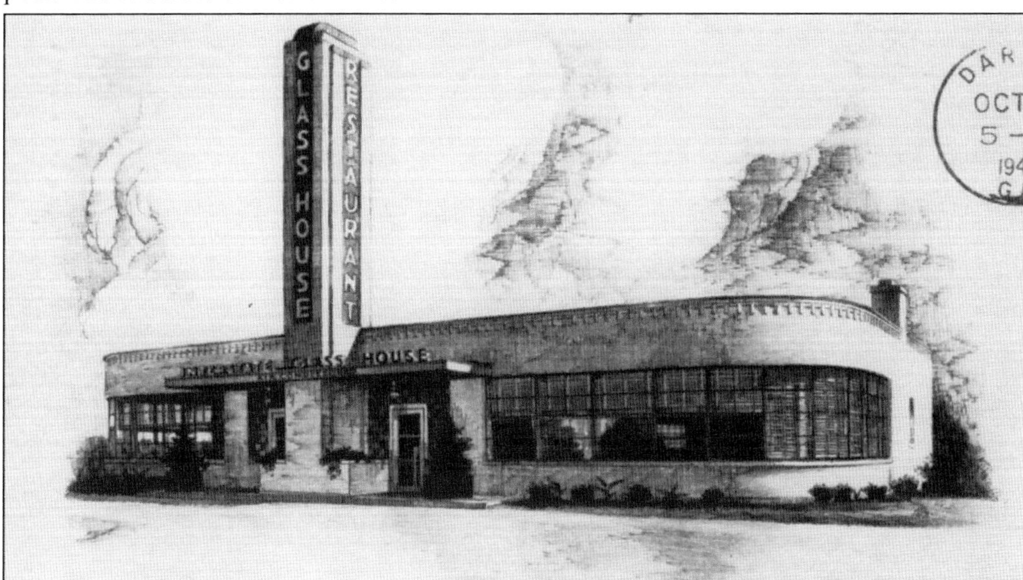

When it opened in March 1940, the Interstate Glass House Restaurant at 629 South Green Street boasted outer walls of plate glass and glass brick, a hemispherical main dining room, bleached walnut woodwork, a modern cocktail lounge that seated 60, and air conditioning. In an article in the *Gleaner*, the Glass House's Chef Mitchell noted the restaurant would feature charcoal broiled meats "for the masculine favor" and "rich newbergs, intriguing casseroles, and savory patties" for the ladies. The restaurant closed in the early 1950s.

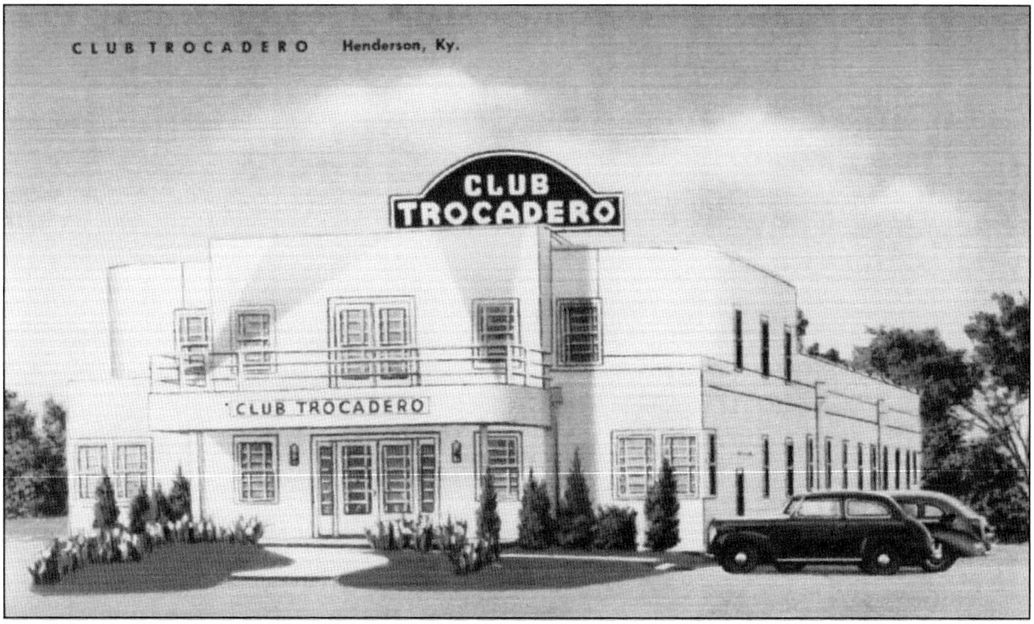

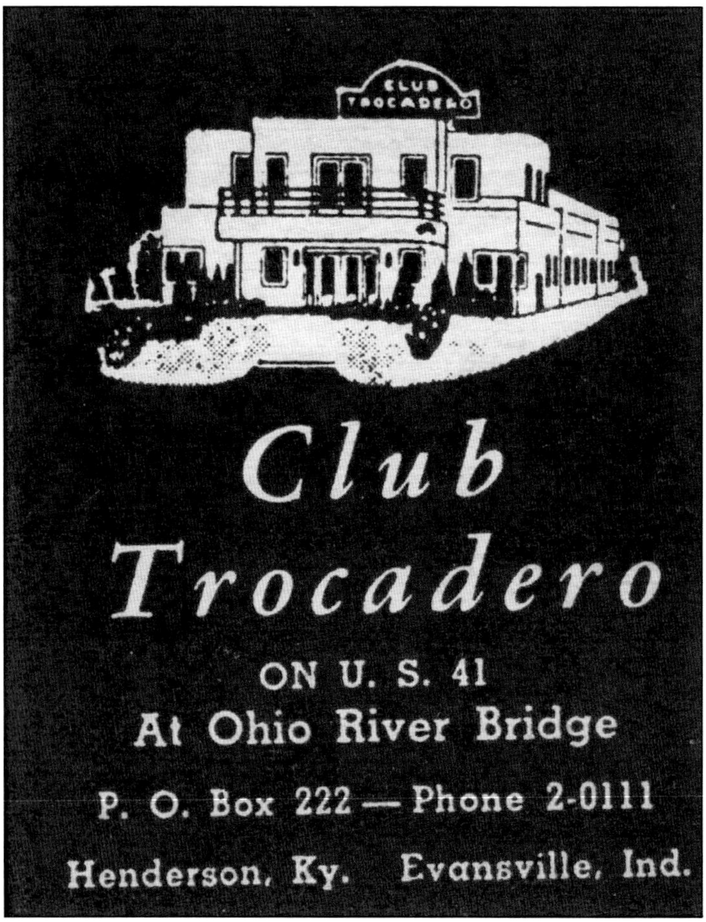

In its heyday, the Trocadero was the premier nightclub (and premier gambling establishment) in the area. Located across U.S. 41 from Dade Park Race Track, the 14,000-square-foot Trocadero opened in August 1939 at a cost of $120,000. It soon became the place to go for tristate couples. "The Troc" played host to such musical greats as Duke Ellington, Cab Calloway, Gene Krupa, Woody Herman, and the Ink Spots. After a crackdown on illegal gambling in the early 1950s, the club closed. In 1983, it opened as an antique mall but was consumed by fire on January 7, 1990. Today the site is home to a gas station and convenience store.

Located on the north side of U.S. 41 South just past the south Y, the Kasey Klub was another of Henderson's swanky nightspots. The club opened in the 1930s and lasted through the gambling and anti-gambling era, closing in the early 1960s. Ernie Hayden (known as "The Little Maestro") and his orchestra were under the exclusive management of the Kasey Klub. (Courtesy of Martin Studio, Maclean Dameron Collection.)

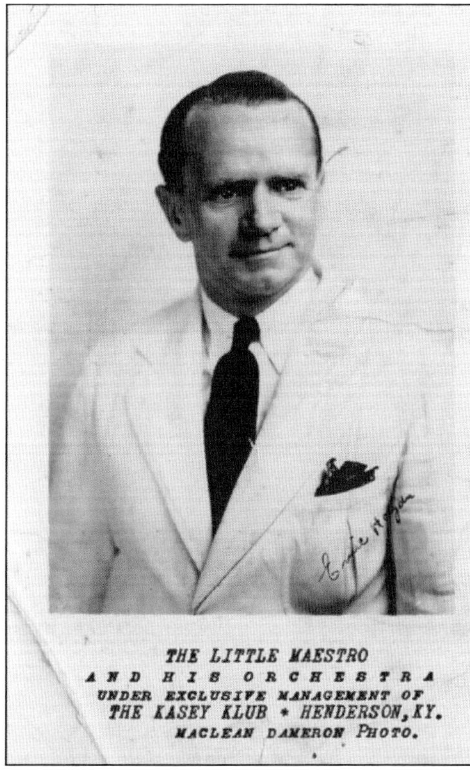

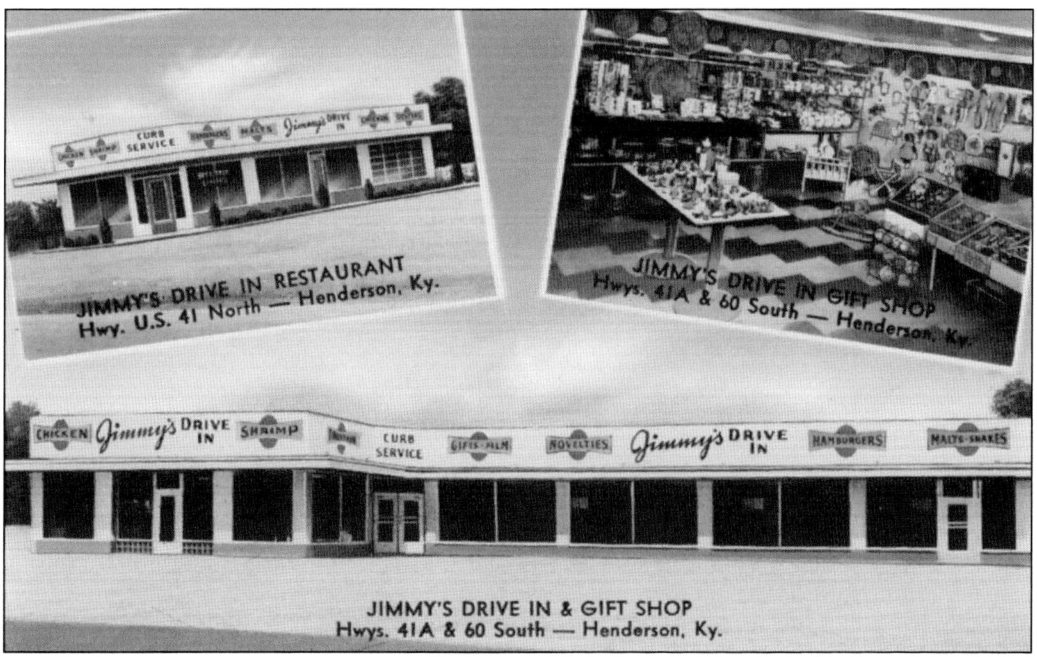

The largest of the Jimmy's Drive-Ins (bottom and top right), located at 1205 South Green Street, opened in the early 1950s and quickly became a trendy dining spot for locals and travelers. Owner Jim Mortensen also opened other sites for Jimmy's, including one at 2119 U.S. 41 North (top left). "Colonel Jim's" chicken became famous in the tristate area.

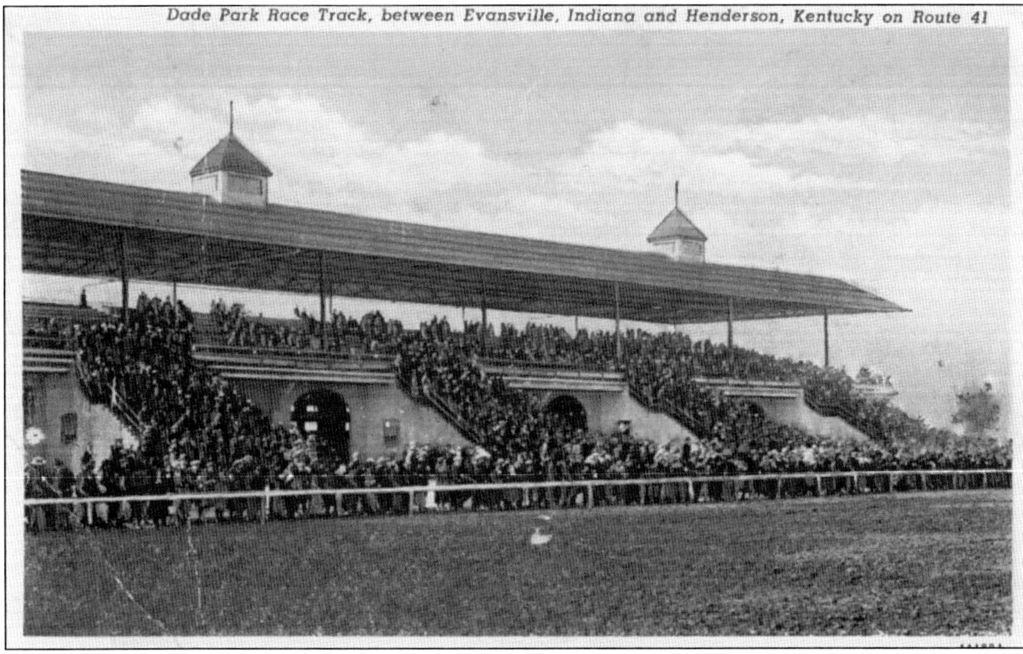

Horse racing has been a part of Henderson's history since the town's early times. In fact, racing was banned from its popular Elm Street location in the 1840s but continued in numerous tracks in the county. In October 1922, an estimated 4,000 to 5,000 people took part in the opening of the Dade Park racetrack (named for A. B. Dade, the track's first director), located on Highway 41 North across the Ohio River. Horse racing at Dade Park was not immediately successful and gave way to car racing the next two years. In 1924, James C. Ellis bought the track for $35,000 and reopened it—with horses again—the following year. Thirty years later, the track was renamed in Ellis's honor.

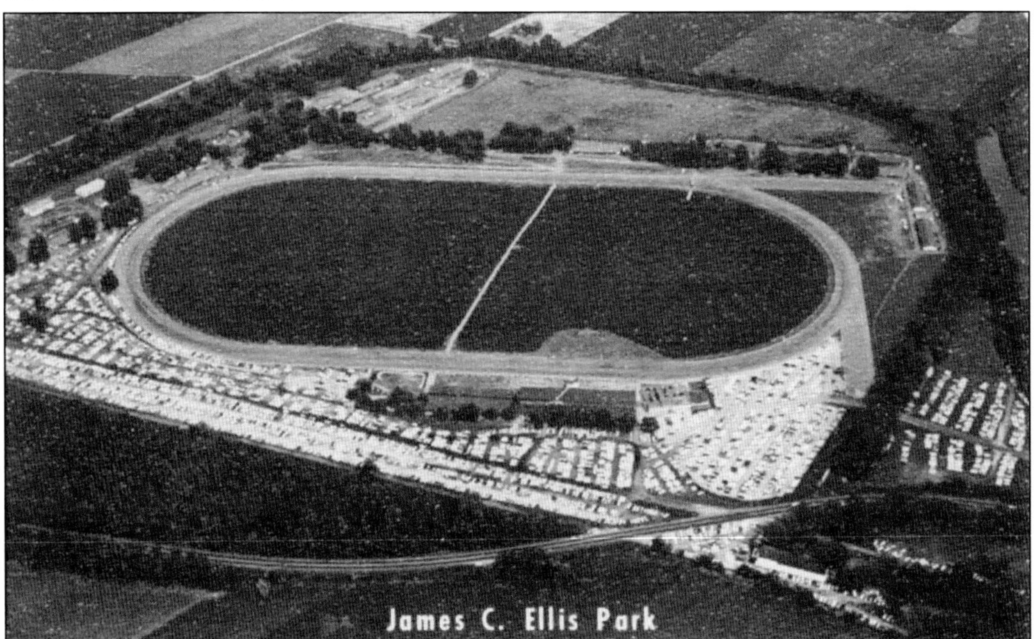

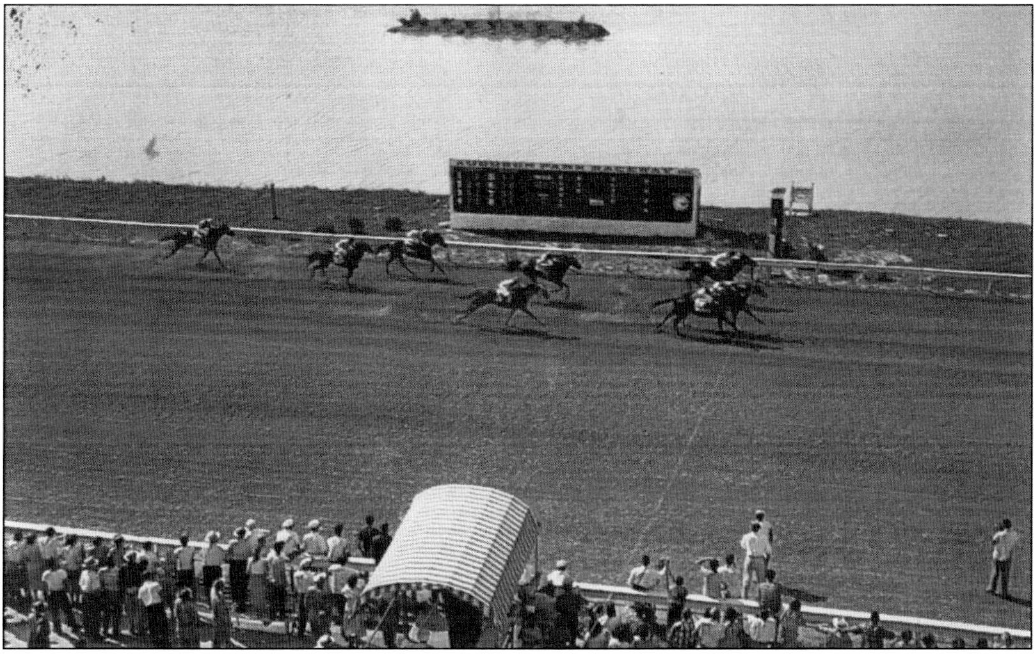

In addition to Dade (Ellis) Park, Henderson was home to a second track, Audubon Raceway. The facility opened on July 4, 1955, but racing did not prove lucrative. The track was closed from 1958 to 1964, and after that, it changed hands a number of times and also switched to harness racing. Later names included the Midwest Harness and the Riverside Downs. The last race was run the mid-1990s.

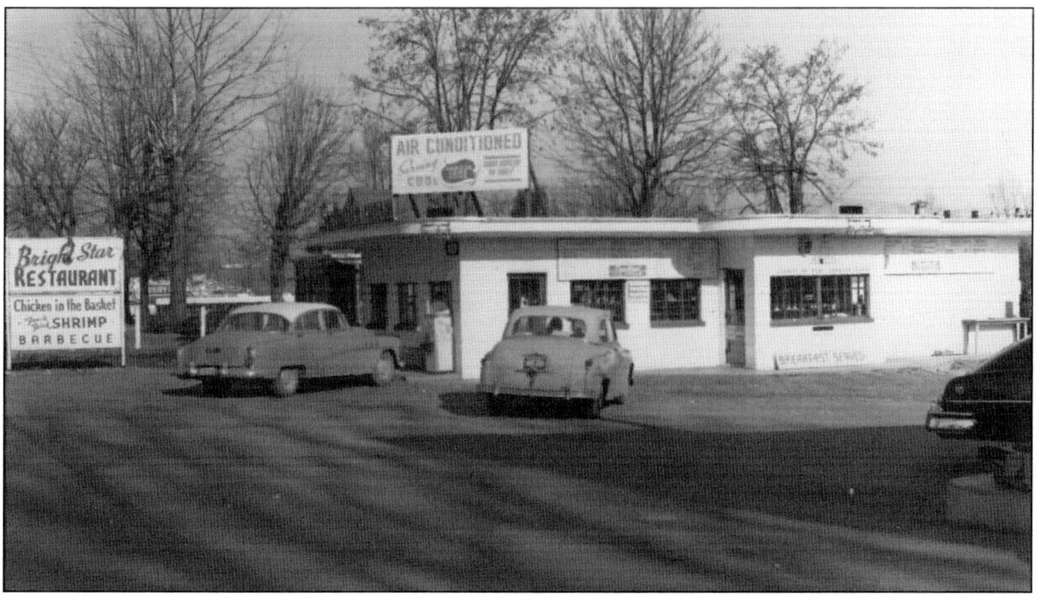

The Bright Star Restaurant, located at 1304 North Green Street, opened in the early 1950s and operated through the end of the decade. Managers included Lyle Magnus and Harry Fawcett. The restaurant featured chicken in the basket, French-fried shrimp, and barbecue, along with American Dairy products (Good Health to You!) and Sealtest ice cream. Customers who wished to dine in their cars were asked to turn their lights on for service. (Courtesy of Pam Austin.)

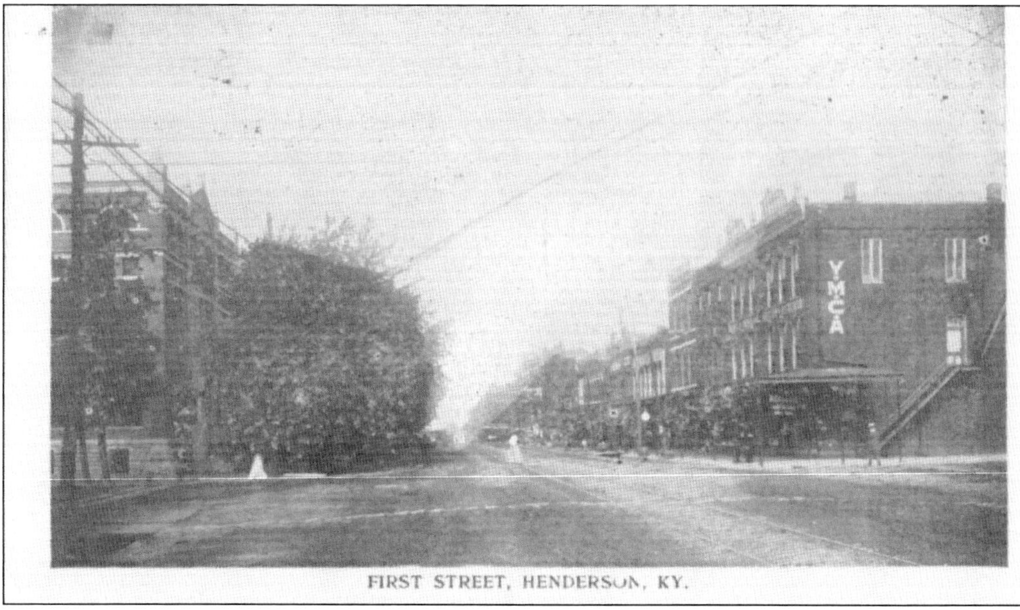

In 1894, efforts were begun to establish a local YMCA. The organization briefly met in a Presbyterian church on Second Street and then found quarters in the third floor (no longer in existence) of the Wise Building on the southeast corner of First and Elm Streets. After that, the YMCA moved diagonally across the street to the 1868 Merritt Building. The top postcard shows the YMCA, then open on the second floor at that location. (Courtesy of Henderson County Public Library.)

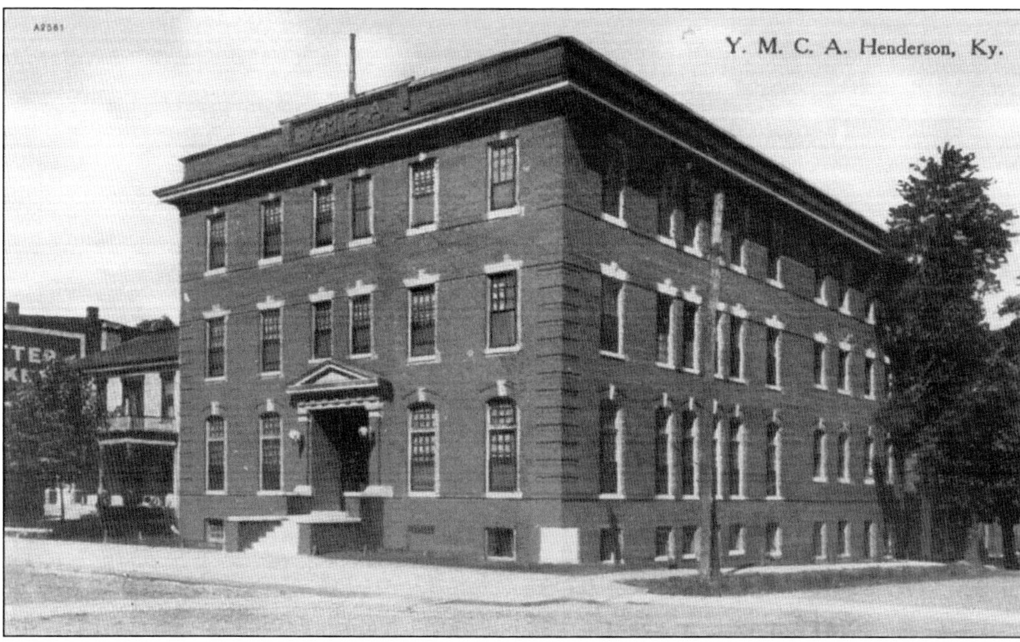

Construction of a permanent YMCA building, seen here at the southwest corner of Third and Main Streets, began in 1905. The cornerstone, complete with a history of the local YMCA, as well as the names of officials and building contributors, was laid in 1907. The building stood three stories tall and also had a basement.

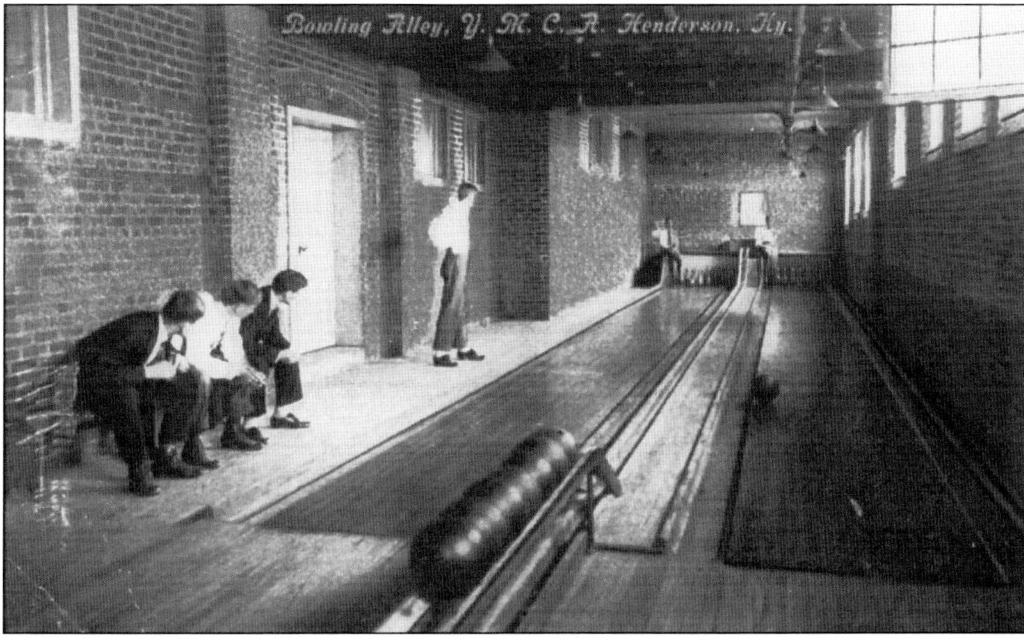

In the basement of the YMCA were the bowling alley, the baths, the members' dressing rooms, and the swimming pool. The main floor housed the lobby, reading rooms, offices, and a gymnasium. The assembly hall, kitchen, men's dormitory living rooms, and gym gallery were on the second floor, and living rooms for 30 were in the dormitory area on the third floor.

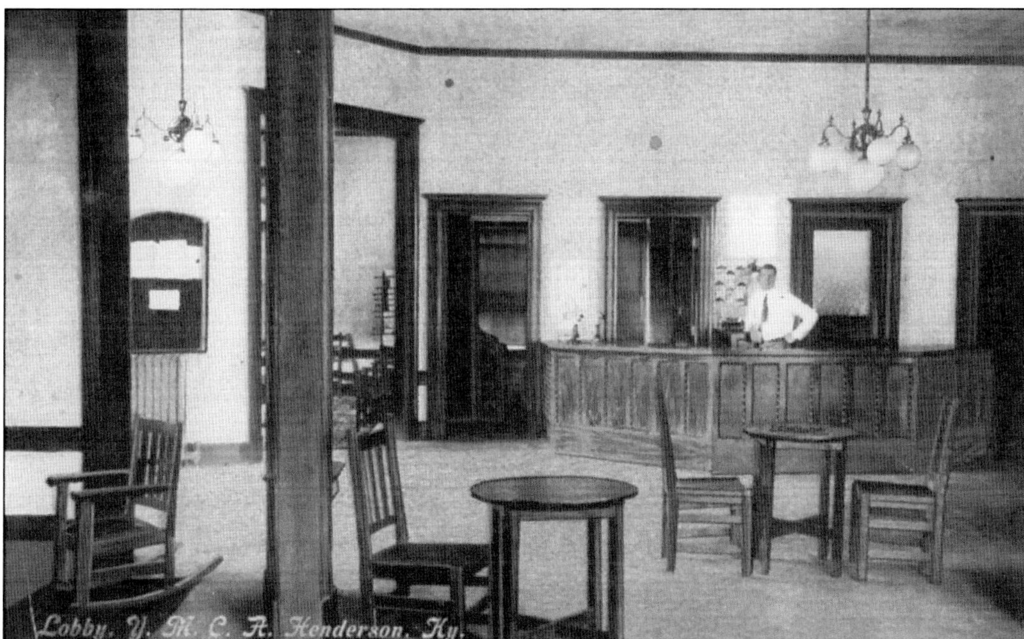

In later years, the YMCA sponsored various clubs for community members, as well as lessons in dancing, crafts, and weaving. After the 1973 construction of the current YMCA (located on Klutey Park Plaza), this building and an adjacent house were sold at auction in 1974 for $45,000. The building was demolished in July 1976.

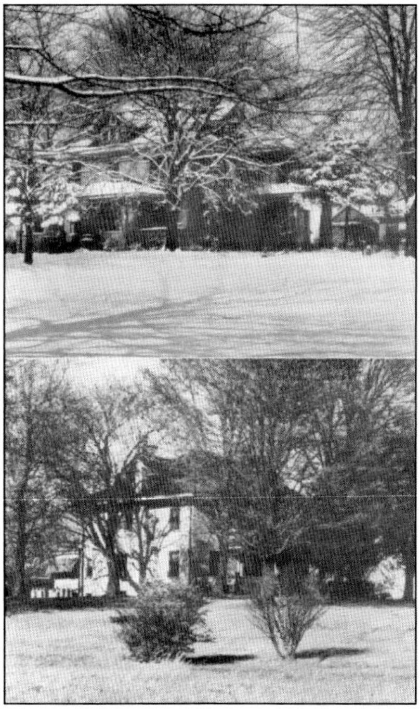

Located in a yellow brick house on U.S. 60 East, the Montgomery Spence Tea Room, established shortly after the end of World War II, was one of the area's most lavish places for parties. Elaborate details about the guests, menus, and decorations for social gatherings held in any of the Spence's three dining rooms were often recounted in the local newspaper.

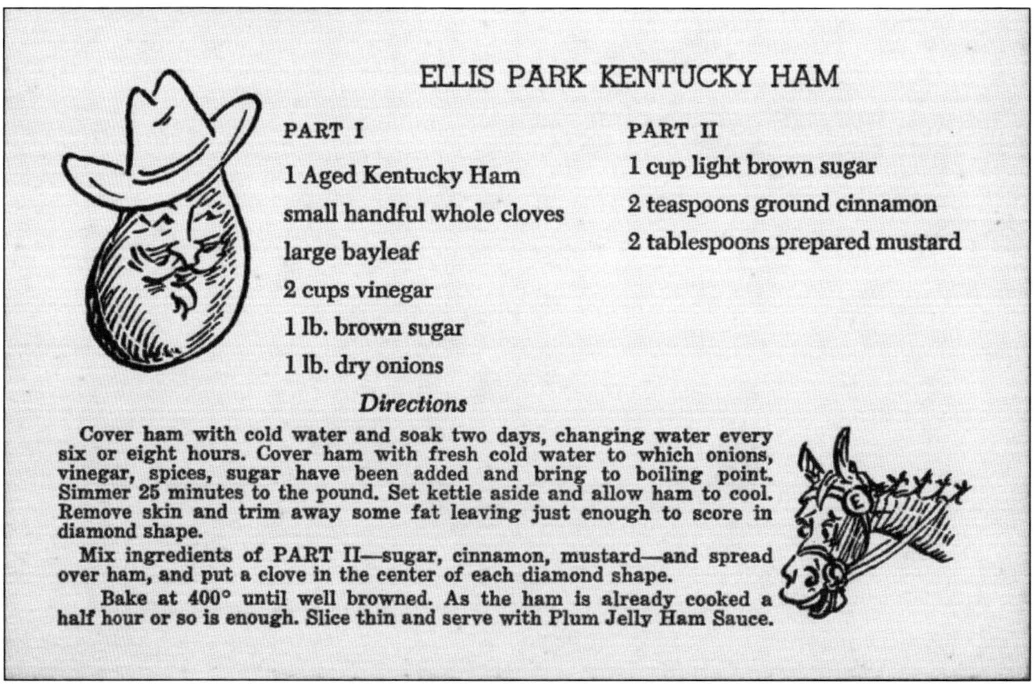

ELLIS PARK KENTUCKY HAM

PART I

1 Aged Kentucky Ham
small handful whole cloves
large bayleaf
2 cups vinegar
1 lb. brown sugar
1 lb. dry onions

PART II

1 cup light brown sugar
2 teaspoons ground cinnamon
2 tablespoons prepared mustard

Directions

Cover ham with cold water and soak two days, changing water every six or eight hours. Cover ham with fresh cold water to which onions, vinegar, spices, sugar have been added and bring to boiling point. Simmer 25 minutes to the pound. Set kettle aside and allow ham to cool. Remove skin and trim away some fat leaving just enough to score in diamond shape.

Mix ingredients of PART II—sugar, cinnamon, mustard—and spread over ham, and put a clove in the center of each diamond shape.

Bake at 400° until well browned. As the ham is already cooked a half hour or so is enough. Slice thin and serve with Plum Jelly Ham Sauce.

The Montgomery Spence Tea Room's owner, Judy Montgomery, offered customers a cookbook with recipes most often requested "by friends who have eaten the specialties here." In addition to Ellis Park Kentucky ham, other recipes included plum jelly sauce, chicken and dumplings, sweet Georgia Brown salad, grits soufflé, scalloped turkey, glazed orange beets, spicy baked cucumbers and onions, eggplant pudding, broccoli mold, Kentucky corn patch, Hawaiian fish basket, Kentucky bourbon pecan cake, and honey butter.

Three

Readin', 'Ritin', and 'Rithmatic

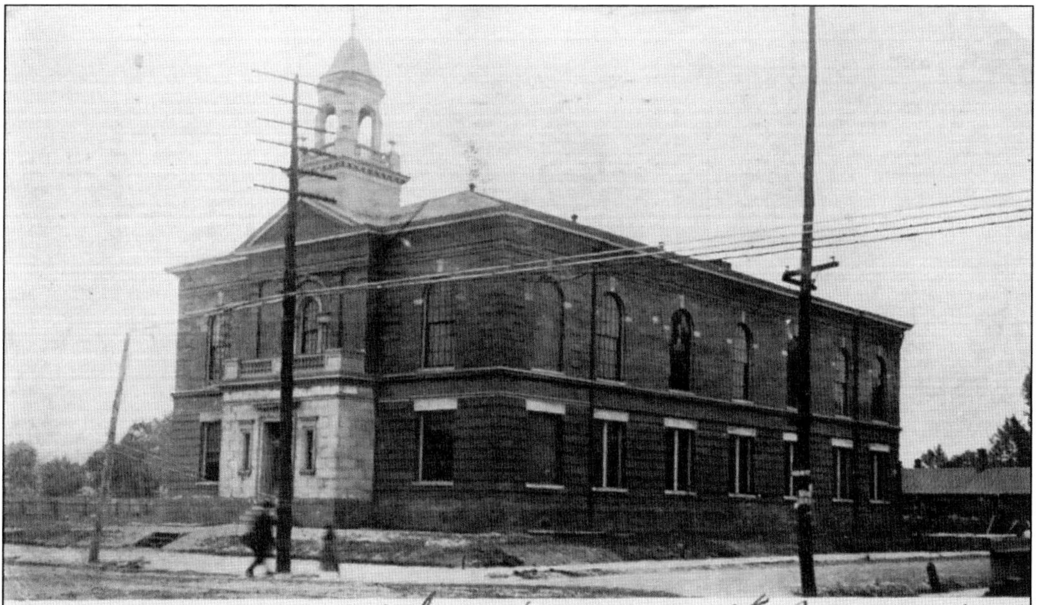

Henderson's first Catholic school was located in a three-room building on the corner of Third and Ingram Streets. After a 1903 fire destroyed the Robards Tobacco Company on the southeast corner of Second and Alves Streets, local Catholics purchased the site the following year and built a two-story redbrick school, complete with towering cupola, which opened on December 6, 1905. The school housed grades one through 12 until the 1950s and grades one through eight after the completion of a separate high school. The building was razed in 1969.

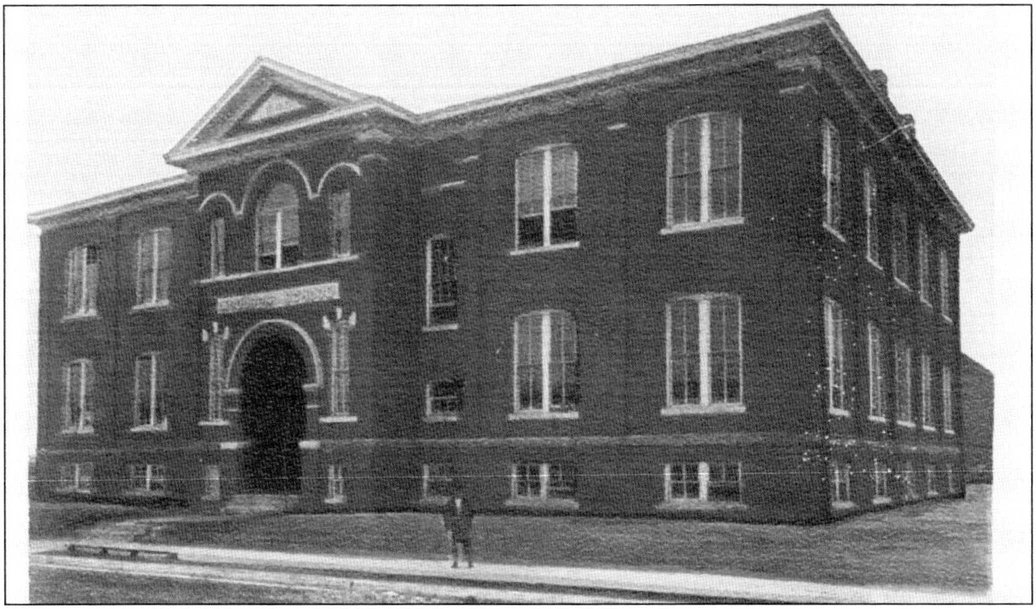

When Henderson annexed the Audubon area in 1905, East End residents requested a new school. The board of education spent $2,675 for a church and lot on the southeast corner of Letcher and Clay Streets and hired Spalding Trible as the architect of a new school. Construction began in 1906, and the school opened in 1907. At one time, it boasted the largest enrollment in the public school system. The school closed after its furnace exploded in 1976.

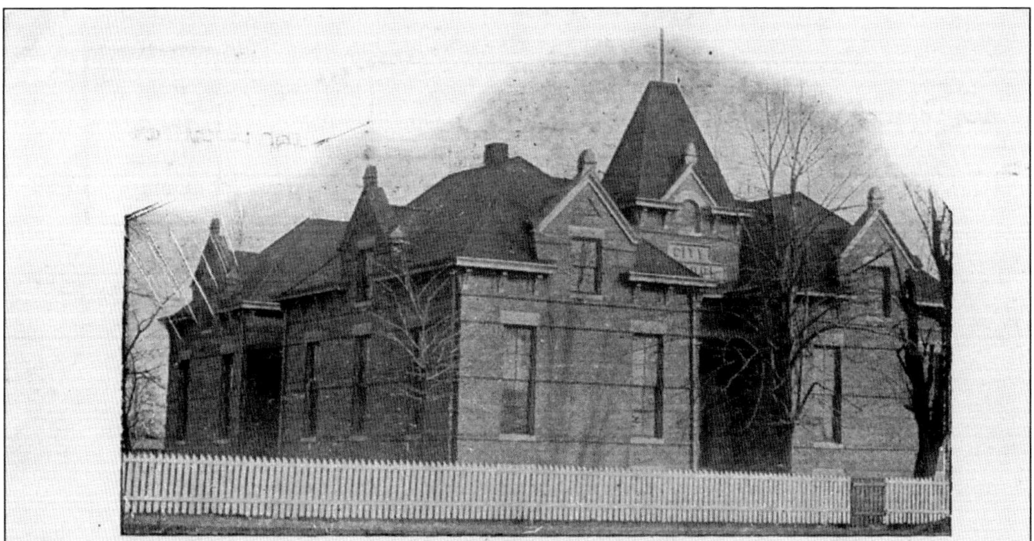

Public education for Henderson's African American students began with a two-room school that opened in 1872. This was followed by Eighth Street School, erected on the northeast corner of Eighth and North Elm Streets. In 1904, a room in this school became Kentucky's first public library for blacks; 100 volumes were sent to the school when Henderson's public library (initially segregated) opened downtown. This branch of the library continued to be used until 1950.

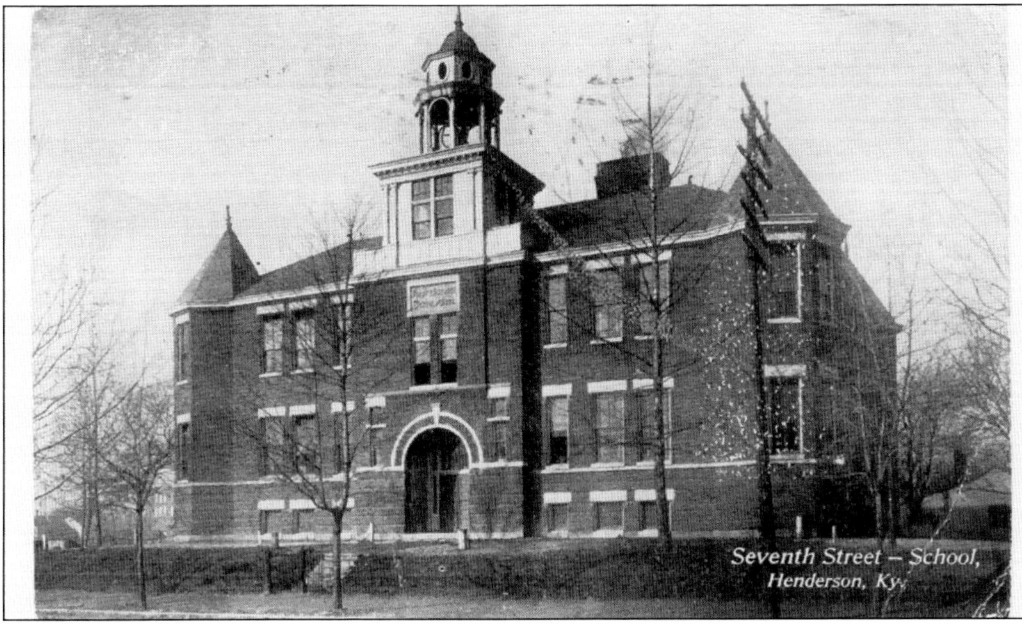

As the population of Henderson grew in the late 1800s, school officials determined that a second elementary school (in addition to the Center Street School) was necessary. Seventh Street School, located on the southwest corner of Seventh and North Green Streets, opened in 1893 with an enrollment of 250 pupils. The 1913 faculty included Lucy Rives, Josie Bennett, Abbie Cooper, Fannie Kimmel, Hazel King, Ellenora Buegger, Mrs. J. P. Smith, and Ethel Riley.

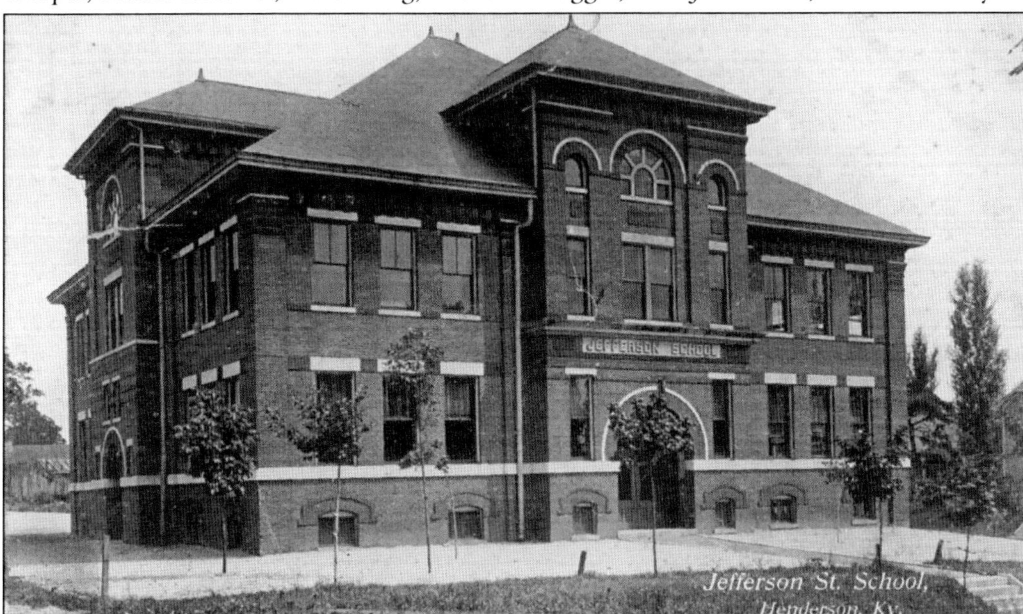

Even after the completion of a second elementary school, Henderson's population continued to grow, and soon a third school was deemed necessary. In 1901, Jefferson Street School opened on the southwest corner of Jefferson and South Elm Streets. In 1913, the faculty included Dazey Baskett, Corinna Satterfield, Frances Riley, Ruth Niles, Emma Arnett, Beulah Lockett, Mary Kellner, and Florence Clark (all unmarried).

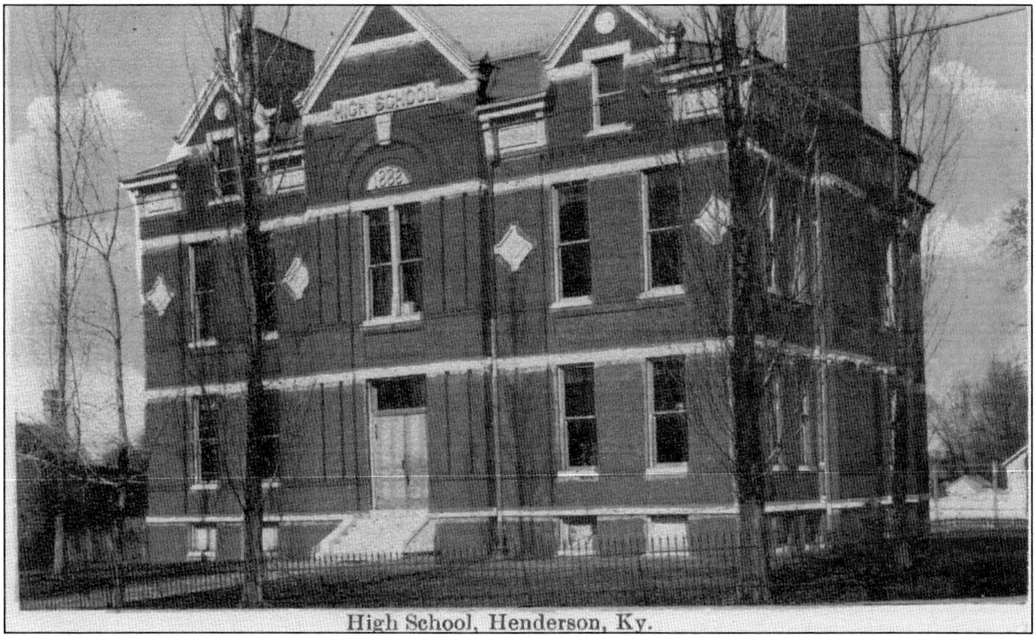

Opening in 1870, Henderson's first high school, which in the days of segregation served only white students, was a three-story brick building at the corner of Green and Center Streets. The school pictured on this postcard, Henderson High School, opened in 1888 at 531 Washington Street. After Barret Manual Training High School opened in 1910, this building served as a junior high and later as Central School, an elementary school. (Courtesy of Pam Austin.)

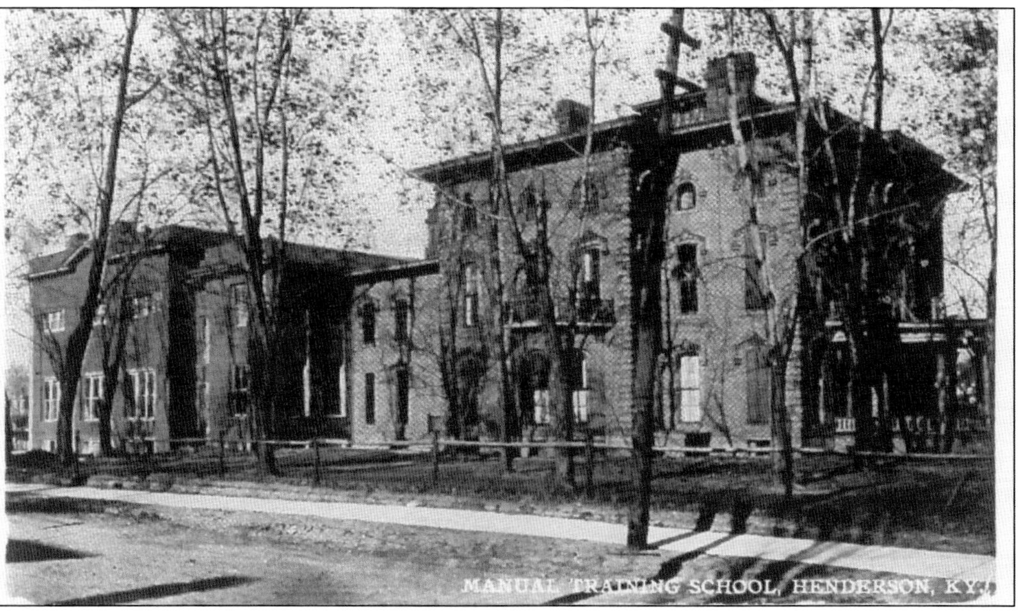

In 1906, Hendersonian James Barret surprised a local education committee by donating the deed to property on Adams and Washington Streets, including a stately 1865 three-story home that had been built for around $100,000. Barret's only stipulation for the deed was that the land be used for both manual training and teaching home economics. In 1910, the former Adams residence opened with 148 pupils as Barret Manual Training High School.

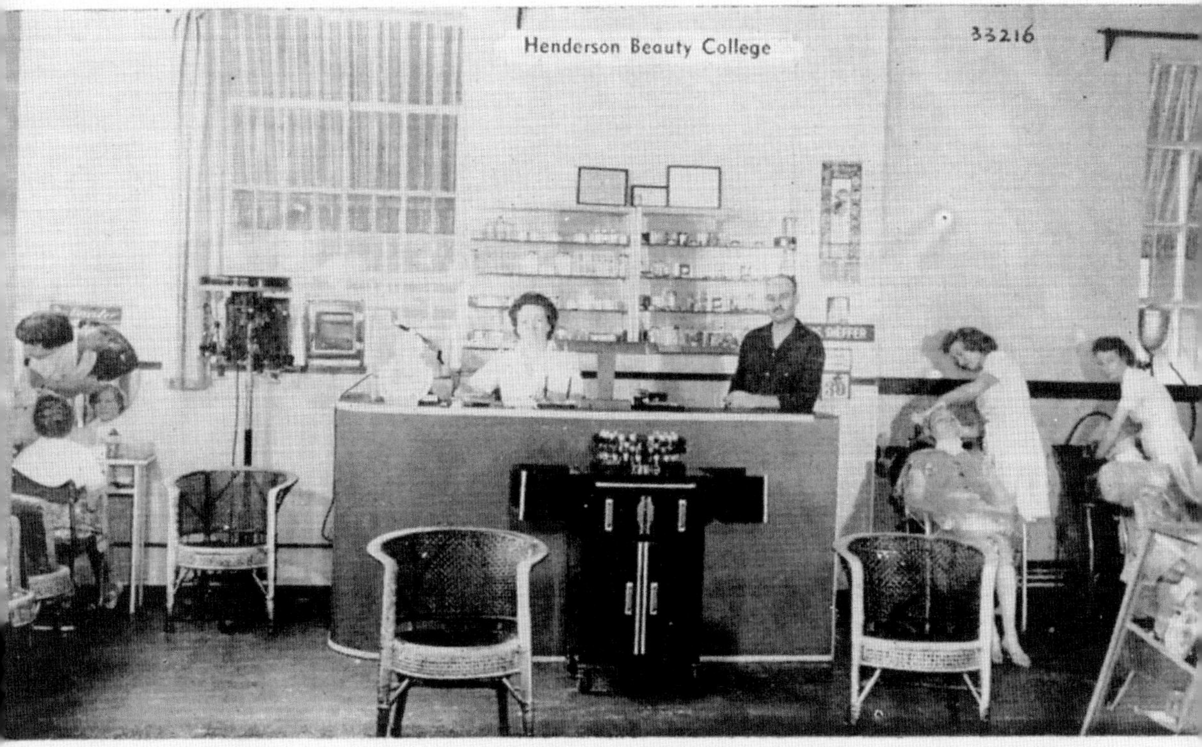

When it opened in 1943 at 129 North Elm Street, Henderson Beauty College encouraged students to enroll at any time. Tuition was $125 (cash), which included books and a manicure kit for the course that lasted 1,000 hours over five to six months. Applicants with an eighth-grade education were accepted with an IQ test approved by the board of examiners. The contact person at the college was Mrs. H. S. Sheffer.

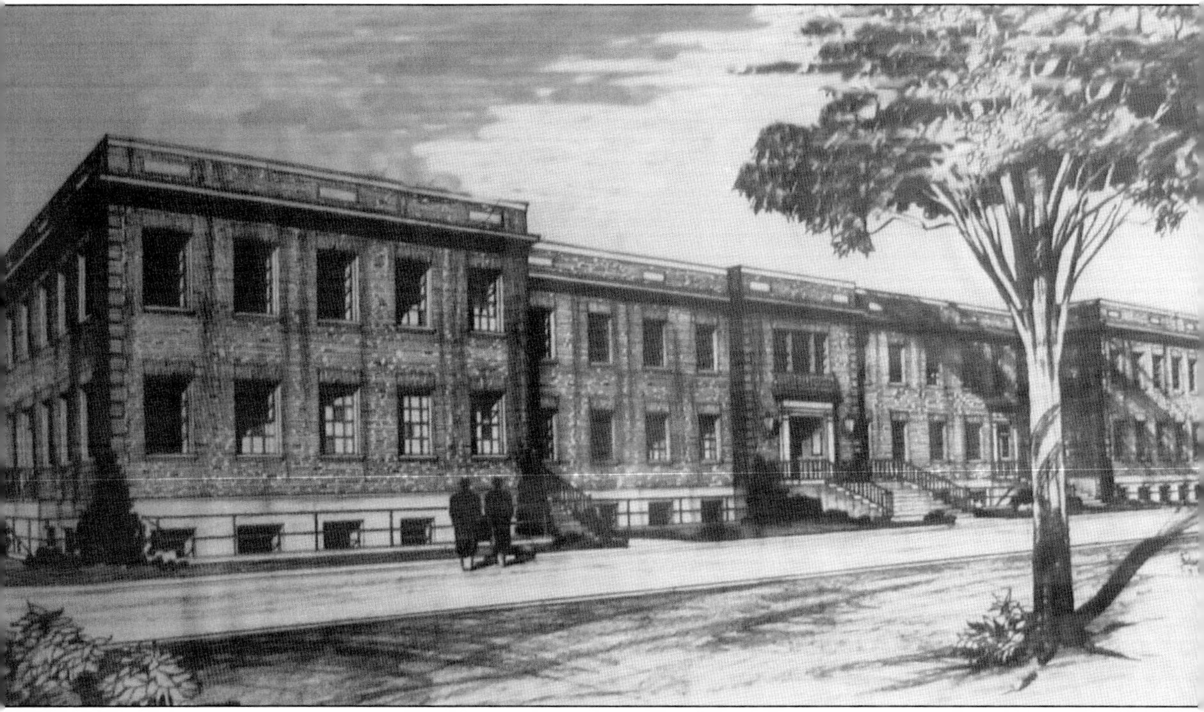

In July 1957, local citizens established a college foundation to solicit money for a site for a local college. Two months later, the University of Kentucky voted to approve a two-year college in Henderson, to be located on Highway 60 West. The school opened in 1960 as the University of Kentucky Northwest Center, and in 1964, it became the Henderson Community College. The institution is now part of the Kentucky Community and Technical College System. (Courtesy of Henderson Community College.)

Four

Working Hard

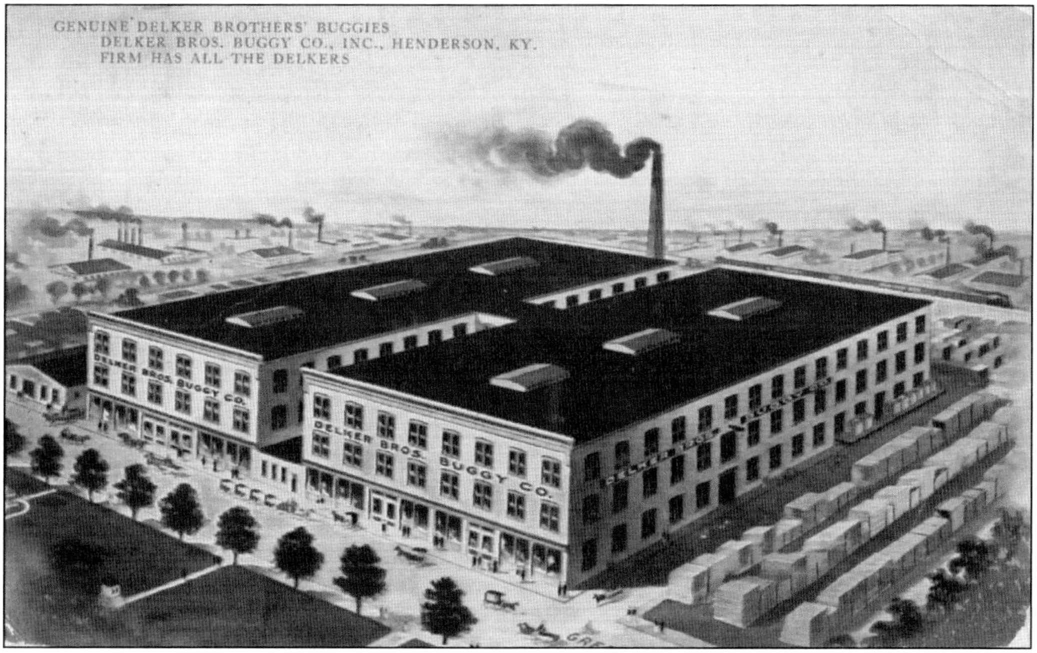

Delker Brothers Manufacturing Company was a huge three-story brick factory and outlying buildings located on the block bounded by Green, Ingram, First, and Second Streets with additional buildings at other sites in town. The company was organized in 1900 and was incorporated five years later. It began its history by manufacturing light buggies, most of which were shipped to markets in the South. In 1913, its average number of employees was 150. After the introduction of automobiles, the buggy business dwindled, and the company switched to the production of fine-quality hardwood maple furniture in an early American style. The factory closed in 1973.

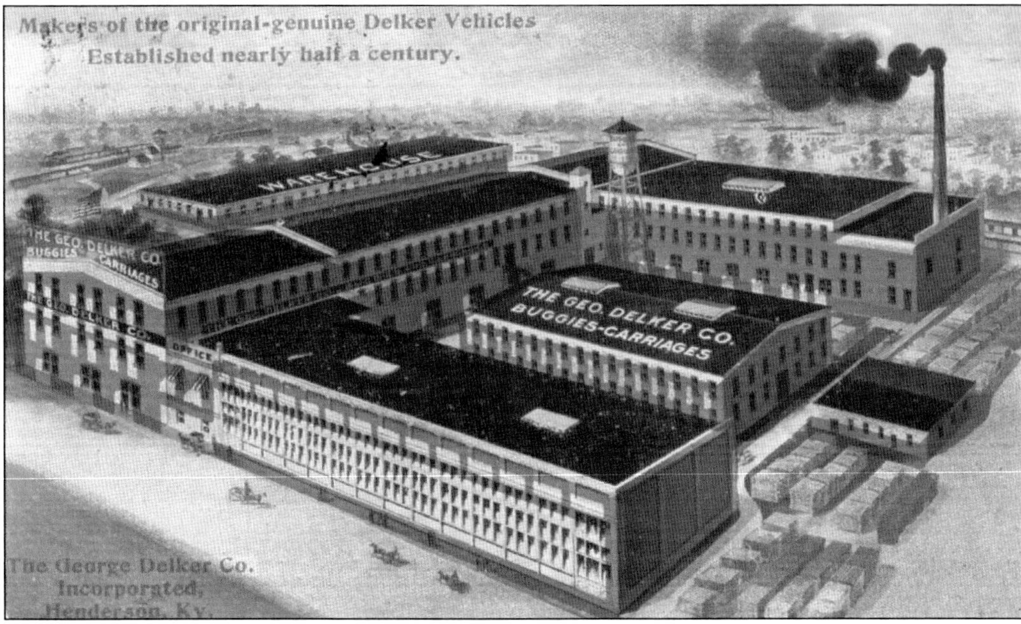

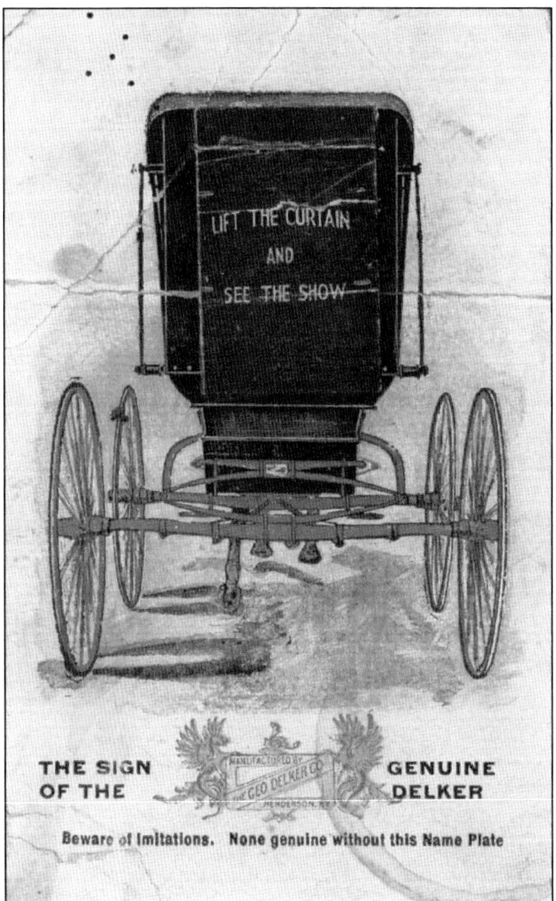

In 1863, George Delker and others began the buggy-manufacturing business that eventually was incorporated in 1887 as the George Delker Company. Just before the turn of the 20th century, the company was producing around 25 buggies each day. By 1904, it had outgrown its building in the middle of the east side of North Elm Street between First and Second Streets and had moved to the location seen here on East Fourth Street near Union Station. At its new location, the company occupied about five acres of ground with a total floor space of about 125,000 square feet. In 1922, the production of buggies was replaced with that of furniture. The company closed in 1929.

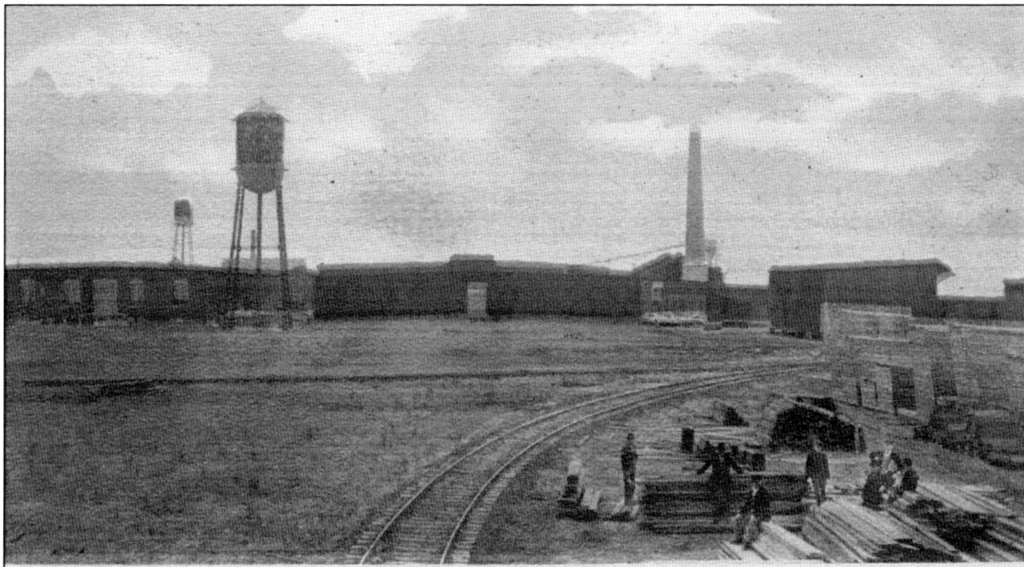

Coquillard Wagon Works, Henderson, Ky.

In the early 1900s, several local merchants purchased stock in the Coquillard Wagon Works, then based in Fort Wayne, and hired local architect Walter Brashear to design a plant, which opened in 1903 on Atkinson Street. Soon the plant manufactured 300 horse-drawn wagons annually. After Coquillard closed, the building housed the H. J. Heinz Company and then the Atlas Tack Corporation. Fire destroyed the building in 1978. (Courtesy of Pam Austin.)

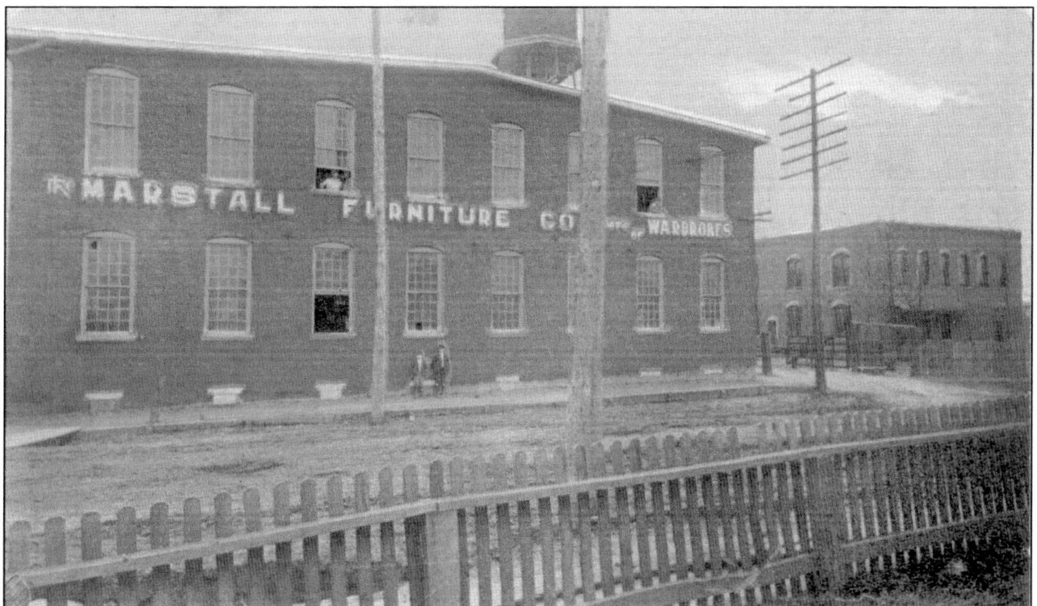

The Marstall Furniture Co., Henderson, Ky.

In 1895, Herman Marstall reorganized and incorporated his furniture business, specializing in the manufacture of medium and better grades of wardrobes. By 1913, the Audubon-area business was spread across seven acres and housed a number of buildings with a total floor space of nearly 60,000 square feet and employed 75 men. The company's motto was "Not the Cheapest, but the Best." (Courtesy of Henderson County Public Library.)

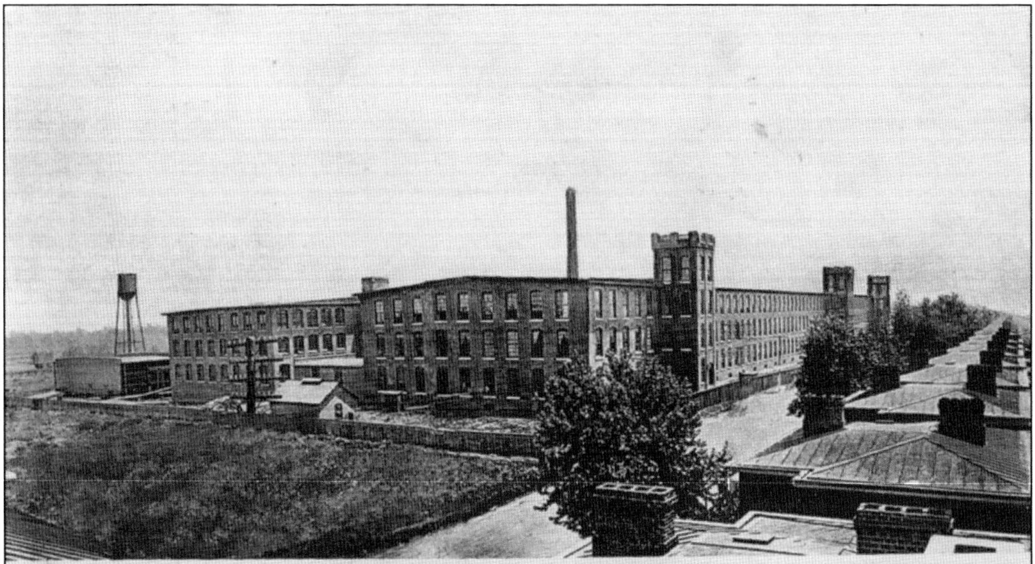

Henderson Cotton Mills. Henderson, Ky.

At one time, the Henderson Cotton Mills was both the largest (covering almost 13 acres in the 1300 block of Washington Street) and the oldest manufacturing plant in Henderson. In its heyday, the mill employed nearly 1,000 people. The business continued until the early 1930s. In 1937, the Bear Brand Hosiery Company—impressed by the fact that Henderson had not suffered damage during the infamous 1937 flood—purchased the plant (along with nine of the nearby workers' houses) and replaced its dated equipment with new hosiery machinery. When the plant reopened in 1937, it employed only 20 people, but that number rose to more than 300 by the early 1950s. In 1969, Elmer Korth bought the mill and operated it under the name the Audubon Hosiery Mill until it finally closed in 1982. The building was razed in the mid-1980s.

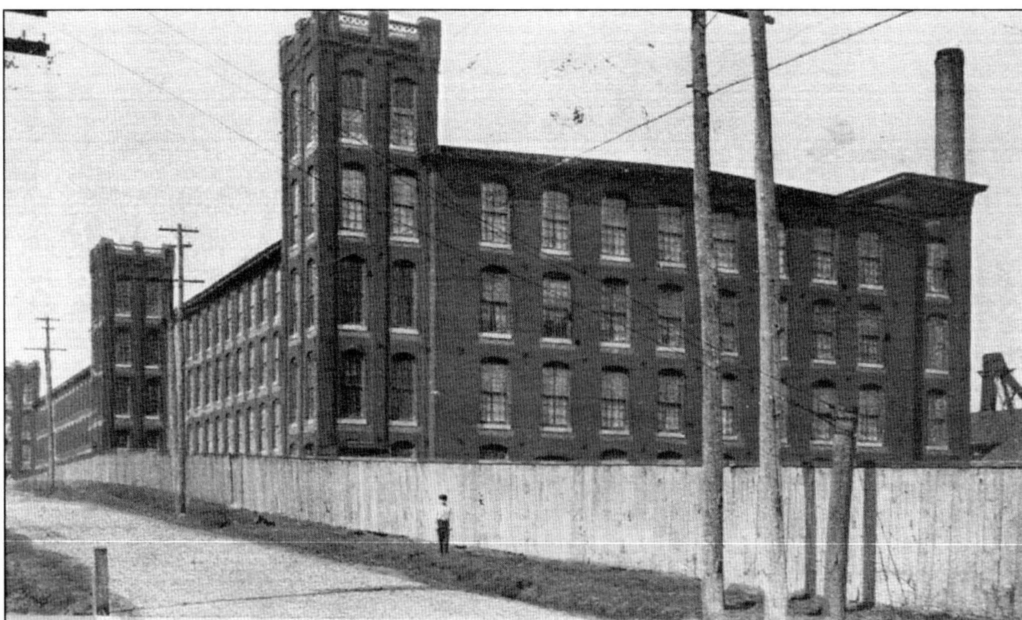

Henderson Cotton Mills, Henderson, Ky.

Prior to the establishment of a city waterworks, water was obtained from cisterns or wells, or it was hauled from the river at $1 a barrel. In the fall of 1872, a petition was presented to Henderson's city council asking that body to establish a system of water supply for the town. Two years later, on August 29, 1874, the city paid $7,438 to W. T. and John H. Barret, executors of the A. B. Barret estate, for grounds located on the Ohio River near the present Methodist Hospital. The site was in an area that came to be known as Water Works Park. On July 1, 1876, the city first began piping water, but not until 1915 did the plant begin treating water from the Ohio River.

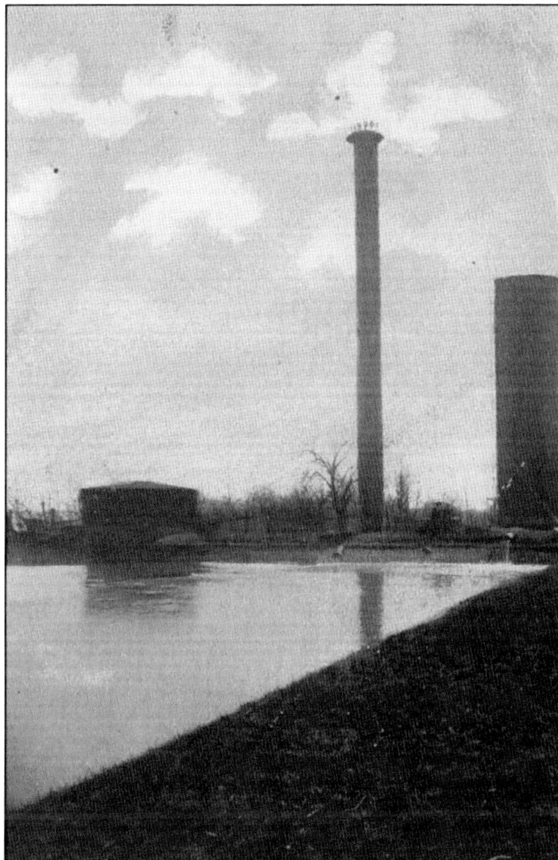

City Water Co. Reservoir and Stand Pipe, Henderson, Ky

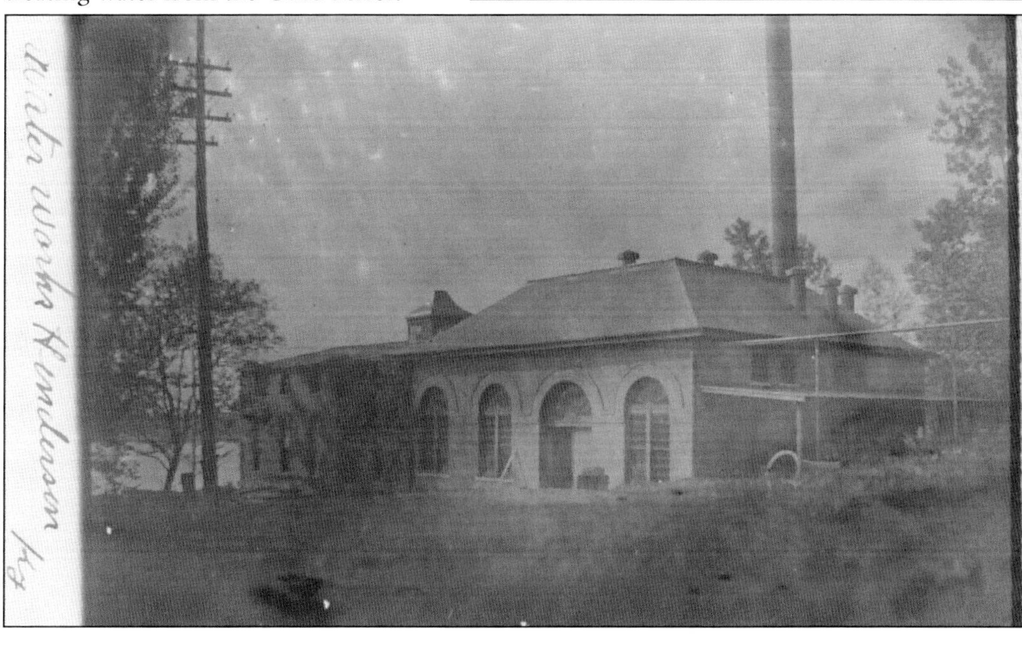

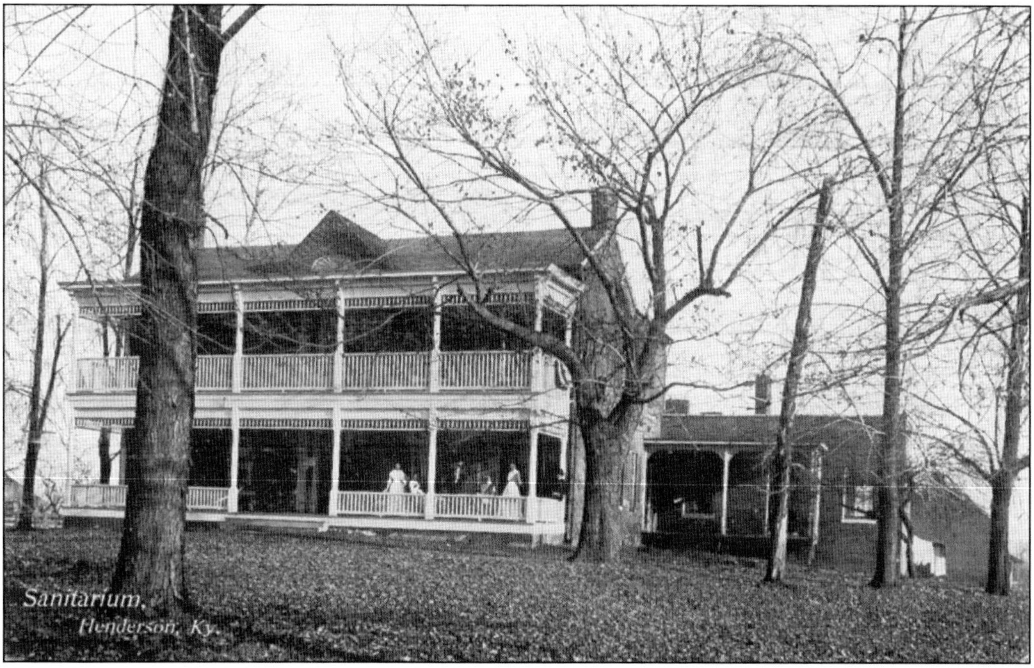

At various times labeled both a hospital and a sanitarium, this extant Federal structure at 424 Ray Street was built in the early 1850s by Capt. William B. Vanzandt (Henderson's first mayor) along with three teenage apprentices and six slaves. Its architecture is said to have helped patients feel as if they were in a private home. Today it has been restored and serves as apartments.

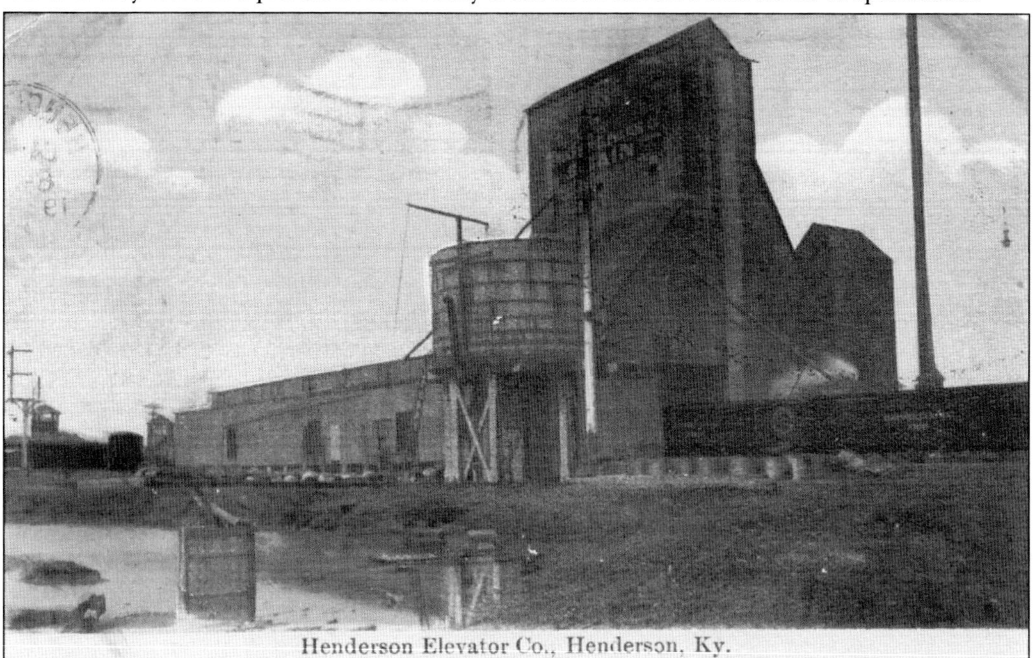

The Henderson Elevator Company was located on the north side of Third Street east of Clark Street and the railroad tracks, which are visible on the left. In this postcard, postmarked 1912, an Illinois Central railroad car looks poised to leave, loaded with grain from the company.

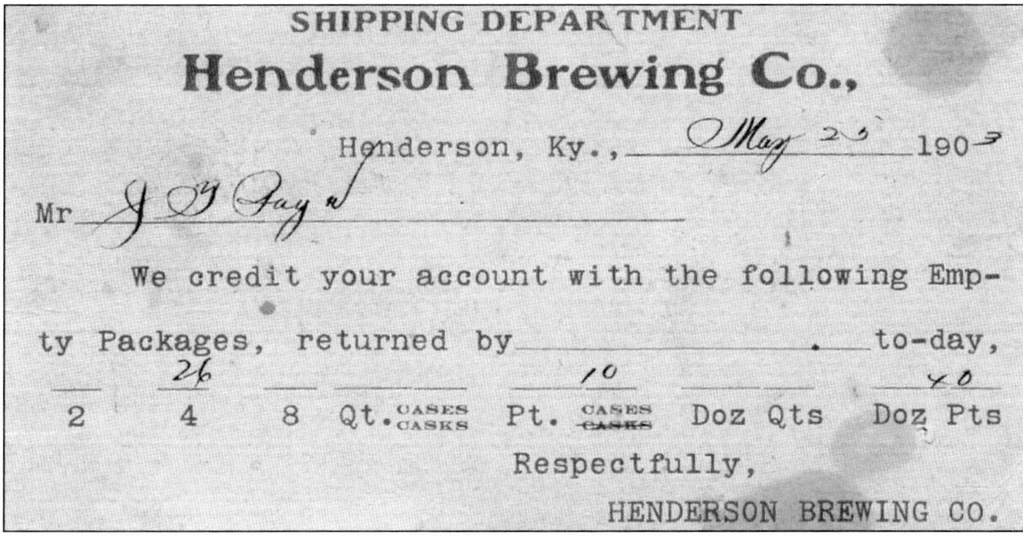

SHIPPING DEPARTMENT

Henderson Brewing Co.,

Henderson, Ky., May 25 1903

Mr J G Gay

We credit your account with the following Empty Packages, returned by ________ to-day,

2	4	8	Qt. CASES CASKS	Pt. CASES ~~CASKS~~	Doz Qts	Doz Pts
	26			10		40

Respectfully,

HENDERSON BREWING CO.

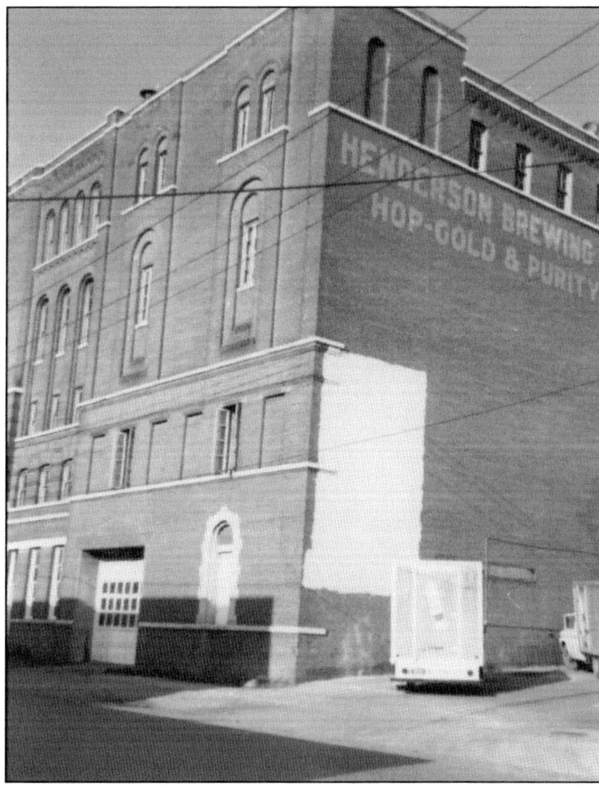

In the 1850s, the Henderson Brewing Company began operating at North Main and Eighth Streets. The business prospered, and in the late 1890s, it moved to the larger and more modern brick, stone, and steel plant—complete with 100-foot smokestack—shown here. The building covered half the city block on the southeast corner of North Water and Fifth Streets. Initially the brewery was run by Jacob Reutinger and George Klauder; later the ownership changed to Reutinger and a Mr. Isefelder. In 1885, a boiler explosion caused the company to cease operations, and two years later, the company was purchased by George Devlin. Beers produced by the company were marketed under the Sphinx brand with individual beers named "Purity" (made with Bohemian hops and Canadian malt) and "Hop Gold" (made with New York hops and American malt). The building was demolished in 1982.

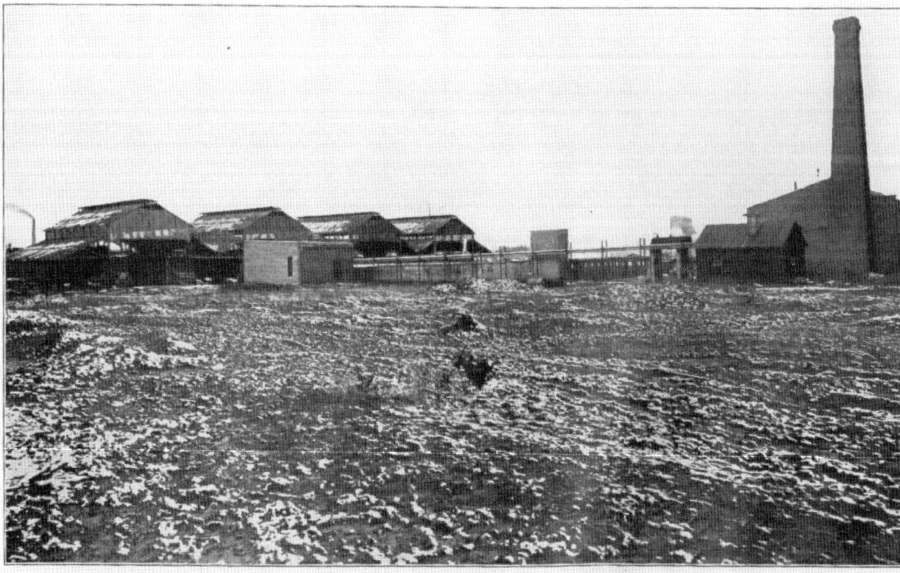

Kleymeyer & Klutey Brick Yards

Established shortly after the end of the Civil War, the Kleymeyer and Klutey Brick and Tile Works was one of the largest companies of its kind in this part of the country. The company operated two yards—a 100-acre yard off Second Street and a 50-acre yard on Corydon Road. The two plants had a capacity of about 10 million bricks a year and averaged 60,000 feet of tile a day.

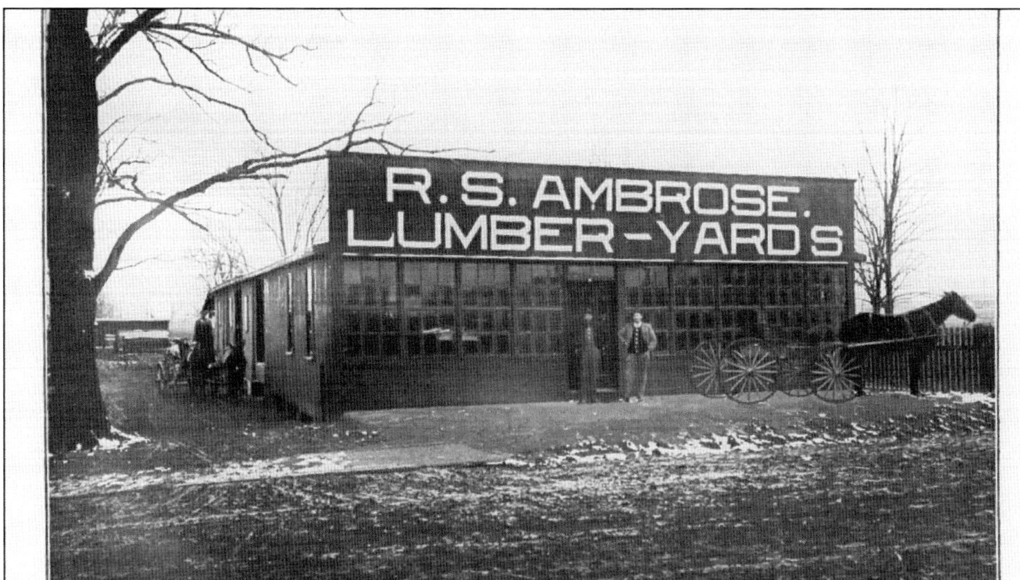

The R. S. Ambrose Lumber Yards was located on Madisonville Road in the Weaverton section of Henderson. It was established around the beginning of the 20th century by R. S. Ambrose (touted in advertisements of the day as "a young man of advanced ideas" who "sells his goods on their merits, and at the lowest possible price commensurate with quality"). The lumberyards included an office, a warehouse, a mill, covered sheds, and stables.

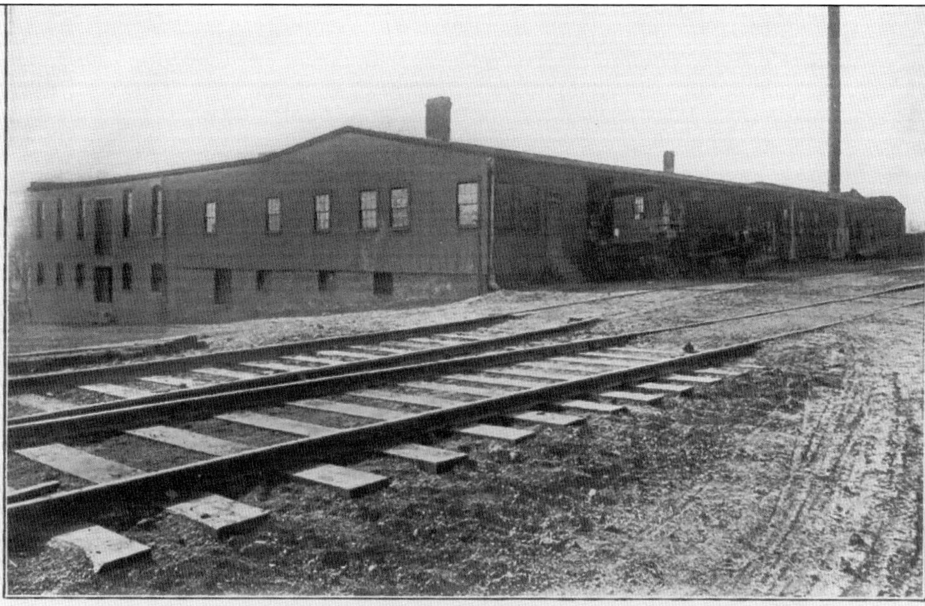

Anderson Box and Basket Company

Located on the corner of Alves and Vine Streets, the Anderson Box and Basket Company, Inc., manufactured woven wire receptacles and shipping cases for bankers, launderers, grocers, and meat markets, as well as baskets for offices and clothes. The company boasted that it had "probably done more to advertise the city of Henderson than any one concern here, as our goods are used practically throughout the entire country."

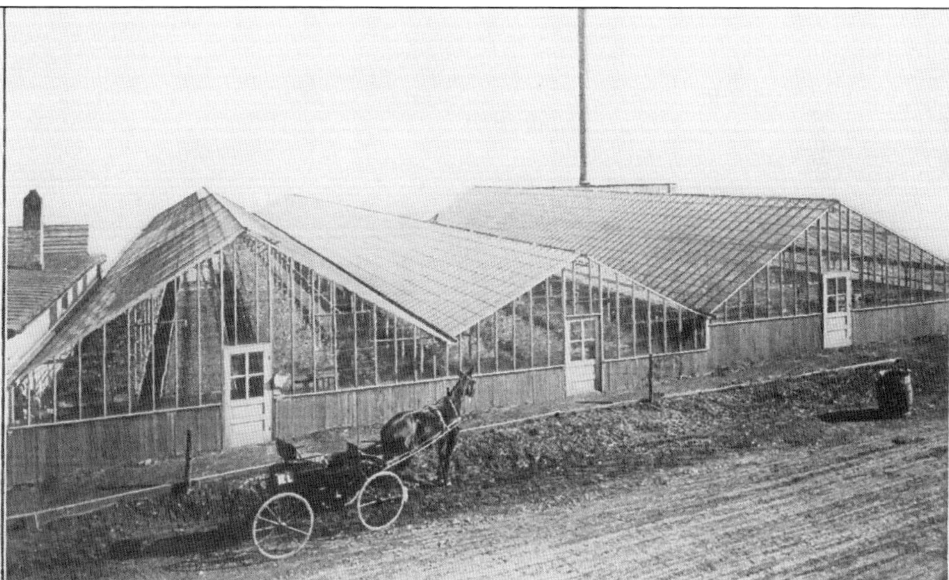

The Morgan Floral Company was incorporated in 1907, and the next year, the company erected its glass greenhouses, covering almost 19,000 square feet, and its office on the corner of Second and Clark Streets, a block from the new Union railroad station. The company advertised that it grew "all descriptions of flowering plants, shrubs, and ferns" with particular attention to the cultivation of carnations.

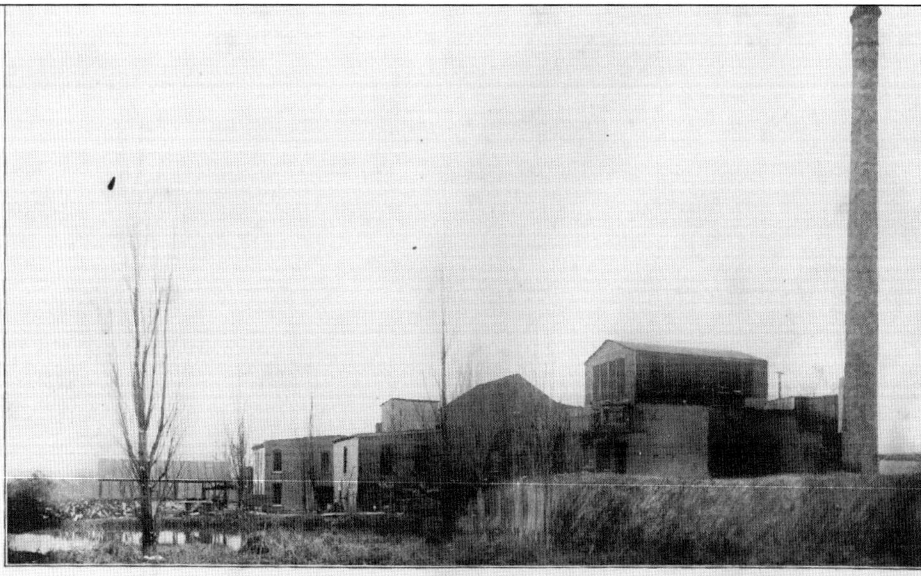

Eckert Meat Company

Established in 1871 by Joseph Eckert, this wholesale meat company grew from modest means and moved in the early 1880s to its location around the 1400 block of South Green Street. By 1913, the brick plant covered almost 35,000 square feet and could accommodate 150 hogs and 30 head of cattle in a day in the ultimate manufacture of meats, sausages, and lard. To store meat freshly, the company maintained its own ice plant.

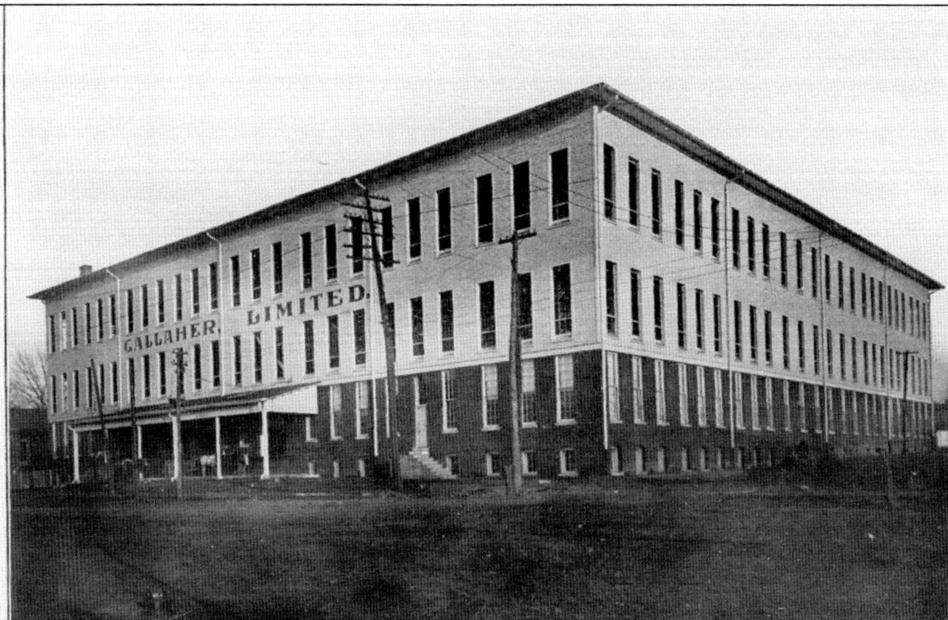

This is the Henderson branch of the Gallaher Limited tobacco company, which had headquarters in Belfast, Ireland. William Michaels, the nephew of company owner Thomas Gallaher, managed the Henderson plant. The plant's capacity was around six million pounds a year, and that amount was shipped from Henderson to Belfast and from there to a number of other foreign factories.

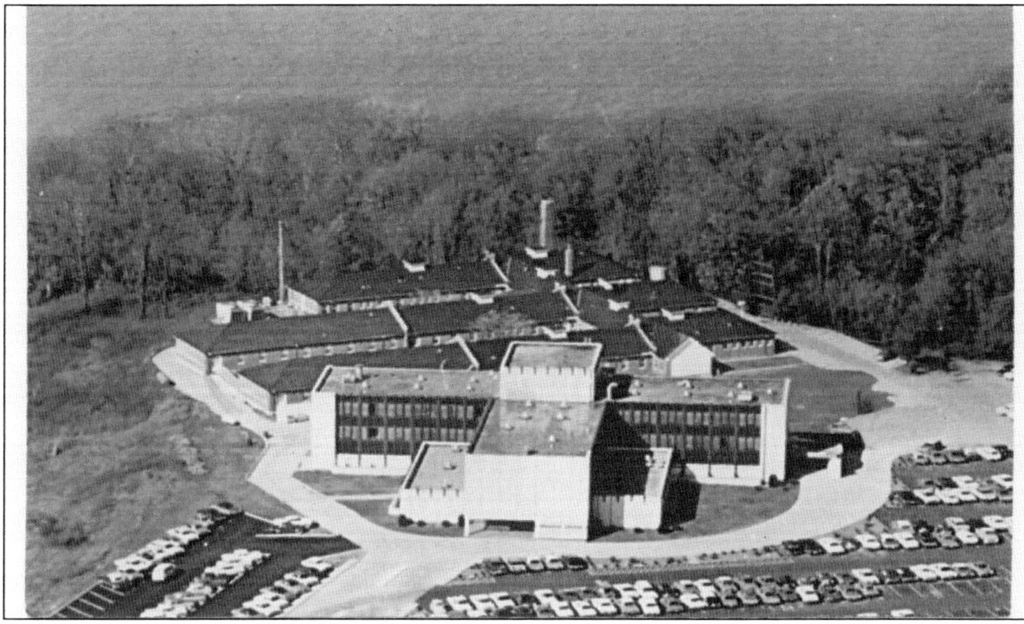

In 1874, the city spent $7,438 and purchased almost 17 acres of land known as Water Works Park from the estate of A. B. Barret. Shortly after the end of World War II, the 60-bed Henderson Hospital was erected on the site that spans the area bounded by Twelfth Street, Atkinson Park, Water Street, and Elm Street. Henderson Hospital, built with help from the federal government, is in the background of the above postcard. In the foreground is Community Methodist Hospital, "a community owned–United Methodist Conference operated Health Care Center," which was completed in 1968. In the bottom card are pictured an x-ray room (top left), a patient's room (top right), and the front lobby (bottom) of Community Methodist Hospital. (Below, courtesy of Pam Austin.)

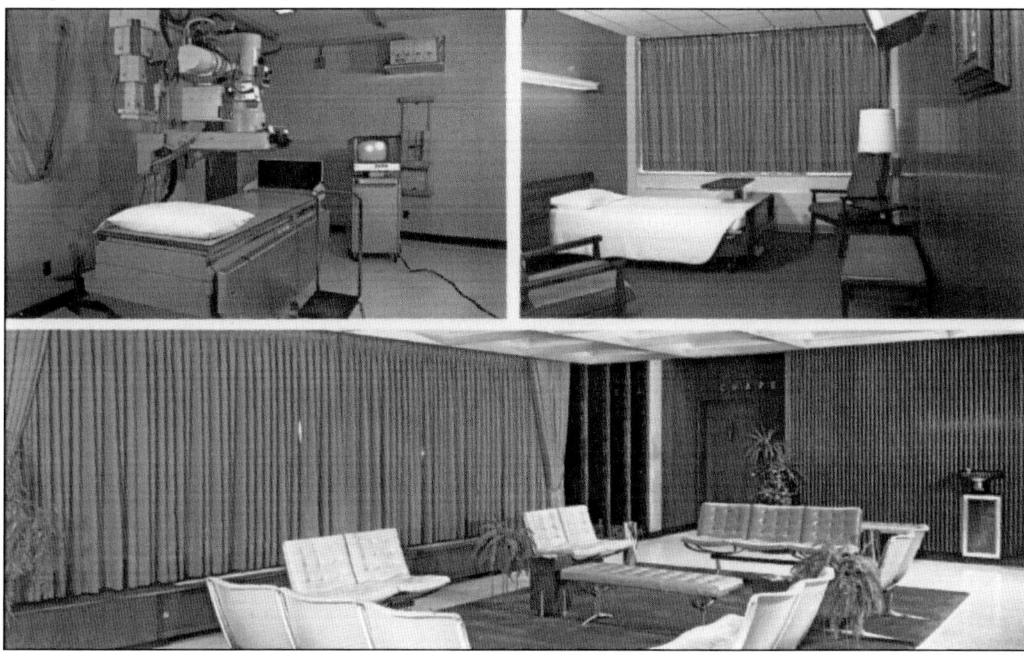

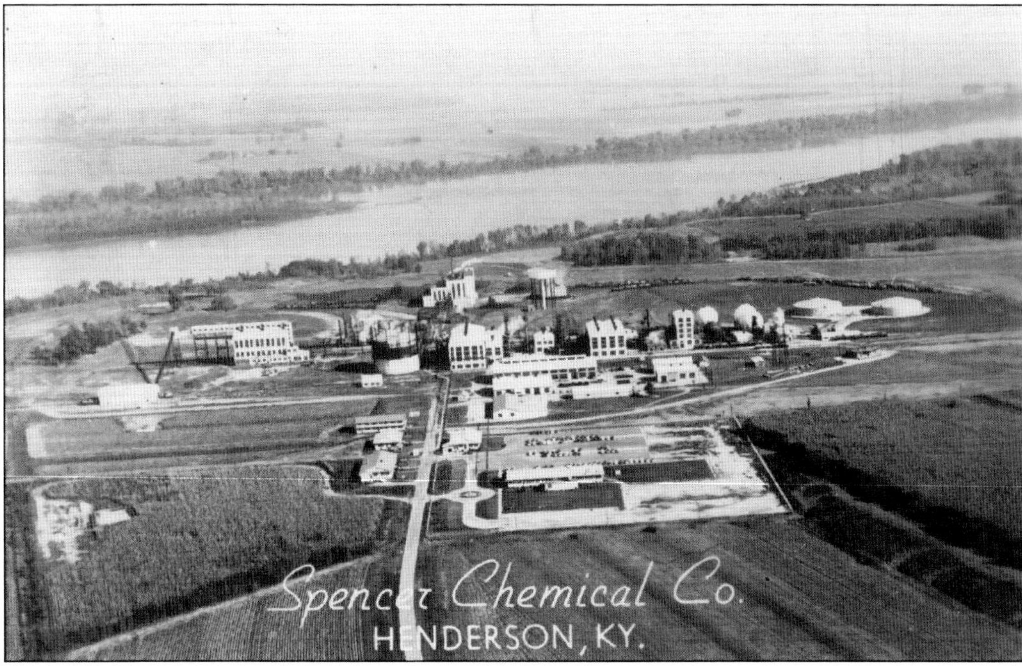

Five years after the end of World War II, Spencer Chemical bought the ammonia plant that had been built by the federal government during the war. After spending $3 million to renovate the factory, Spencer Chemical became a leading area employer for the next 18 years. In 1968, the company was sold to Gulf Oil. Customs Resin acquired the plant in 1978 and remains there today.

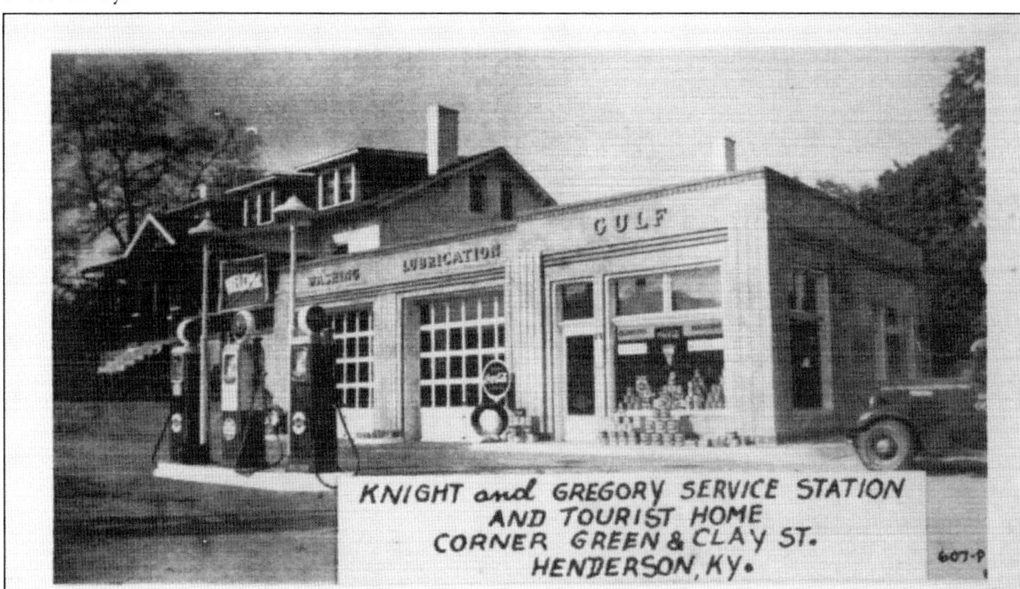

The Knight and Gregory Service Station and Tourist Home was a frequent stop for many motorists who were traveling major highways through Henderson. Located at 329 South Green Street, it opened in the late 1930s and, under different ownerships, was in business for most of the 20th century.

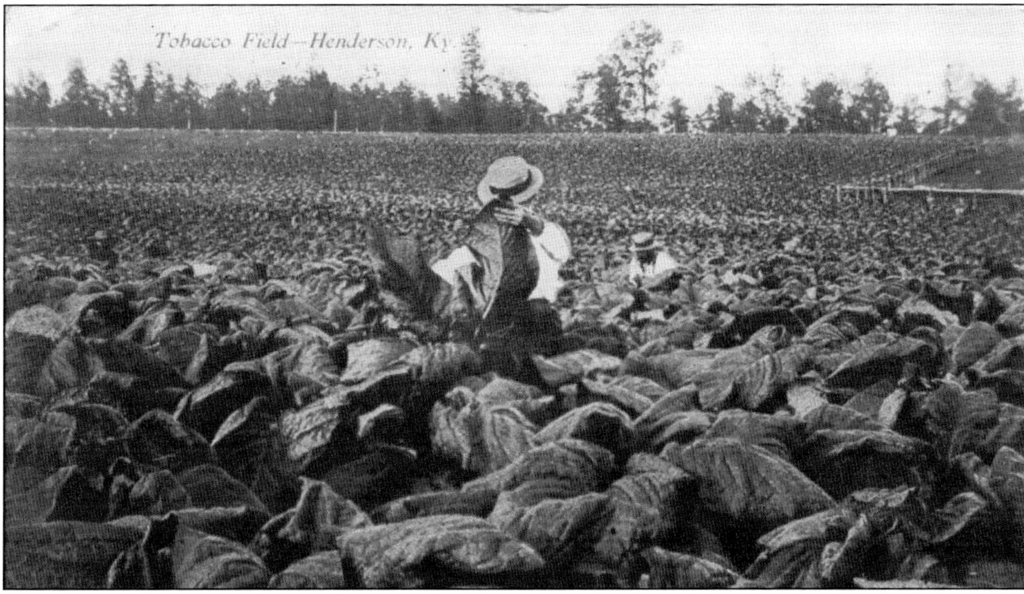

Tobacco has been an integral part of Henderson's history almost since the town was founded. In 1801, Henderson was designated to be one of the state's new tobacco inspection points. By the end of the 1890s, fifty-one tobacco processing factories or stemmeries were located in the county. Dark tobacco, used for smoking and chewing, was grown in Henderson County on many farms, especially prior to World War I.

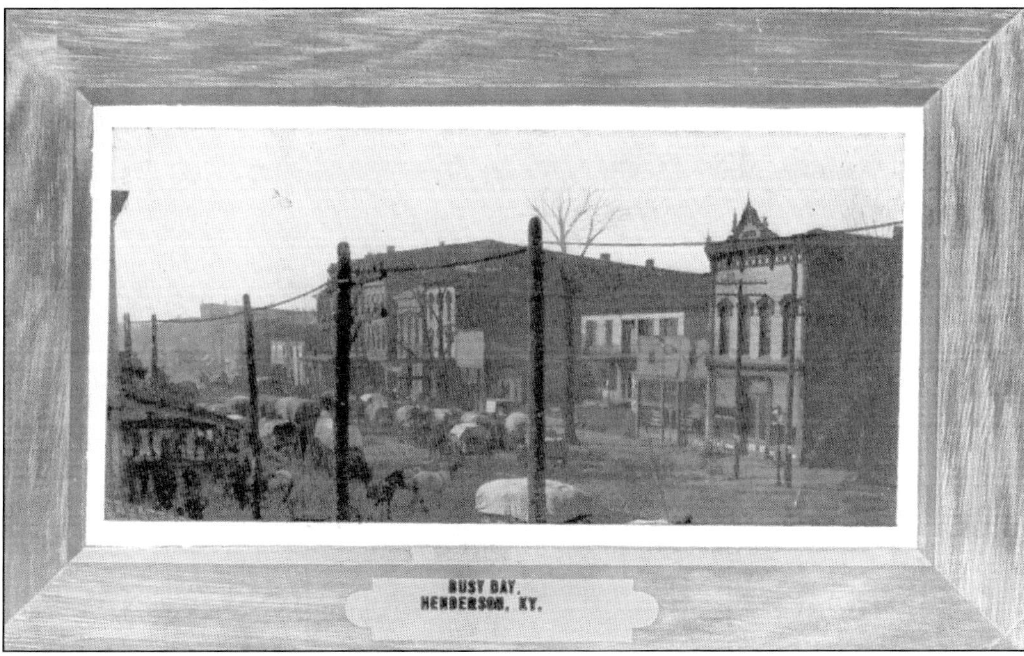

When harvested, tobacco was put up in local factories before being sent to New Orleans and then overseas, especially to markets in Liverpool, England, and Glasgow, Scotland. Tobacco became the dominant industry in Henderson, and demand for local tobacco resulted in Henderson's status as having one of the largest per capita incomes of any town in the United States. This scene shows tobacco wagons on Main Street, looking south from Third Street.

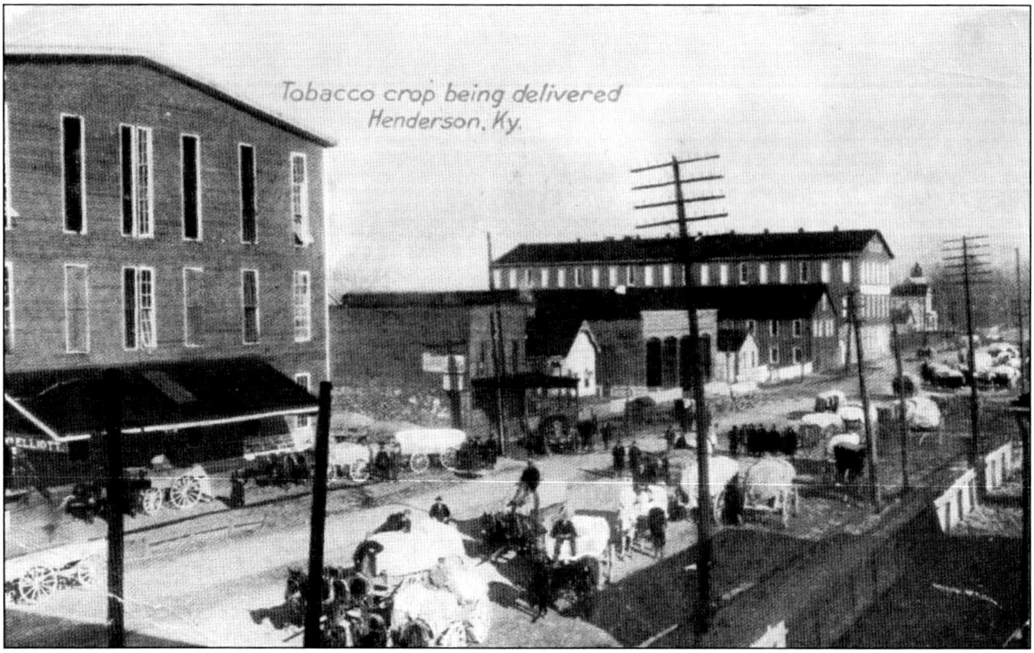

Tobacco was first shipped by hogshead down the Ohio River, but stemmeries (facilities that processed tobacco to produce re-dried tobacco as a customer specified) and factories in Henderson were soon erected. Farmers delivered their crops to these businesses by wagon. This scene, dated before 1909, shows wagons lined up near the William Elliott Tobacco Factory on the west side of South Main Street between Dixon and Jefferson Streets.

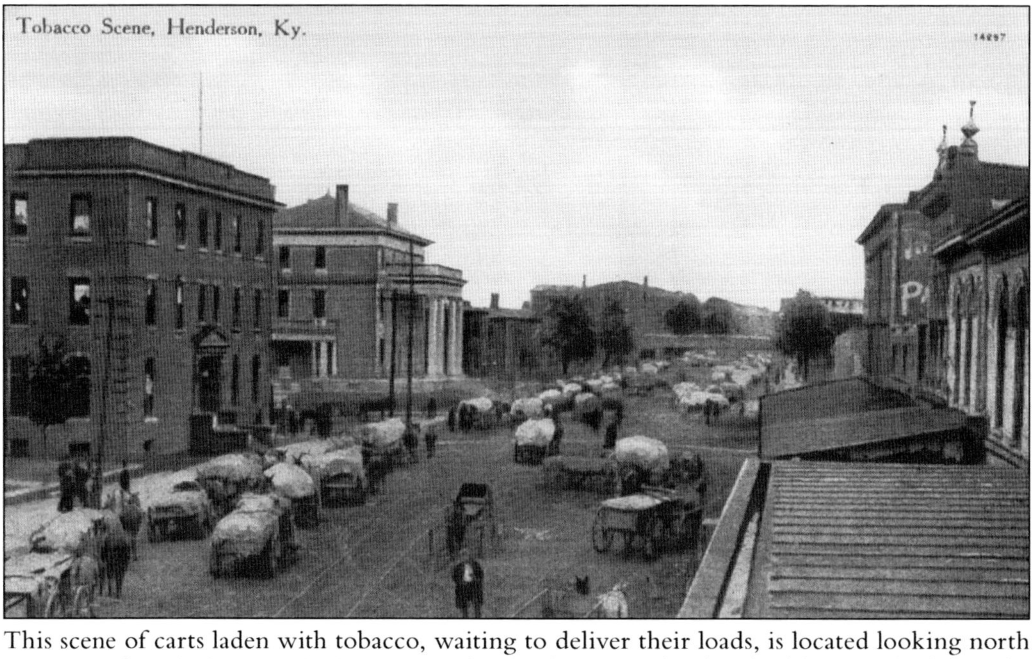

This scene of carts laden with tobacco, waiting to deliver their loads, is located looking north on unpaved Main Street at its juncture with Third Street. The first building on the left is the YMCA, and the second one is the Elks Lodge. The railroad overpass is in the far right, and a tobacco warehouse on Fifth and Main Streets sits past the railroad overpass.

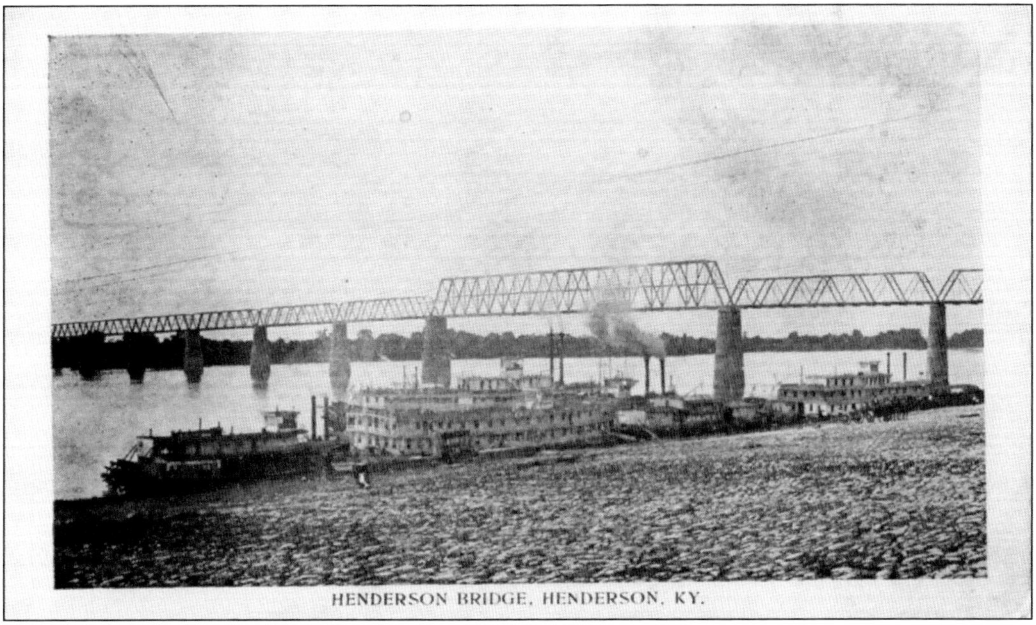

Although the 1885 railroad bridge signaled the beginning of the end for Henderson-Evansville boat traffic, river traffic continued to thrive for some time, as can be seen in this postcard that shows at least four different boats lining the Henderson wharf. The revenue brought in by river employees was a great boon to the local economy.

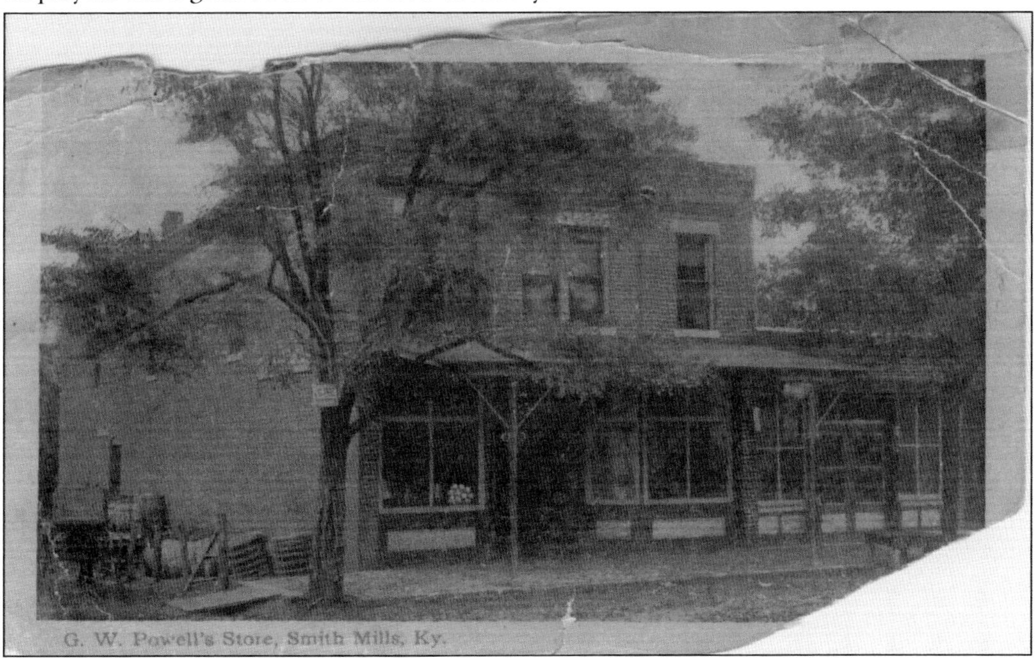

"No store can supply your needs like G. W. Powell's Big Store, Smith Mills, Ky." reads the back of this postcard, postmarked 1911. In later years, the top half of the building burned, and the right side was destroyed in a storm. The bottom half of the building has been renovated and is now the home of the Smith Mills Market and Meals. (Courtesy of Sharon Chancellor and April Spore.)

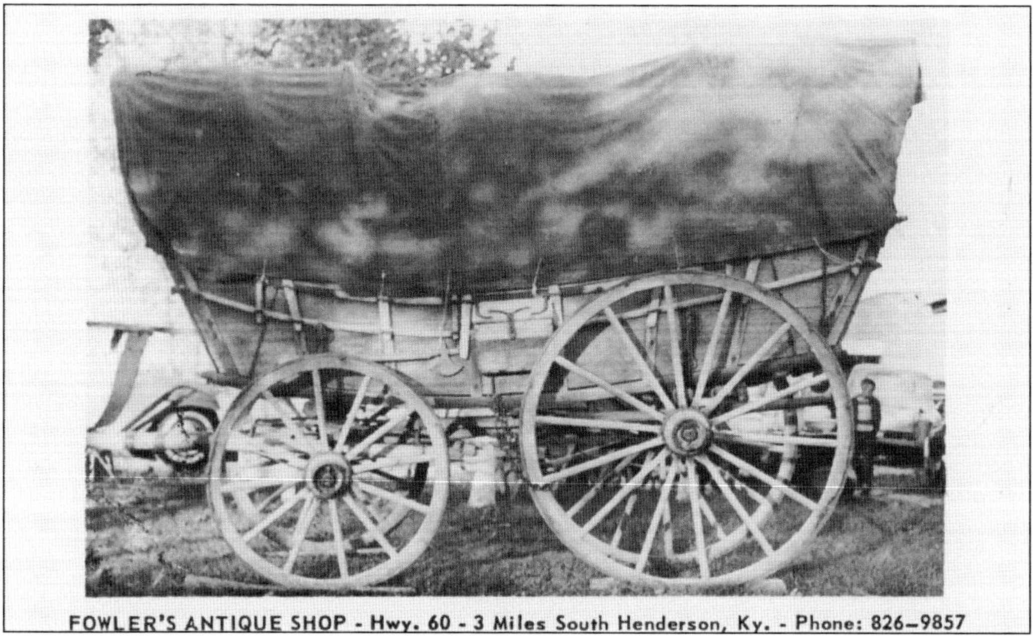

This 1843 prairie schooner, which had been brought from a farm that had been homesteaded, was for sale at Fowler's Antique Shop on Highway 60 three miles south of Henderson. At one time, a number of antique shops dotted the highways around Henderson and other communities in Henderson County.

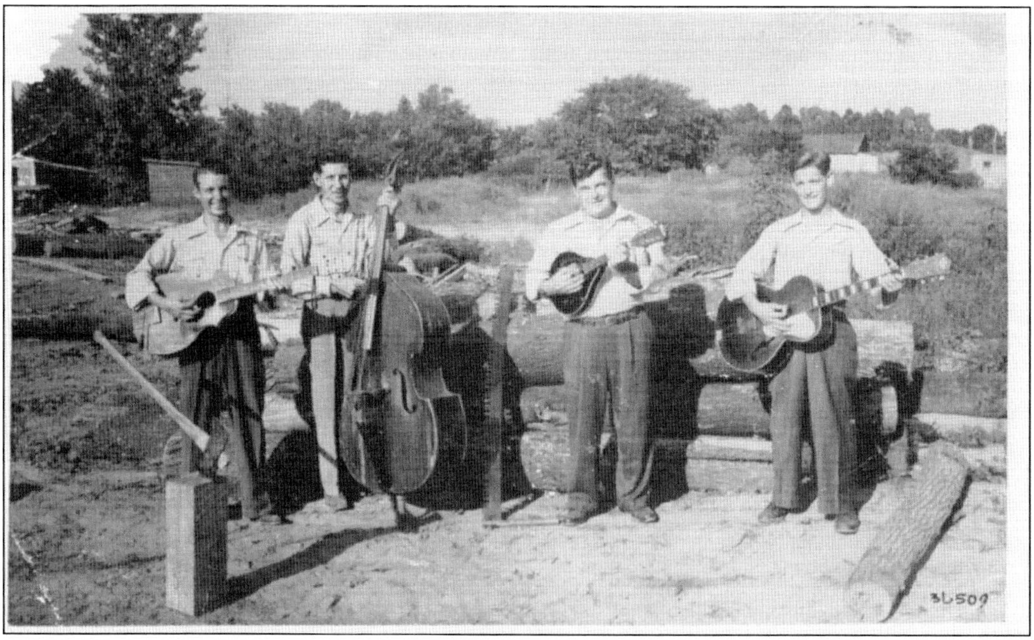

After local radio station WSON began broadcasting on December 17, 1941, it played host to a number of live performers, many of whom performed at the Zion Road station while en route to Nashville. Featured on this postcard are Oscar Yates and the Woodchoppers. Other popular bands included Les Smithhart and the Super X Cowboys, and Bob Berry and the Country Showboys.

Five

Praying Hard

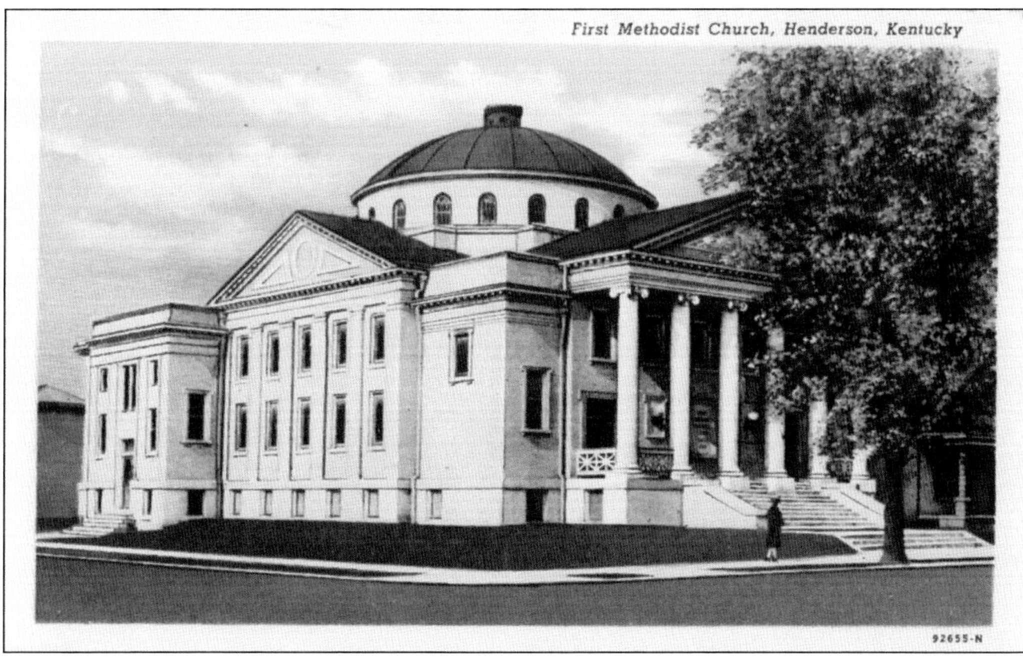

After organizing locally in 1805, Methodists worshiped in several places until the middle of the 19th century when the congregation paid $1,500 to George Atkinson for a lot at the southwest corner of Third and North Green Streets, land once owned by John James Audubon. Their first church in that location was completed in 1859. In 1913, the congregation paid Nettie Royster Murphy $1,400 for an adjacent lot. The cornerstone of the present church was laid on Thanksgiving Day in 1914, and the First Methodist Church (now the First United Methodist Church) was dedicated in 1917.

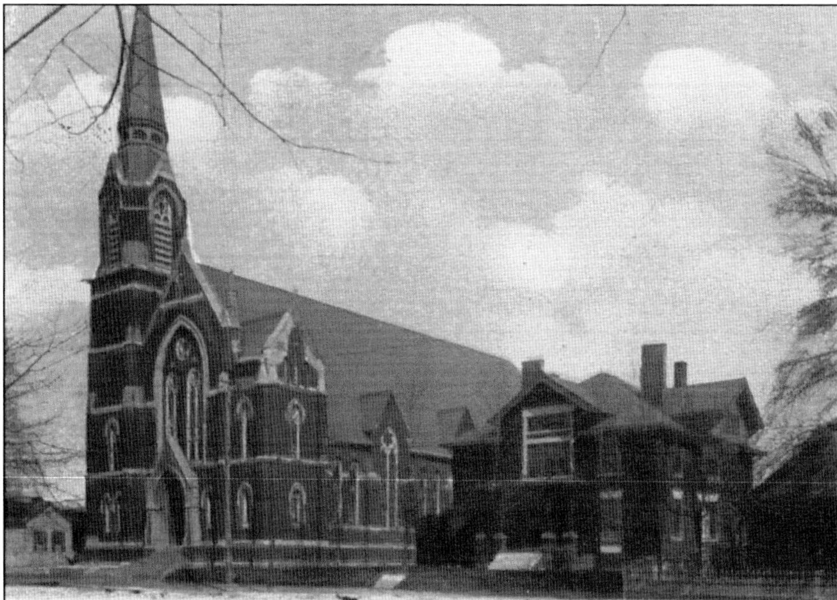

Catholic Church and Parsonage, Henderson, Ky.

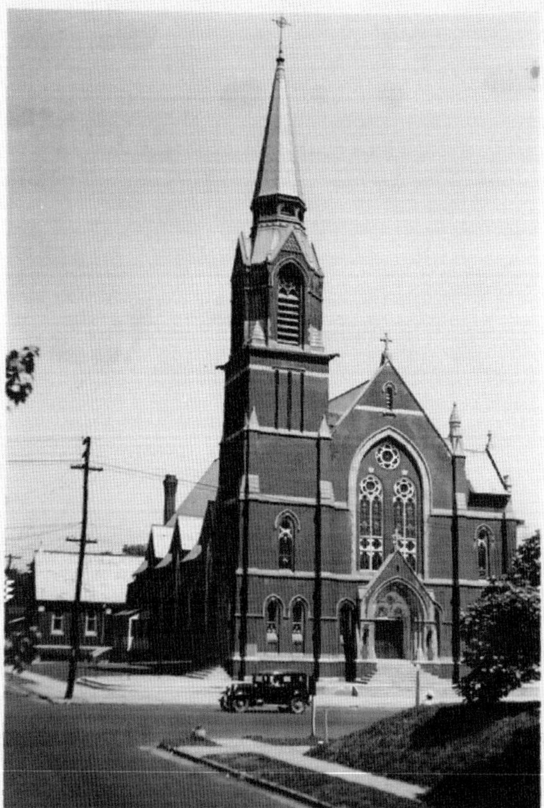

HOLY NAME CHURCH --- HENDERSON, KY.
maclean dameron Photo NO. 303.

The Catholic faith has been a part of Henderson from the town's early years. In 1810, at least 10 Catholic families lived here. In 1855, local Catholics bought land on the northwest corner of Ingram and Third Streets and, in the early 1860s, erected St. Louis Church. Twenty-one years later, church officials purchased the northeast corner of Second and Ingram Streets to build the Holy Name of Jesus Catholic Church, which features a large sanctuary and a spacious side chapel. The cornerstone for the new $50,000 church was laid on October 17, 1886. Designed in the early English Gothic style by Chicago architect J. J. Egan, the church was made of pressed brick with stone ornamentation. It featured a main altar and stained-glass windows imported from France. The first Mass in the new church was celebrated in 1891. (Left, courtesy of Martin Studio, Maclean Dameron Collection.)

The First Baptist Church, with 35 charter members, began as an outgrowth of a revival held in Central Park's old Union Church. The congregation built a church on the northeast corner of Elm and Center Streets. In 1903, that building was replaced by the redbrick structure shown on this postcard. The church's Sunday School annex was added in 1910.

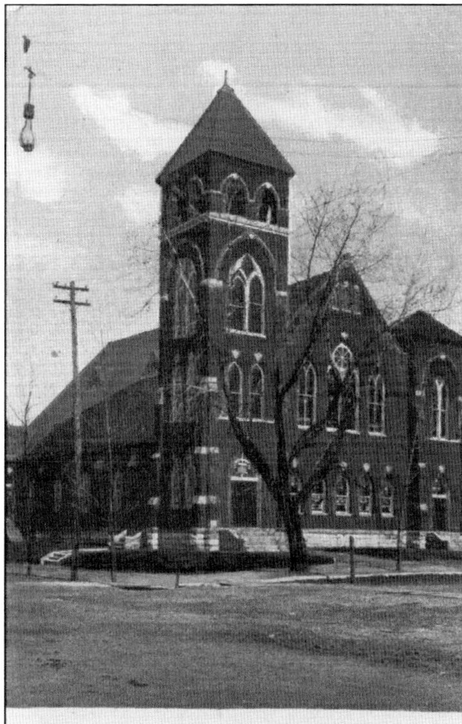

First Baptist Church, Henderson, Ky.

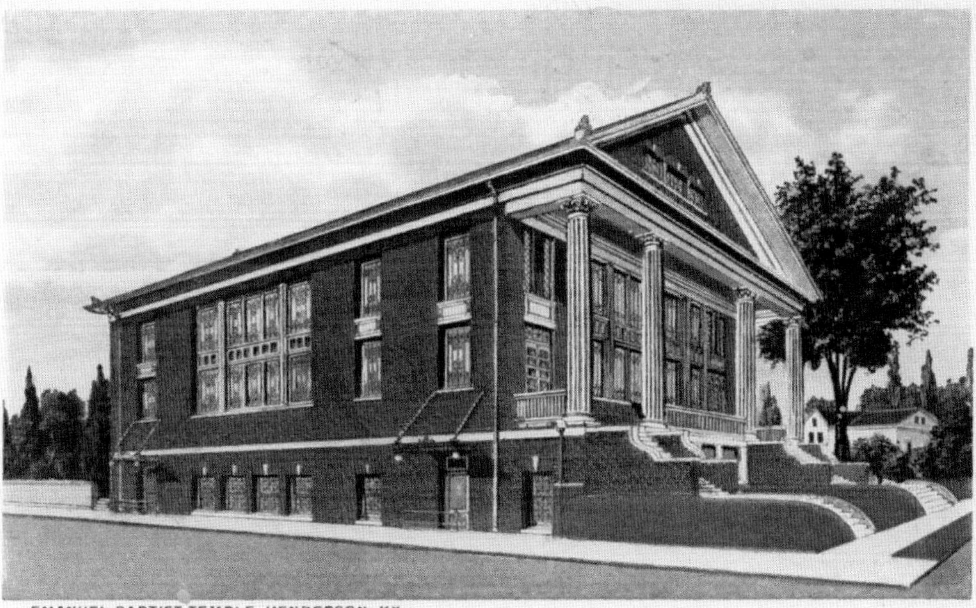

EMANUEL BAPTIST TEMPLE, HENDERSON, KY.

On August 9, 1914, a group of men met in the Jewish synagogue (at the northwest corner of Center and Alvasia Streets) in order to form a new Baptist church. The new congregation unanimously voted to name the church Immanuel Baptist Temple (note the misspelling on the postcard). The first pastor was the Reverend George W. Clarke. This postcard was postmarked in 1916, just after the establishment of the church.

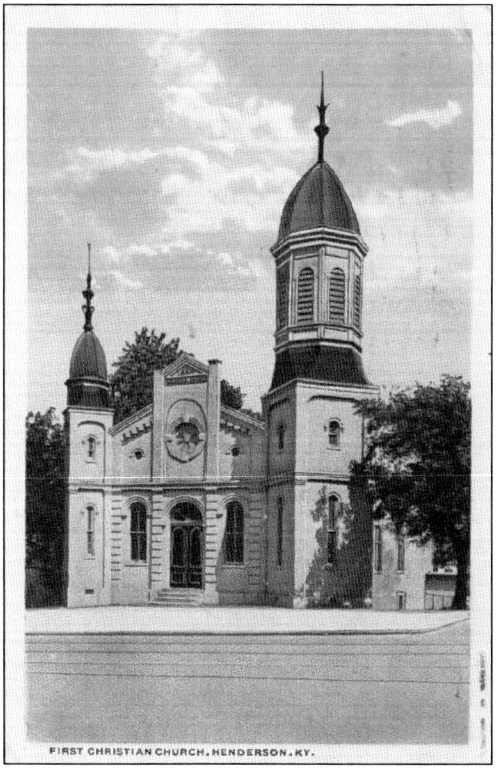

The First Christian Church, the oldest church building extant in Henderson, is located on the northeast corner of South Green and Washington Streets. A 35-by-55-foot building (part of the present church) was constructed in 1854. During the Civil War, the Union army used the building as a military prison and hospital. Over the years, the church has changed denominations a number of times.

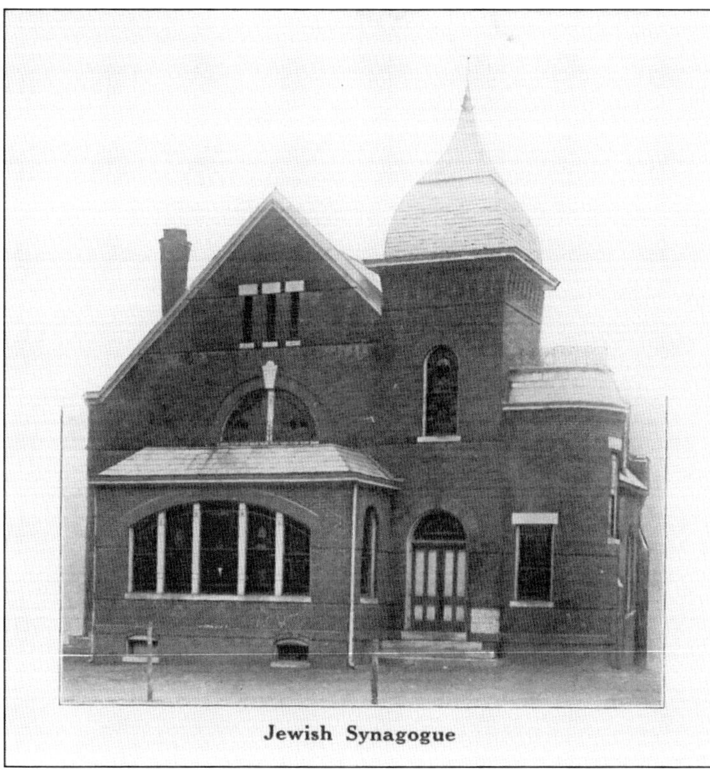

Henderson's Jewish congregation was formed in the mid- to late 1800s and initially met in various members' homes. In 1887, the Adath Israel congregation incorporated, and its members held services in several businesses or local halls. Shortly thereafter, Henry and Maurice Baldauf donated a lot on the northwest corner of Alves and Center Streets for the construction of a temple. The cornerstone was laid in 1891, and the Adath Israel Temple was dedicated in 1892.

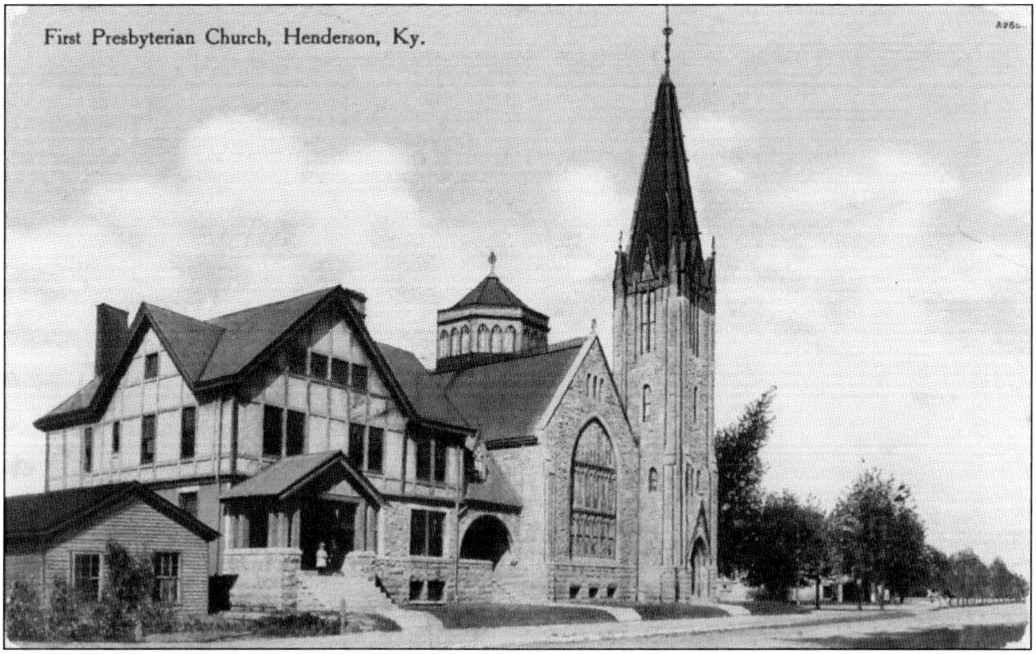

Presbyterians trace their Henderson history back to the beginning of the 1800s when the Reverend James McGready was active in the area. The Presbyterian church pictured here was built on a $5,250 lot purchased in 1891 on the southeast corner of South Main and Washington Streets. The Cincinnati architectural firm of Crapsey and Brown designed the building, which incorporated stone from a Bedford, Indiana, quarry and stained glass created by the firms of A. H. Wallis of St. Louis, Missouri, and Donald McDonald of Boston. The cornerstone for the church was laid in 1893, and the church was dedicated in June 1894. Note the trolley tracks in the lower right-hand corner of the postcard on the bottom. The church burned in September 1972.

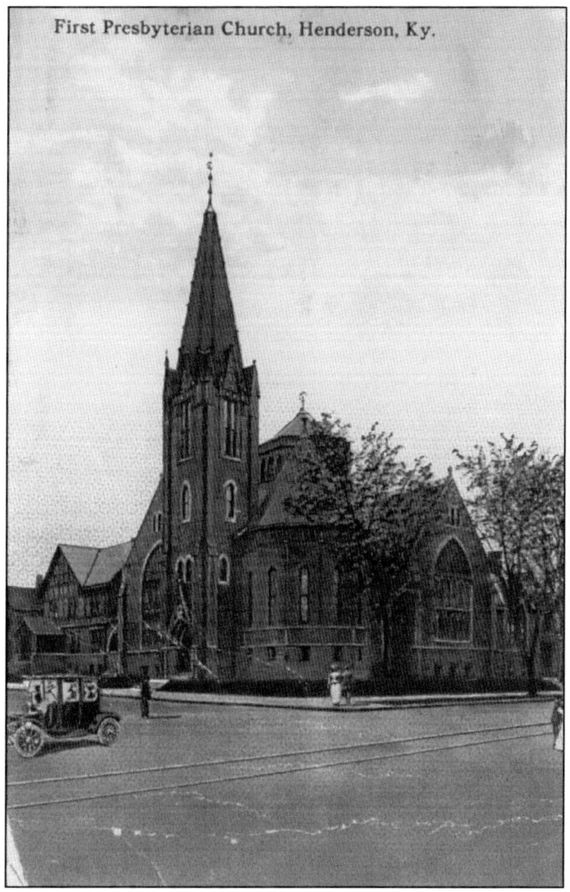

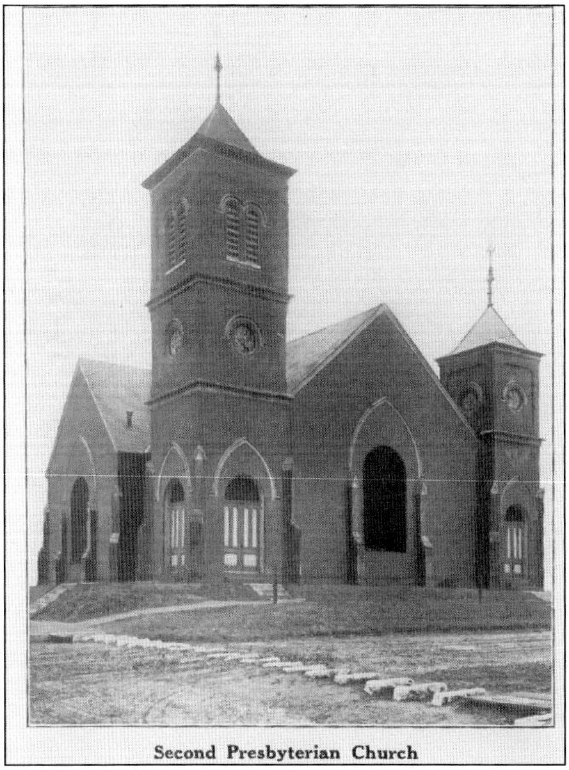

In 1868, a Presbyterian mission Sunday school was established at the northwest corner of Washington and Alvasia Streets. Originally called the Chestnut Hill Presbyterian Church, the name was eventually changed to the Second Presbyterian Church and then to the Central Presbyterian Church. The church building pictured here was completed in 1885. In 1973, the congregation of Central Presbyterian Church merged with that of downtown's First Presbyterian Church.

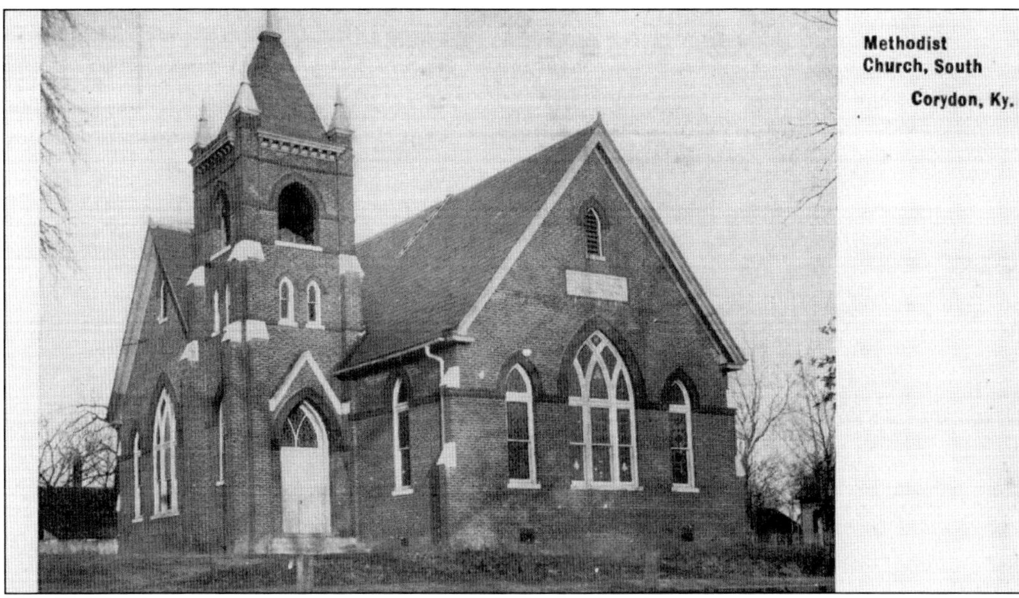

Early Corydon Methodists worshiped at Pleasant Hill Methodist Church, built in 1810 about two miles from Corydon on Rock Springs Road. In 1871, a parcel of land at the corner of Sixth and Hancock was given to church members, and a two-story frame church was built. In 1902, this church was replaced by the redbrick church pictured on this postcard. The belfry once housed a bell that summoned the congregation to come to worship. (Courtesy of Mary Edith Pritchett.)

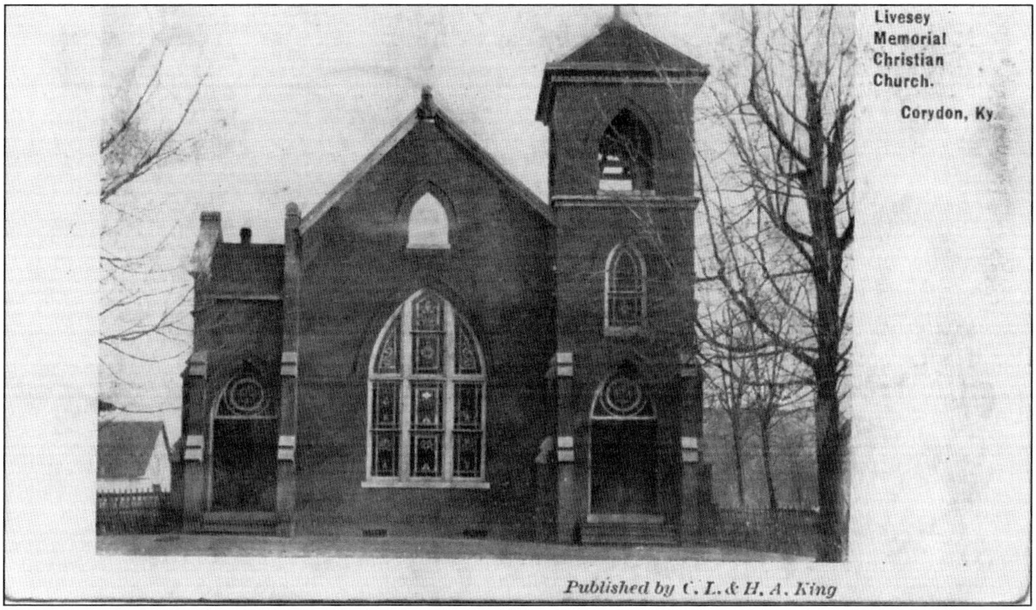

When Brother John Livesey arrived in 1832, he first preached in private homes before organizing a church south of Corydon. Later the congregation moved to the Powell Schoolhouse and then built a church in Corydon. The third church, the one in seen on the postcard, was built in 1897 on land deeded by Mr. and Mrs. C. L. King for the Livesey Memorial Christian Church. The new church and its furnishings cost $8,000. (Courtesy of Mary Edith Pritchett.)

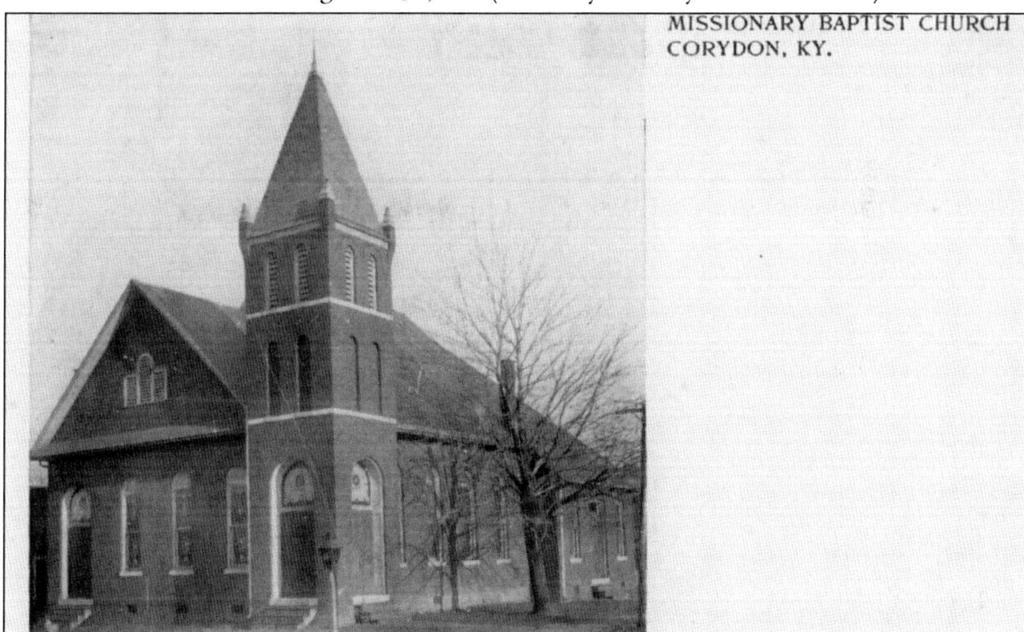

Organized in 1878, the Missionary Baptist Church in Corydon built its first church at the corner of Seventh and Hancock Streets. In the late 1890s, the congregation built a new brick church (seen in this card) at Sixth and Main Streets. The lot was purchased for $500, and the building was estimated to cost a little more than $3,000. By the turn of the 1900s, all of the outstanding notes for this church had been paid. (Courtesy of Mary Edith Pritchett.)

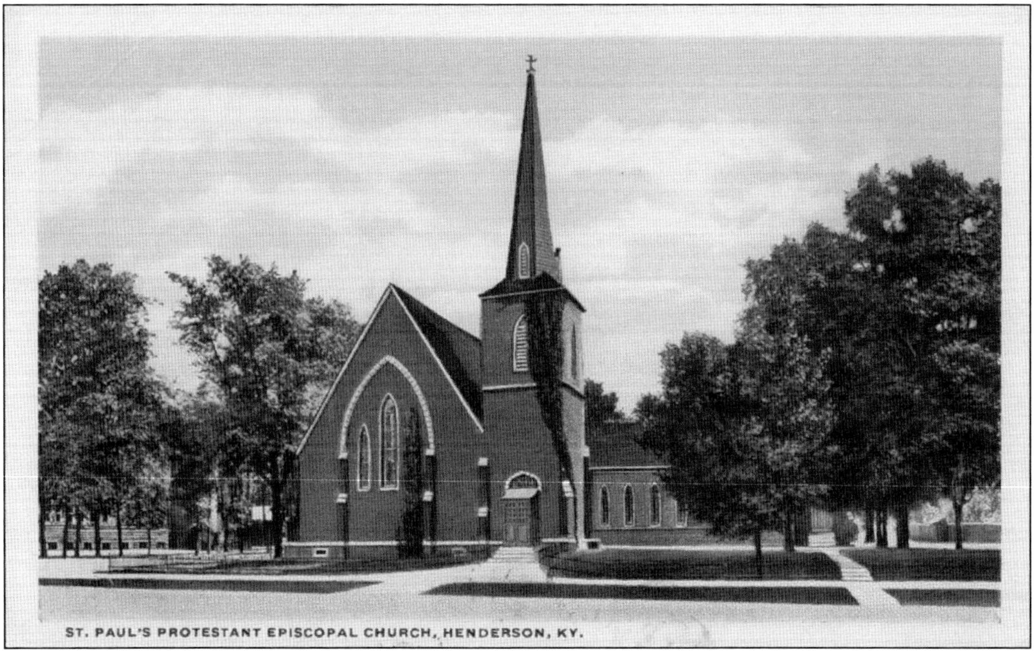

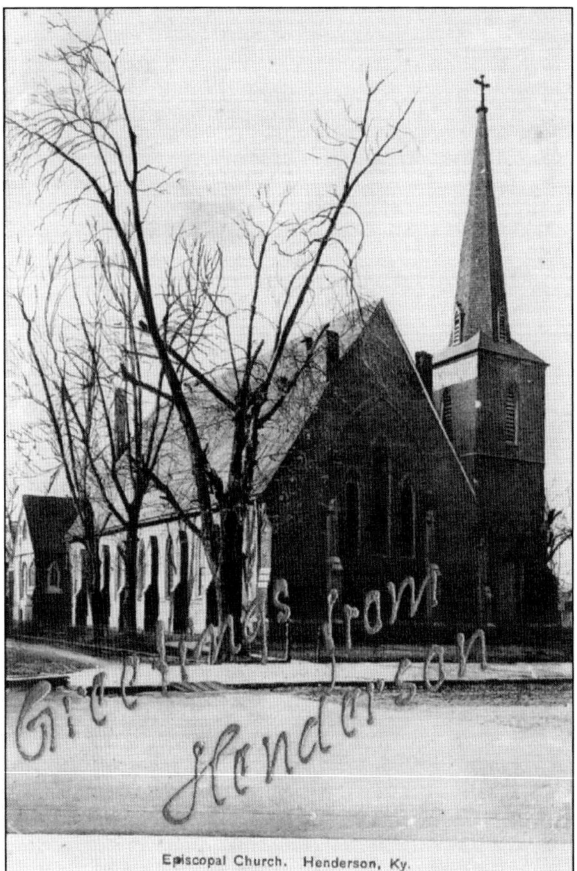

The oldest continuously used church in Henderson, St. Paul's Episcopal Church, located at the southwest corner of Center and Green Streets, is listed on the National Register of Historic Places. The congregation laid the cornerstone for the $12,000 Gothic church in 1858, held its first service in 1859, and consecrated it in 1860. The church features stained-glass windows imported from Munich, Germany. The interior of the church is of plastered brick and frame. When the church opened, Hendersonians were said to have been "shocked" by its organ—the first in the city. Just prior to World War I, stucco was applied to the structure at a cost of $1,675.

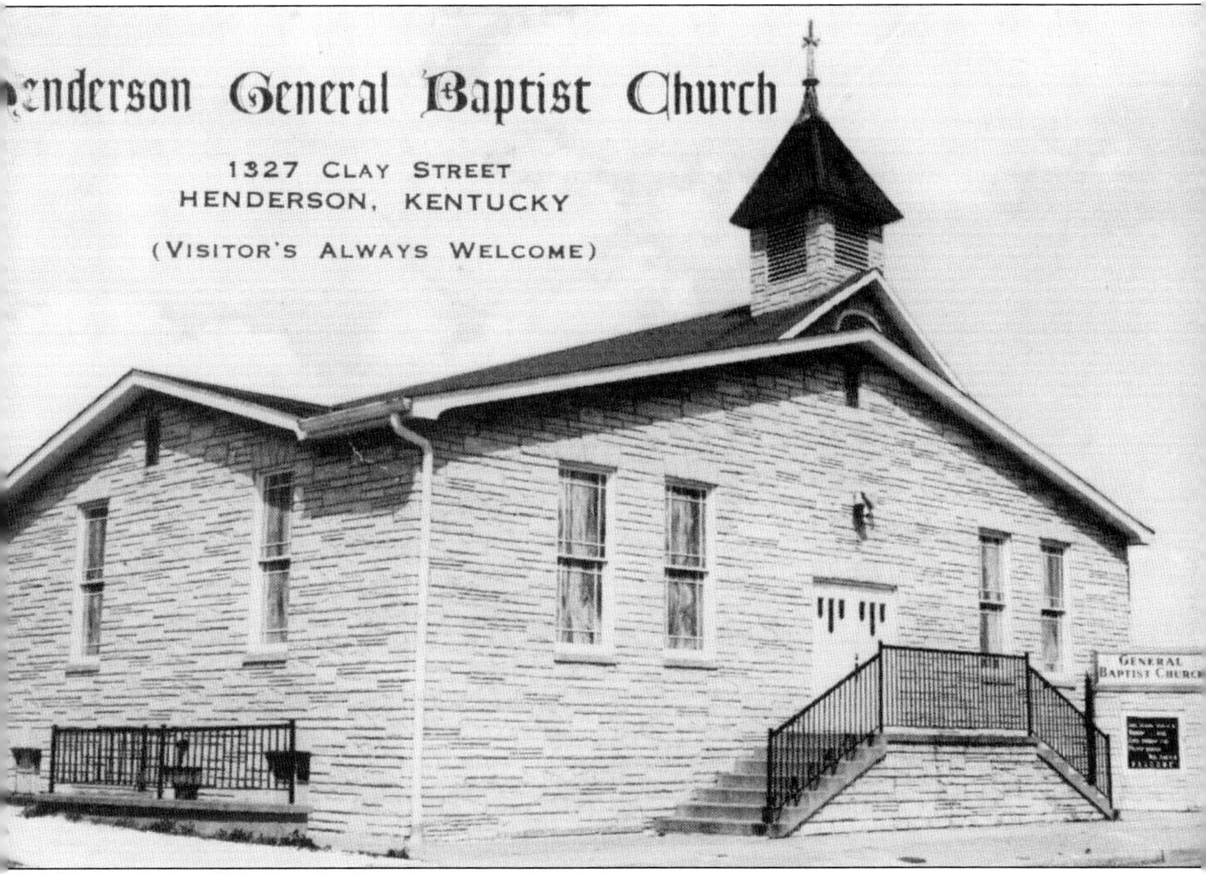

In this undated postcard, the Henderson General Baptist Church welcomed visitors to its services at 1327 Clay Street. Over the years, this building has housed a number of different denominations and is currently home to the Temple of Deliverance Church of God in Christ. (Courtesy of Pat Workins.)

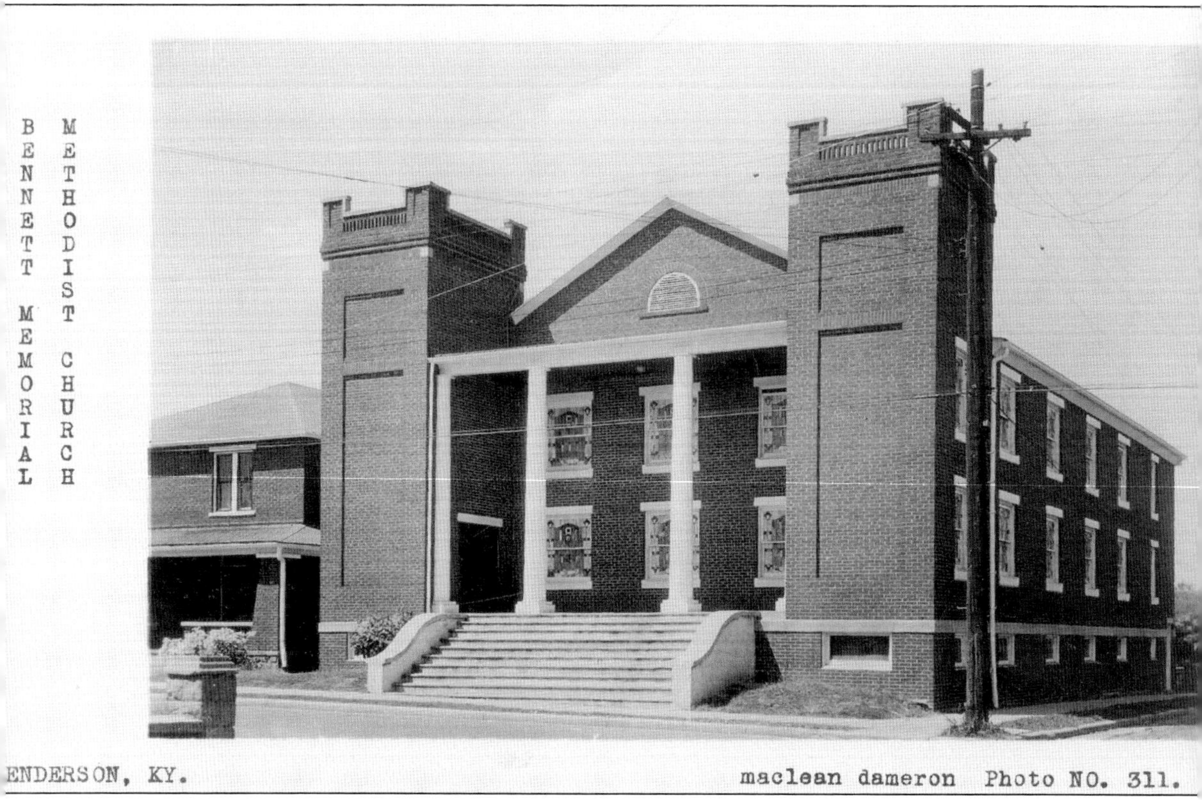

In 1890, Methodists in the Audubon section of Henderson formed their own congregation and procured land for a church on Clay Street. By 1924, that church had become too small, and under the leadership of the Reverend E. R. Bennett, a larger and more modern church was begun at the corner of Letcher and Cumnock Streets. The church is named in Reverend Bennett's honor. (Courtesy of Henderson County Public Library and Martin Studio, Maclean Dameron Collection.)

Six

Just Visiting

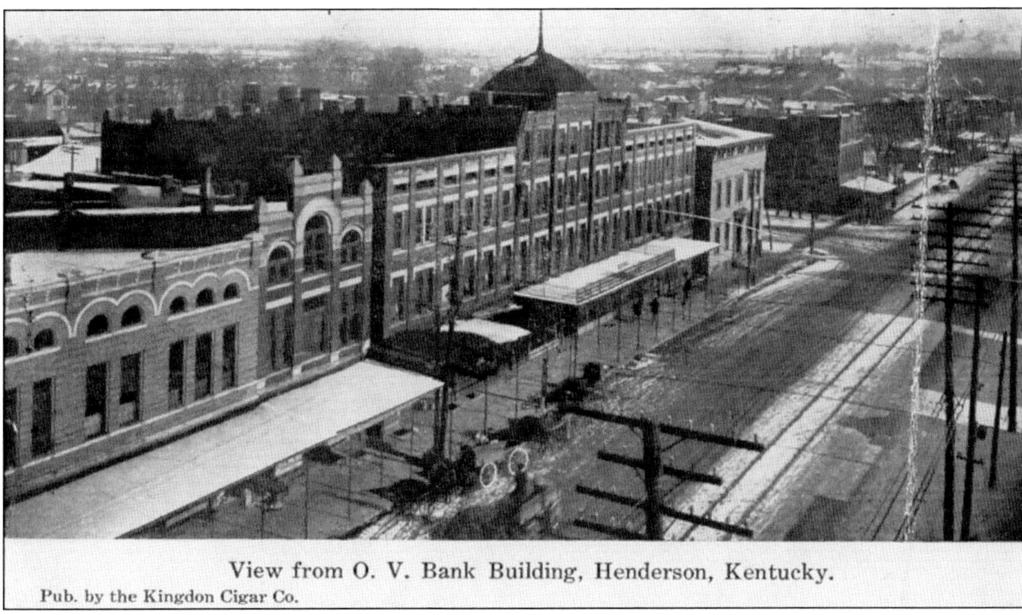

View from O. V. Bank Building, Henderson, Kentucky.
Pub. by the Kingdon Cigar Co.

This aerial view, published by the Kingdon Cigar Company, was taken from atop the Ohio Valley Bank building and shows the north side of Second Street looking east. This may be the only postcard that gives a view of buildings that formerly stood on either corner of Second and Elm Streets, as well as those between Elm and Green Streets on Second. In this scene, downtown streets have not been paved, and streetcars and horse and buggies are still the main modes of transportation. The Kingdon Hotel dominates the middle of the block, and part of the steeple of the Holy Name Church is visible in the far top right.

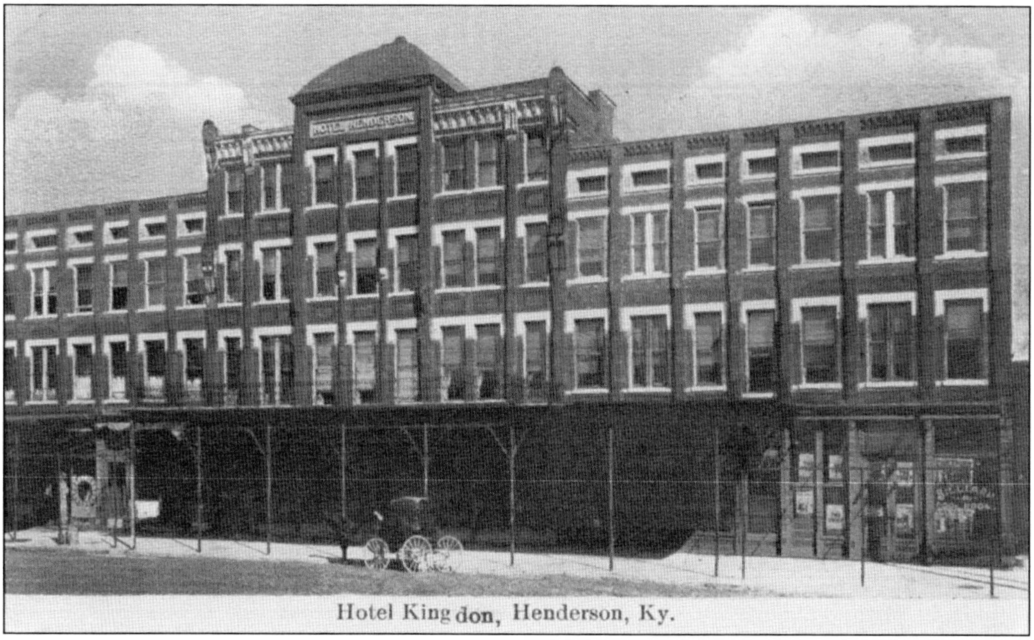

A high-class downtown hotel was the brainchild of Louis and Charles Kleiderer, who paid $12,000 to John and Sarah Mallory for their two-story home and elevated lot in the middle of the north side of Second Street between Main and Elm Streets. The Kleiderers razed the house and constructed the Henderson Hotel, which sported a wooden awning and iron hitching posts. "Hotel Henderson" can be seen in the middle of the building of the postcard.

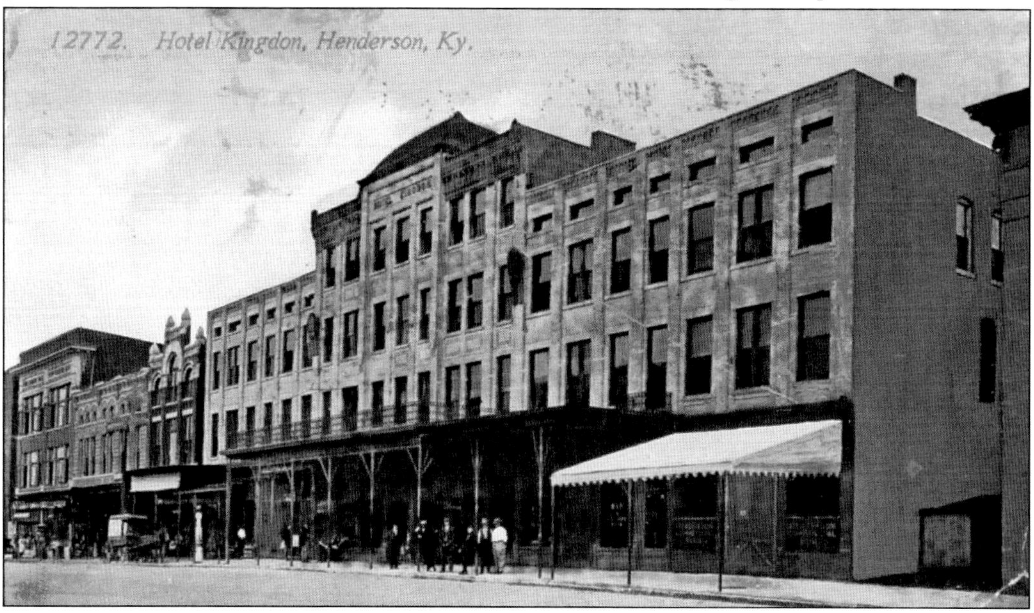

The Kleiderers suffered financially and sold their hotel to Charles King and others for $11,400. King remodeled the building and changed its name to the Kingdon Hotel. In the postcard at the top of the page, the hotel's billiard room is on the street level on the right; in the postcard above (a pre-1907 card that looks west toward Main Street), Henderson's Commercial Club—a forerunner of the Henderson Chamber of Commerce—has established its offices there.

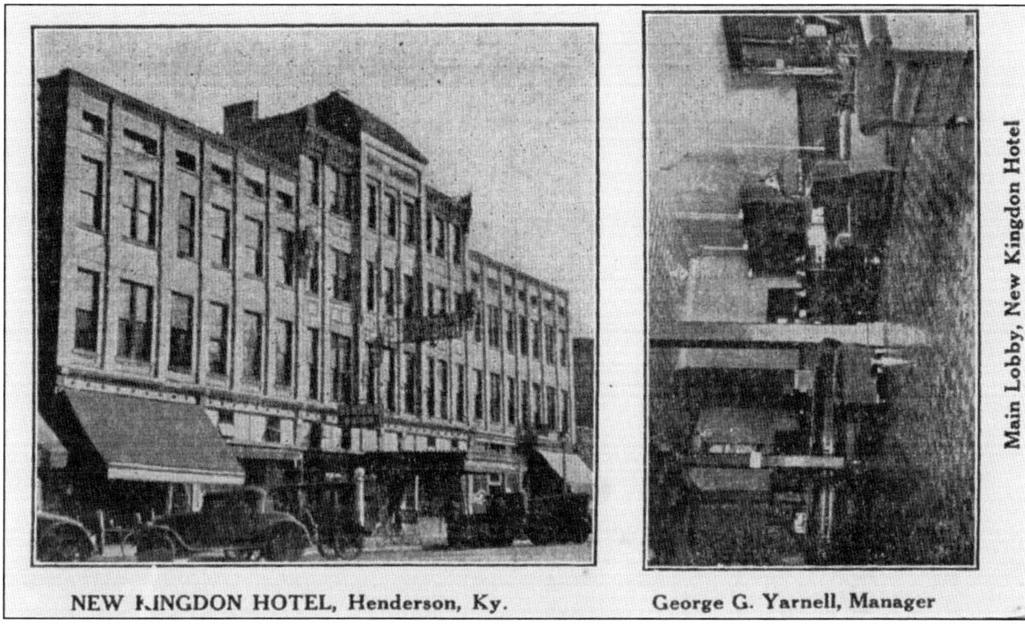

A few years after it changed names, the Kingdon Hotel—Henderson's leading hotel of the day—boasted that it had been remodeled and equipped with private baths "in almost every room." A 1913 newspaper said "the 'Knights of the Grip' [traveling salesmen] always make it a point if possible to Sunday over in Henderson and at the Hotel Kingdon." By the time these postcards were printed, cars had replaced the horse and buggies seen in the earlier cards, and the hotel advertised its Western Union services. The postcard below highlights the Arcade Café (later Galbraith's) and a barbershop where men were "assured of a clean and pleasant shave, stylish haircut or any other tonsorial requirements." Eventually the building, a giant in its day, fell on hard times and was razed in 1973; a parking lot fills its former site.

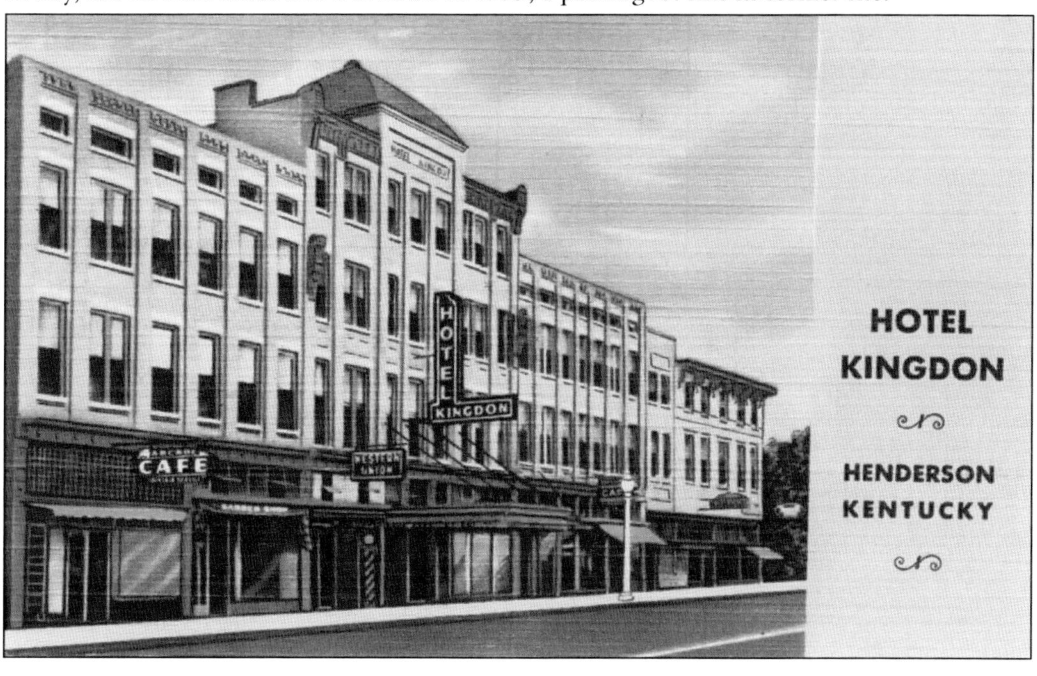

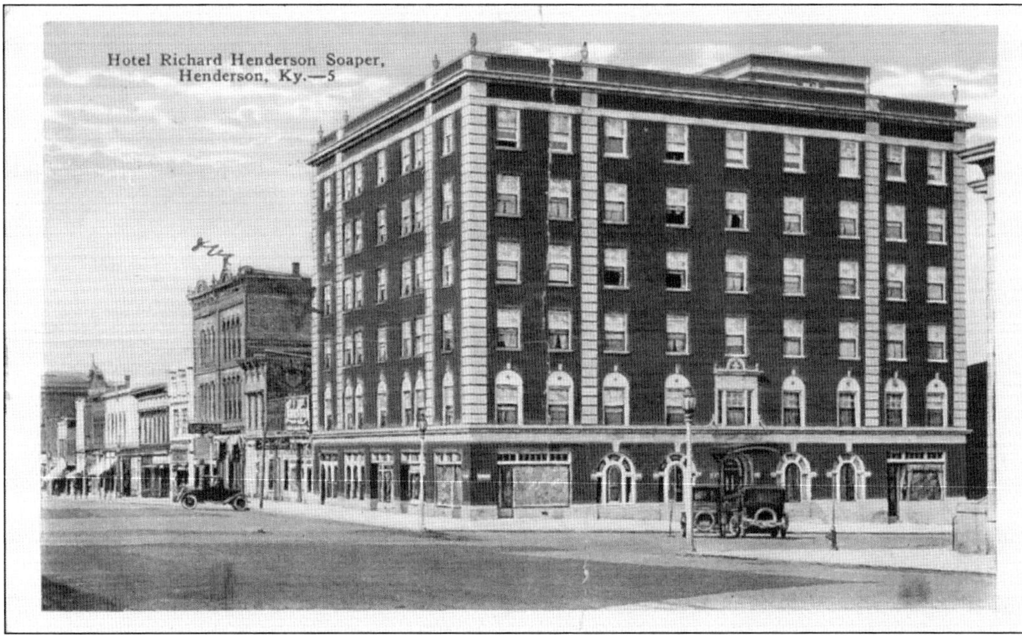

Located at the southwest corner of Second and North Main Streets, Henderson's tallest downtown building, the six-story Richard Henderson Soaper Hotel, was constructed in 1924 and named for the local citizen who helped secure its financing. At various times, the Georgian brick structure was home to a popular coffee shop, a restaurant, a ballroom, a jewelry store, a drugstore, and a beauty parlor. In later days, two large "Hotel Soaper" signs were atop the hotel; the signs were easily visible from Highways 41 and 60 (two blocks east) and from the Ohio River (one block west). The hotel's corner entrance mirrored the corner entrance of the Union Bank located directly across Second Street.

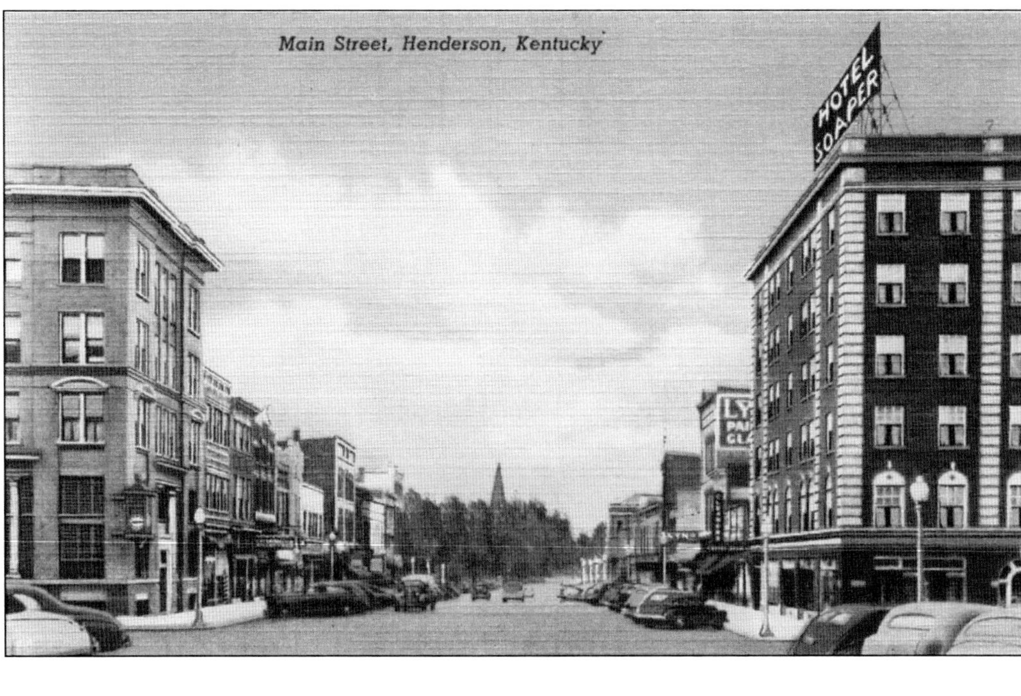

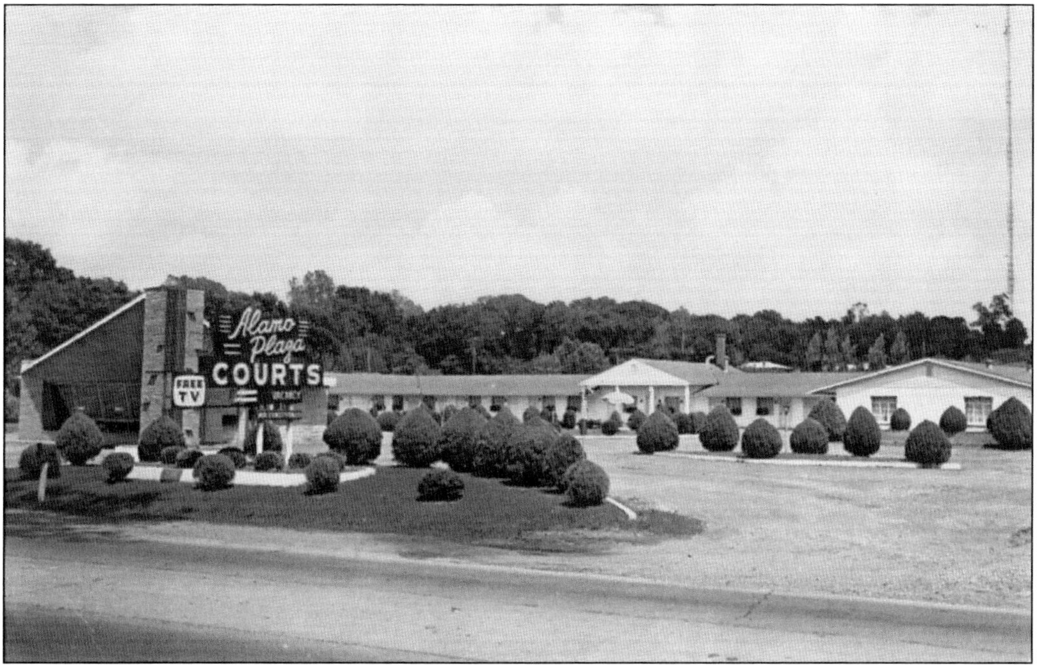

"Southern Hospitality Awaits You" was the motto of the Alamo Plaza Courts, located on the east side of U.S. Highway 41 North south of Marywood Drive. Along with its 50 air-conditioned rooms, it advertised free television, a patio, and "rates that are considerate."

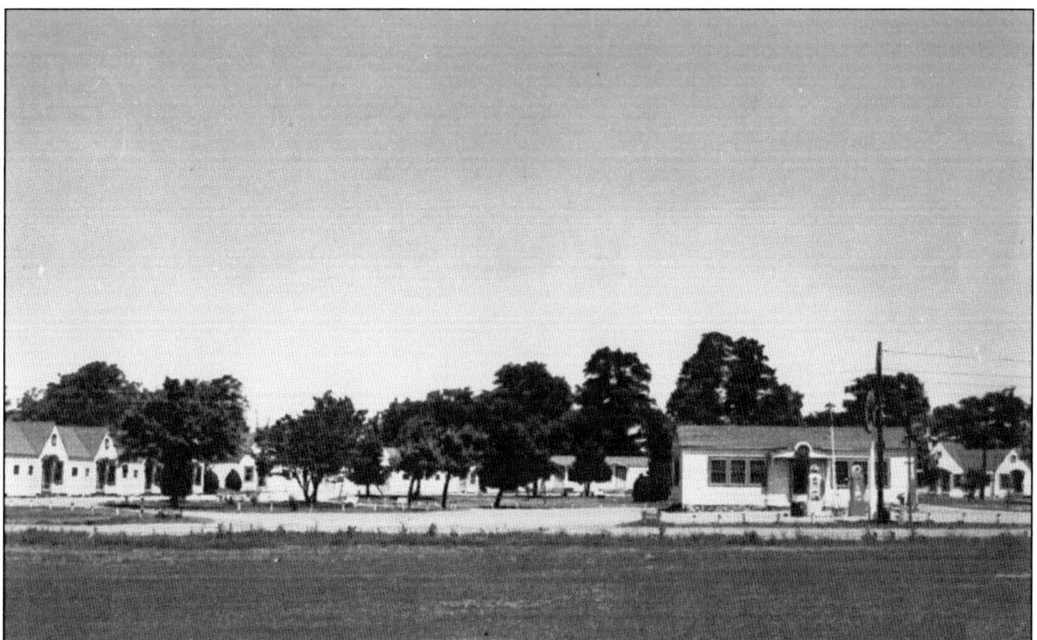

The 25 "strictly modern" cottages of Stone's Motor Court were located a mile south of Henderson on Highways 41 and 60. The postcard promotes Stone's as "a comfortable place to stay, with real Southern Hospitality." At the time this postcard was printed, A. E. Grimwood was the manager.

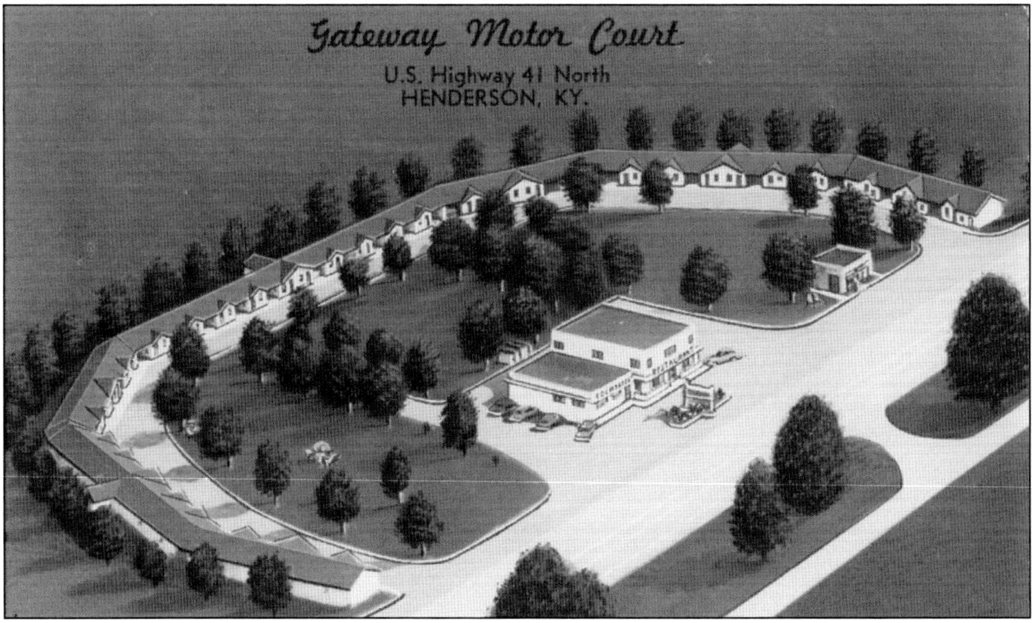

When it opened, the Gateway Motor Court on U.S. 41 North, where Shoney's and the Audubon Village currently stand, had just 10 cottages. After World War II, 32 more were added, making a semicircular structure surrounding the popular Gateway Restaurant, which operated from the late 1940s until 1970. Because of its proximity to Audubon Park, Dade Park, and Evansville, as well as its location on the popular Dixie Bee Highway (later renamed Highway 41), the Gateway Motor Court was a popular spot for travelers and advertised the latest in amenities. Outside each cottage was its own garage; inside the rooms all featured the latest in postwar décor along with steam heat, modern tile baths, radios, air-conditioning "in summer," and room service. After the motel closed in the 1960s, the site was home to a flea market. The motel's cottages were razed in the late 1980s.

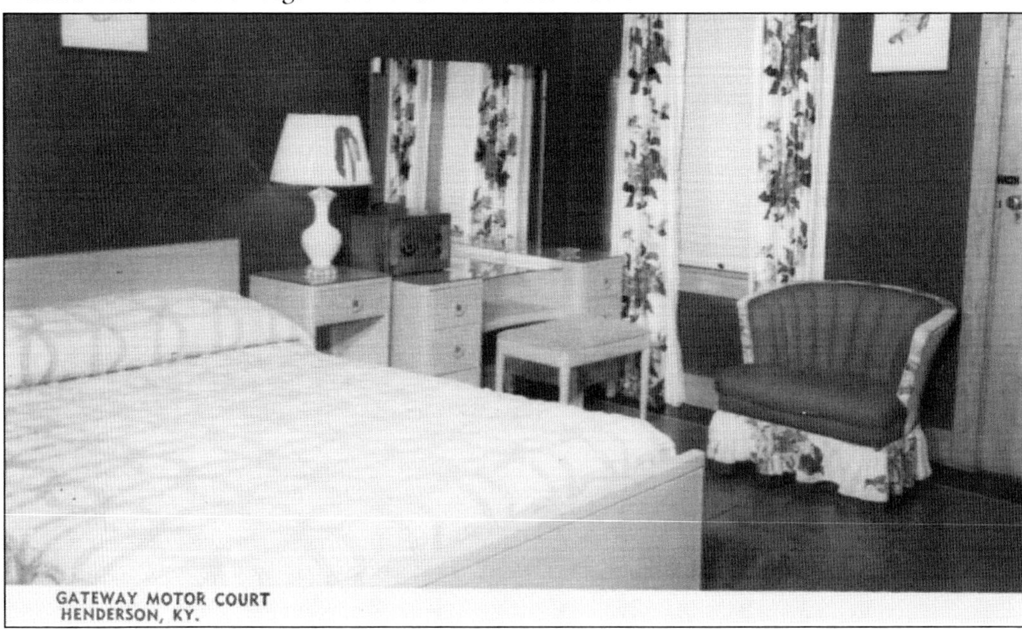

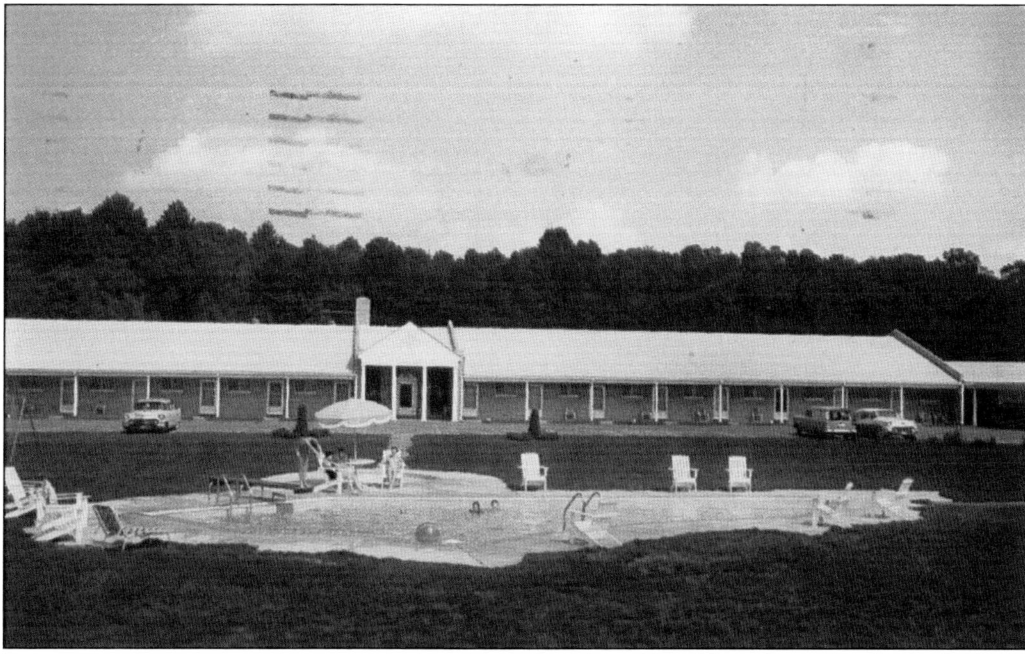

The Kentucky Terrace Motel was located at 2820 Highway 41 North, just south of the entrance to the Audubon State Park and also close to Dade Park. The motel boasted that its air-conditioned 50 units were equipped with individual room temperature controls, as well as wall-to-wall carpeting. Perhaps the motel's main drawing point was its unique swimming pool, created in the shape of Kentucky. A Howard Johnson's restaurant was located at the entrance to the motel's property. The motel later became a part of the Scottish Inns chain; in the 1990s, it was razed to make way for more modern motels.

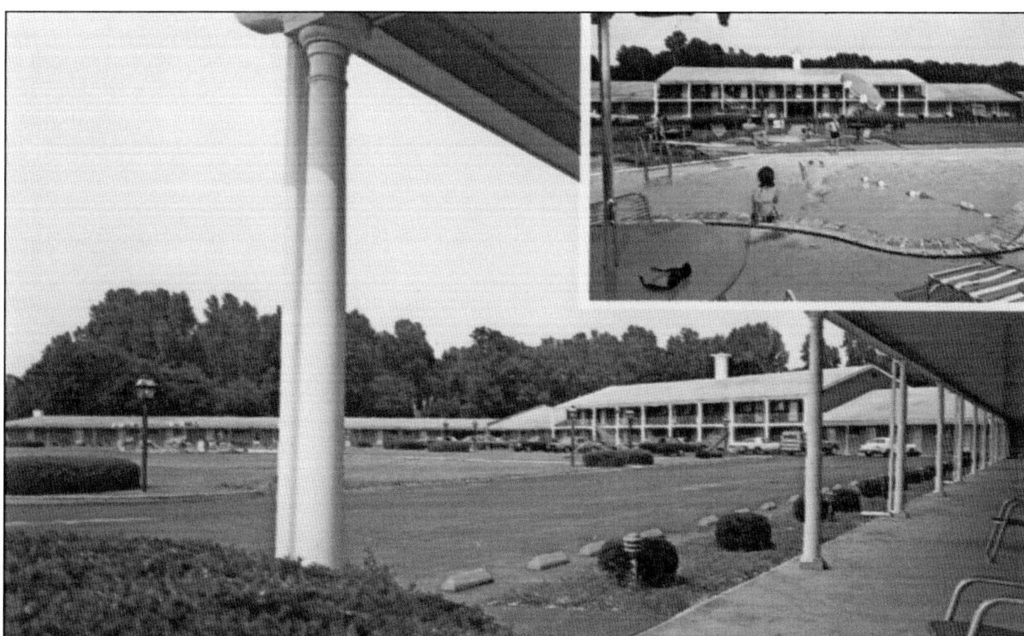

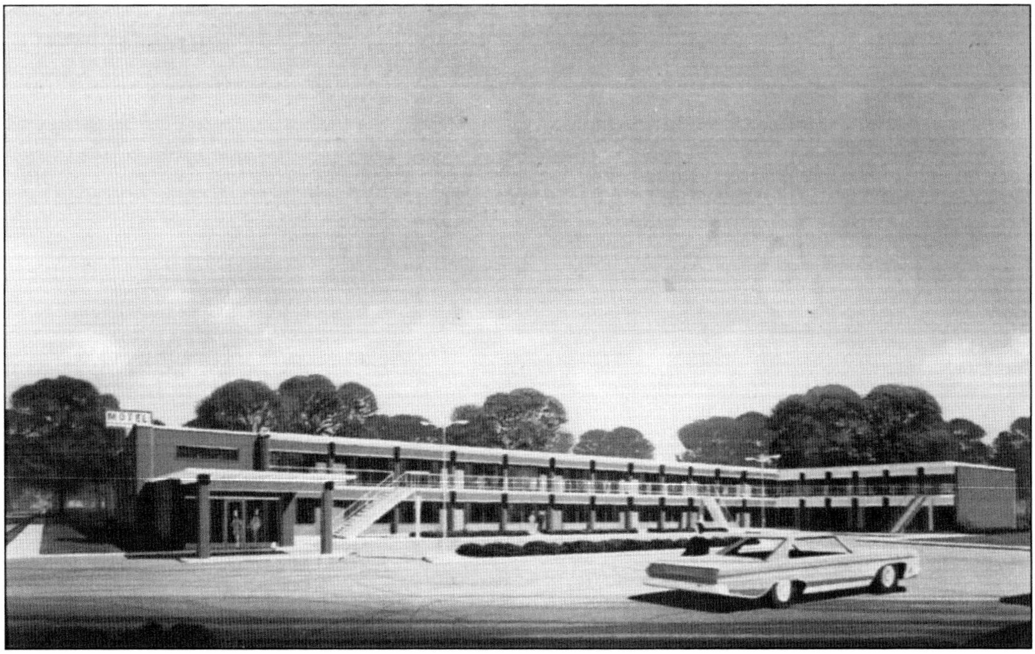

The Downtown Motel at the southwest corner of Fifth and Green Streets along highways U.S. 41A and U.S. 60 was opened by the Hays family in 1968. This postcard advertises the rooms' RCA color televisions, direct-dial phones, and the restaurant on the grounds. The motel is still a popular resting place for travelers.

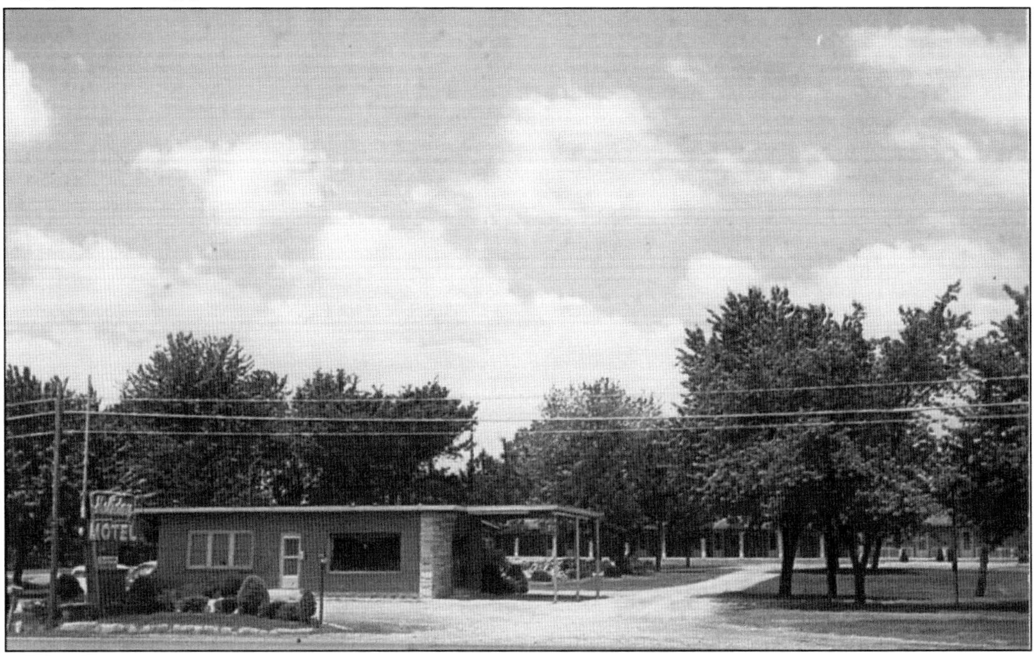

Located at 1759 South Green Street, the Holiday Motel still does a thriving business. Today a restaurant is housed in the building on the left. When this postcard was printed, the motel, then owned and operated by Melba Apperley, advertised that it was located on "a beautiful, quiet, wooded lot."

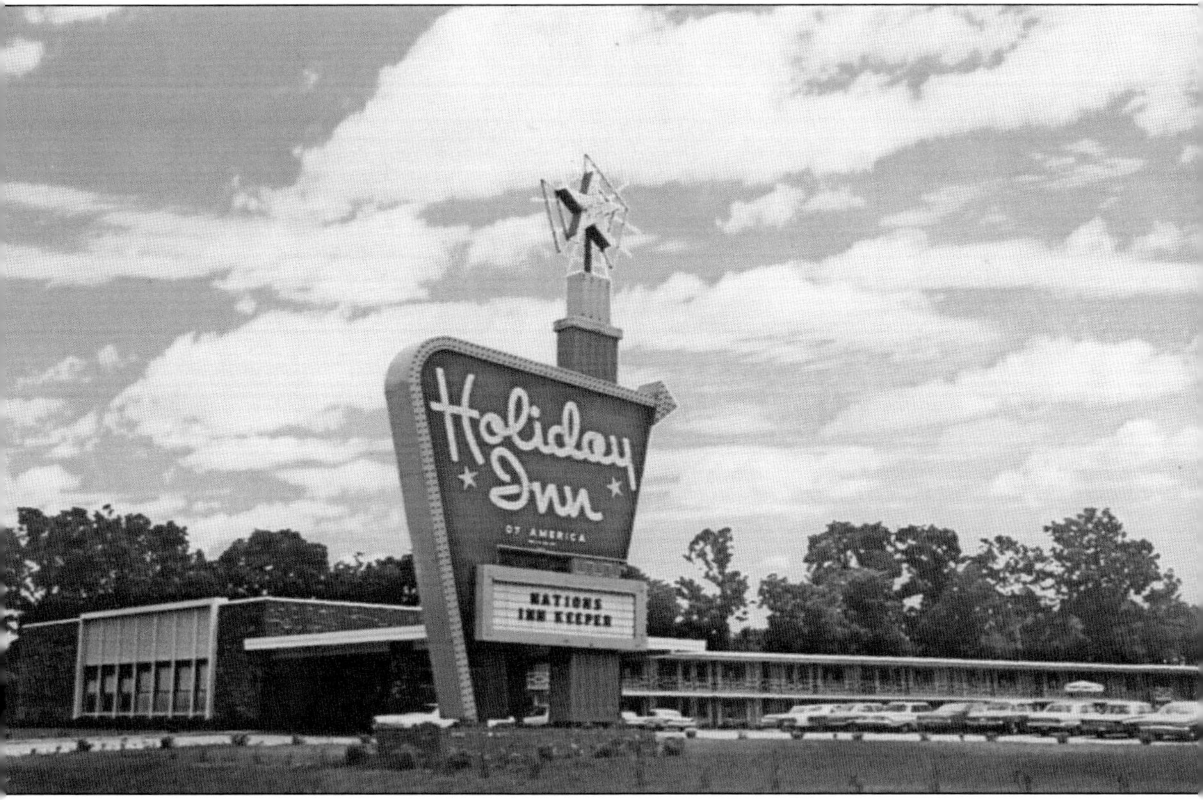

One of the many business that sprang up along what is called "the strip" (the area on either side of the six-lane highway on Henderson's north side), the Holiday Inn at 2030 U.S. 41 North offered the latest in luxury when it was built in the 1960s. Not only did it have modern rooms and a swimming pool, it also featured a popular restaurant.

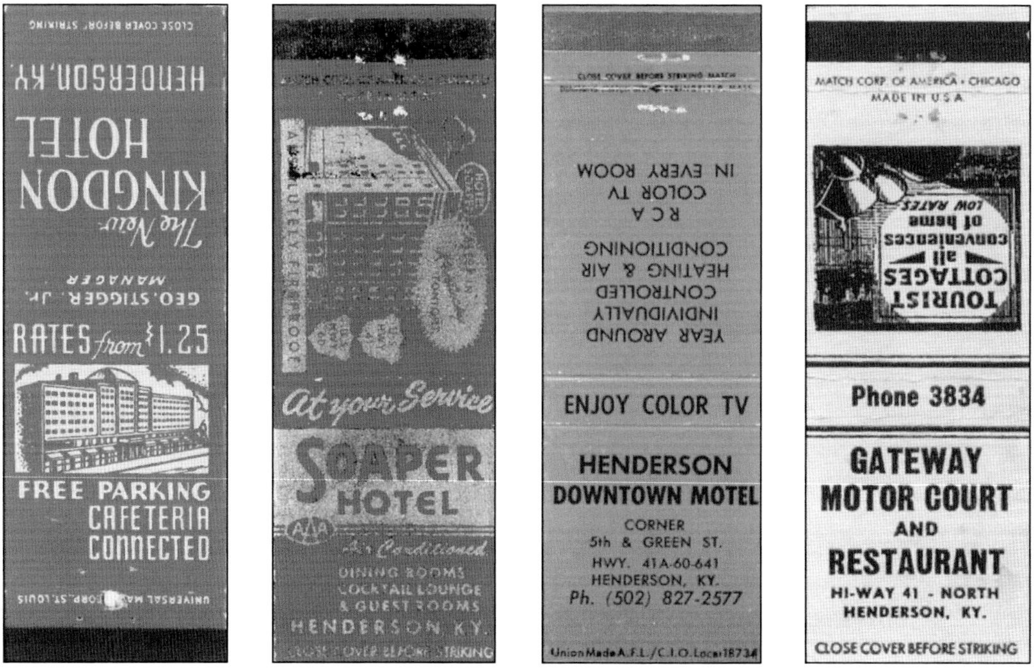

In this collection of matchbook covers, the Kingdon Hotel promoted its low rates (from $1.25), free parking, and cafeteria. The Gateway also boasted its low rates and said its cottages had "all the conveniences of home." The Soaper, where customers could "sleep in Kentucky tonight," wanted patrons to know that the building was "absolutely fireproof." The Henderson Downtown Motel advertised its individually controlled heating and air-conditioning, and the fact that every room had an RCA color television.

Seven

Flooding and Freezing

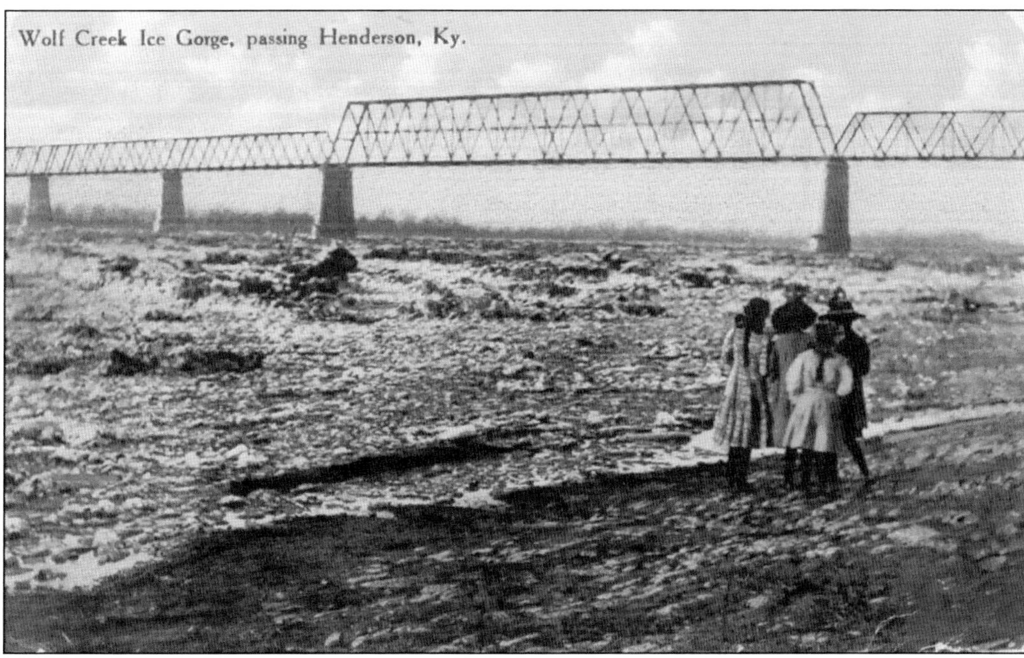

A number of Wolf Creek ice gorges have wreaked havoc over the years, but this postcard, postmarked 1910, probably depicts the huge floating ice drift that swept down the Ohio River in February 1897. The river was covered solid with ice for about 25 miles above Henderson. Logs, trees, and all other sorts of debris were wedged in the ice, which at one point was piled 40 feet high, presenting a great danger to Henderson's railroad bridge. Because captains were afraid their boats would be damaged by the ice, local river transportation all but closed.

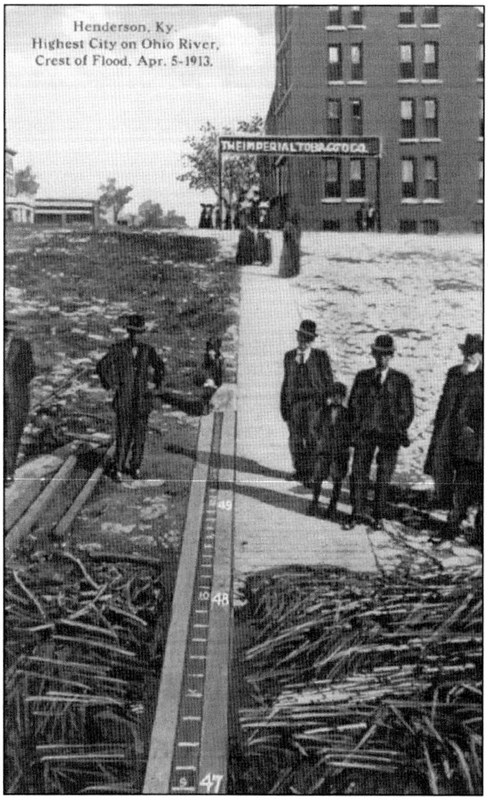

This postcard shows the Third Street gauge that marked the high water mark left when the river crested. Currently, a marker on the Second Street boat ramp indicates the 1913 crest. In the background on the right is the Imperial Tobacco Company; on the left is the side of the Elk's building. Even in 1913, Henderson was promoting itself as the "Highest City on Ohio River."

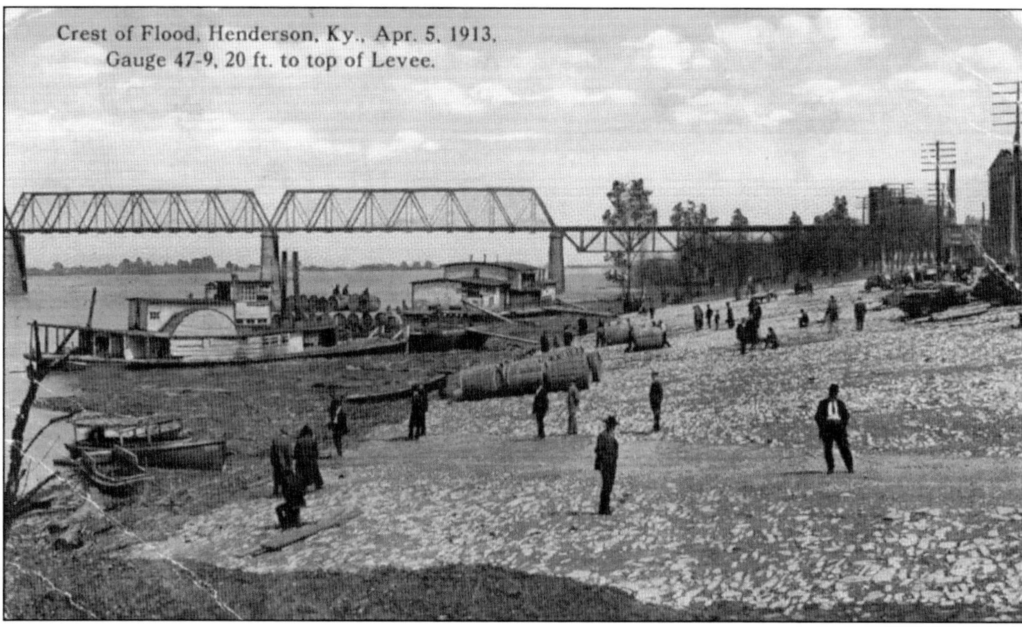

Floods have been a constant problem throughout Henderson's recorded history. At its crest of 48.4 feet on April 5, the flood of 1913 was the city's fourth worst. In the Ohio River Valley, the flood was responsible for the deaths of as many as 700 people and for $100 million in damages.

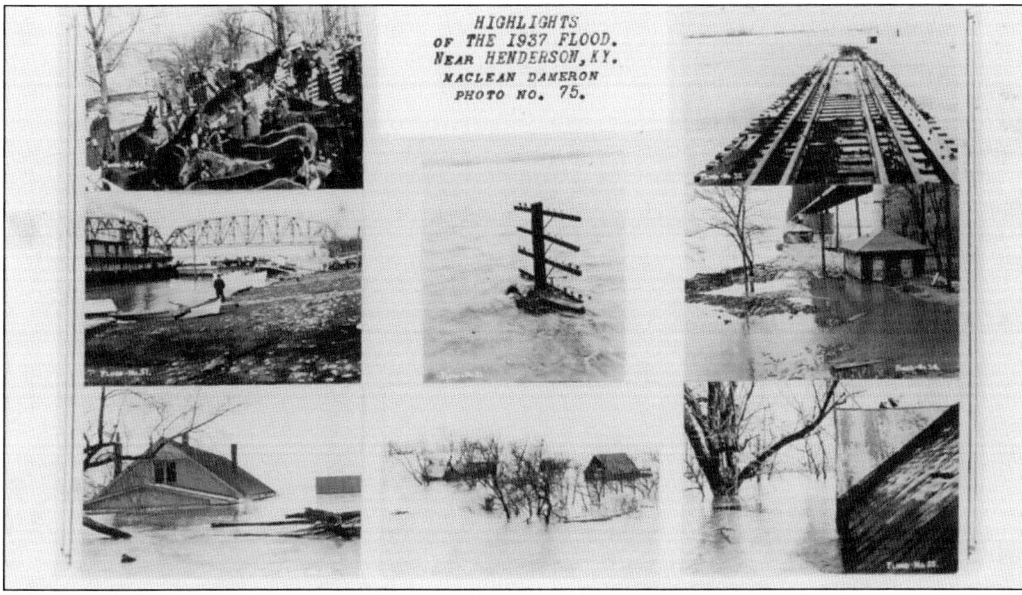

The infamous flood of 1937 was the worst in recorded history. Some form of precipitation fell almost continually between January 5 and January 23, 1937, and the river rose to a record flood stage of more than 53.9 feet. Approximately 45 percent of the county was inundated by water, and eventually 60 people were evacuated. (Courtesy of Martin Studio, Maclean Dameron Collection.)

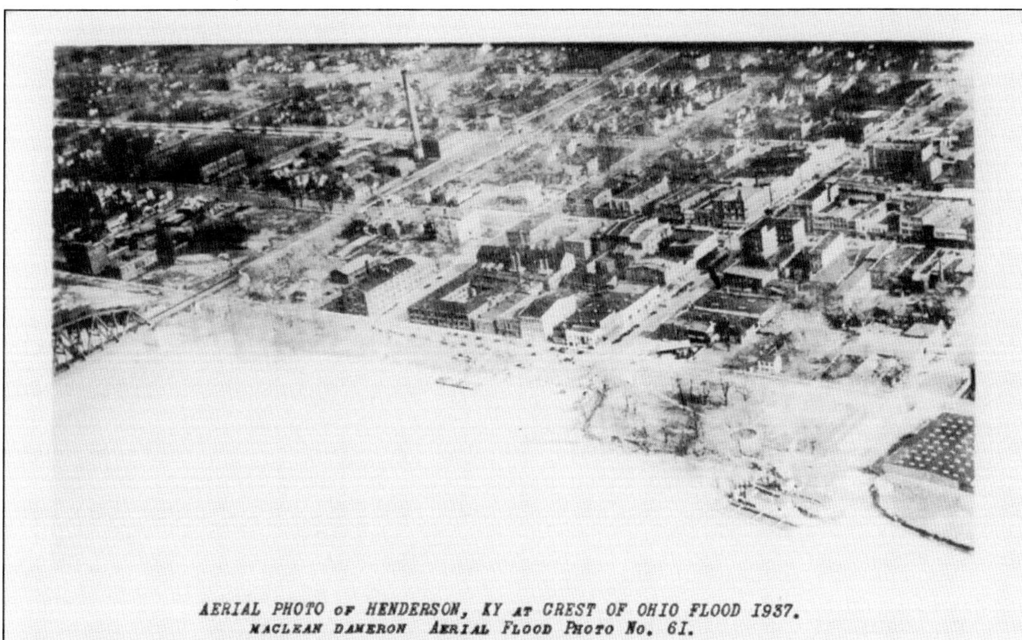

During the 1937 flood, the city of Henderson experienced no flooding and was the only city along the Ohio River that remained dry. The aerial photograph on this postcard shows the river still had many feet to rise before it reached Water Street, the street closest to the Ohio. After the waters receded, Henderson adopted the motto "On the Ohio, but never in it." (Courtesy of Martin Studio, Maclean Dameron Collection.)

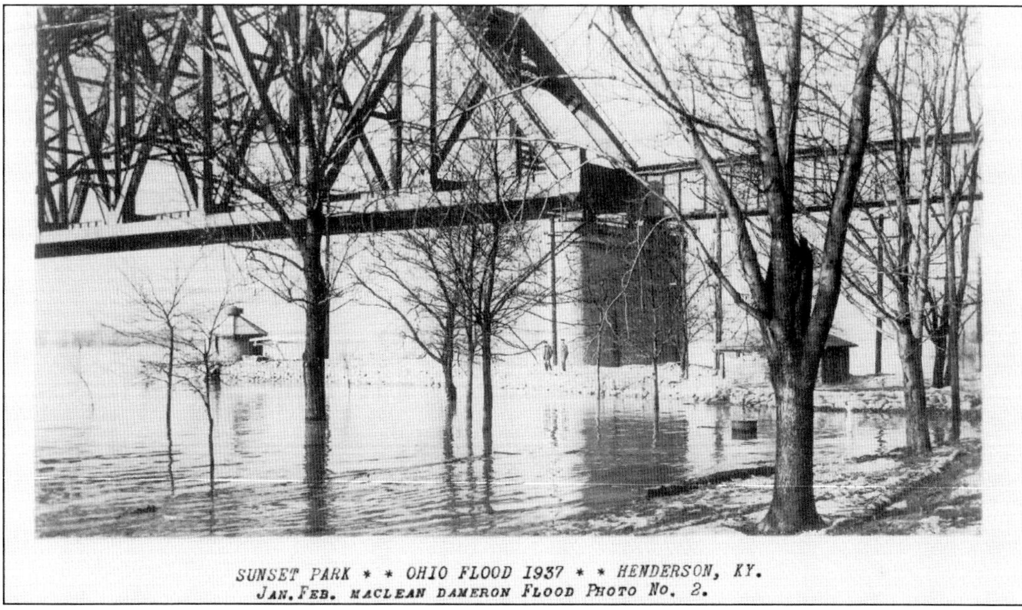

This scene shows the 1937 flood as seen from Sunset Park. Members of the CCC and others sandbagged the area under the railroad bridge to protect the city's pumps and maintain the city's power. Henderson sits 72 feet above the low watermark of the Ohio River, and even at the height of the flood, the city stood 19 feet above the floodwater. (Courtesy of Henderson County Public Library and Martin Studio, Maclean Dameron Collection.)

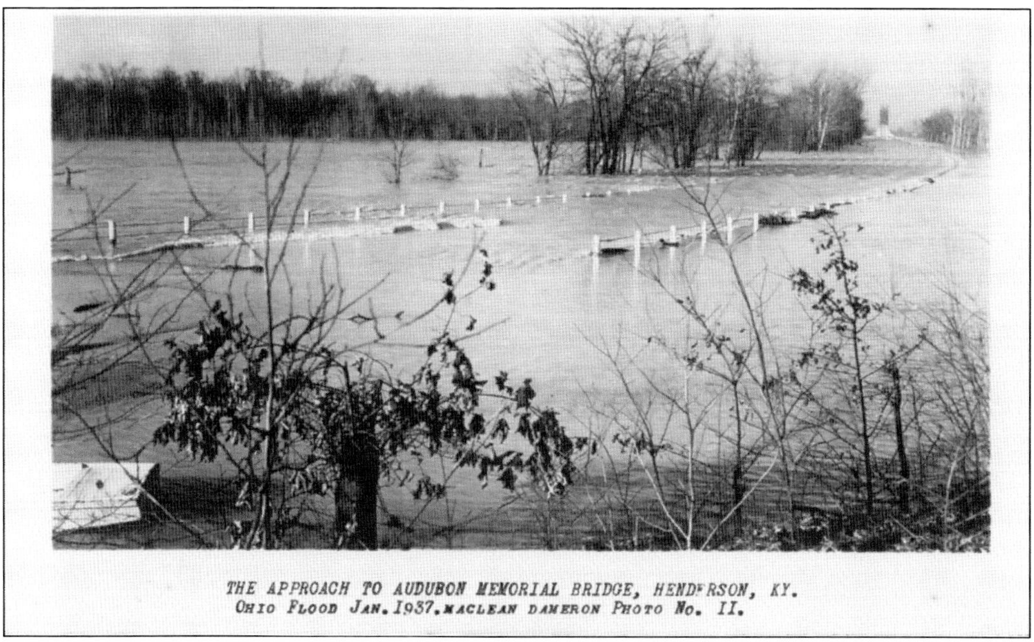

The automobile bridge connecting Henderson and Evansville had been open just under five years when rising waters of the 1937 flood threatened to make the approach along Highway 41 impassable. In an effort to keep the highway open, 100 enrollees from Camp Cromwell spent 20 hours sandbagging the levee. Despite their efforts, the river continued to rise and eventually flooded the highway. (Courtesy of Martin Studio, Maclean Dameron Collection.)

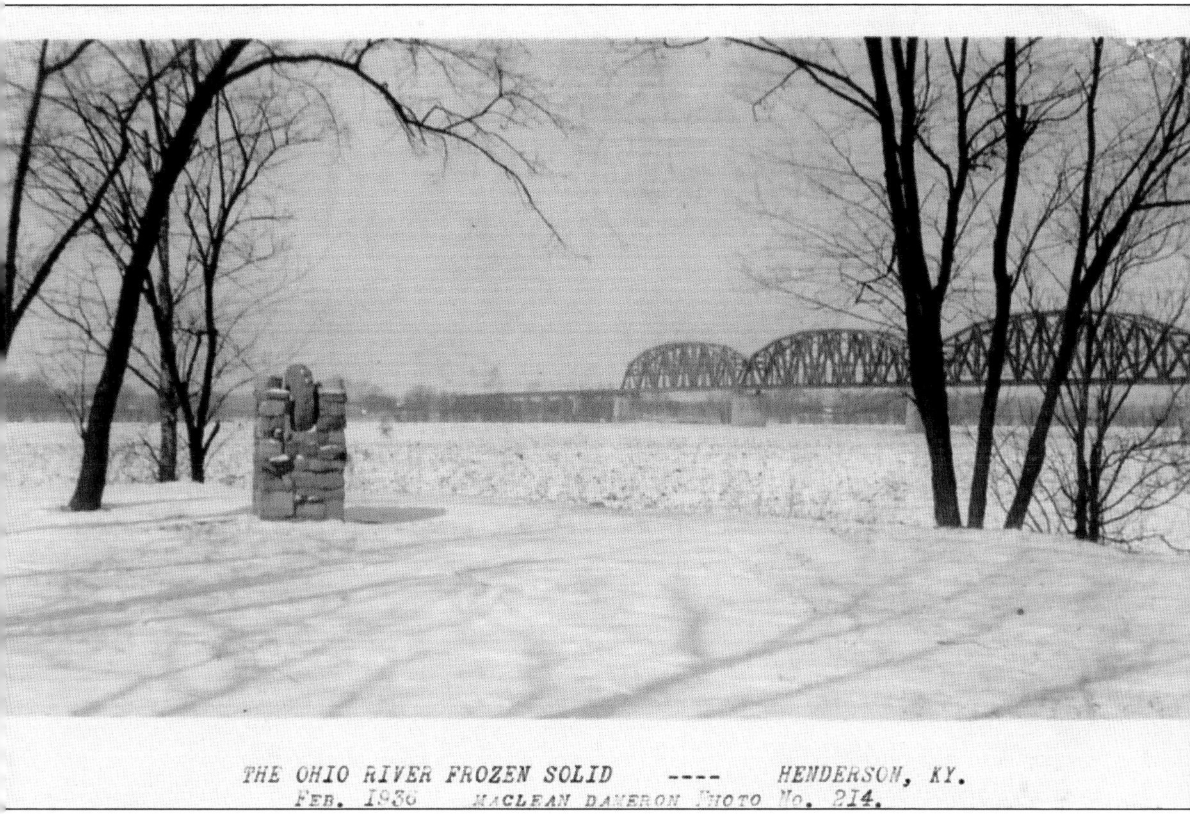

Problems with the Ohio River freezing have plagued locals throughout Henderson's history. In 1812, ice closed the Ohio for 23 days and again in 1845 for four days. Area citizens were reported to have walked across the ice-covered Ohio River in 1856, 1872, 1892, 1911, and 1918. In mid-February 1936, the *Gleaner* reported that the Ohio River was so jammed with ice that its gorge extended for 100 miles. (Courtesy of Martin Studio, Maclean Dameron Collection.)

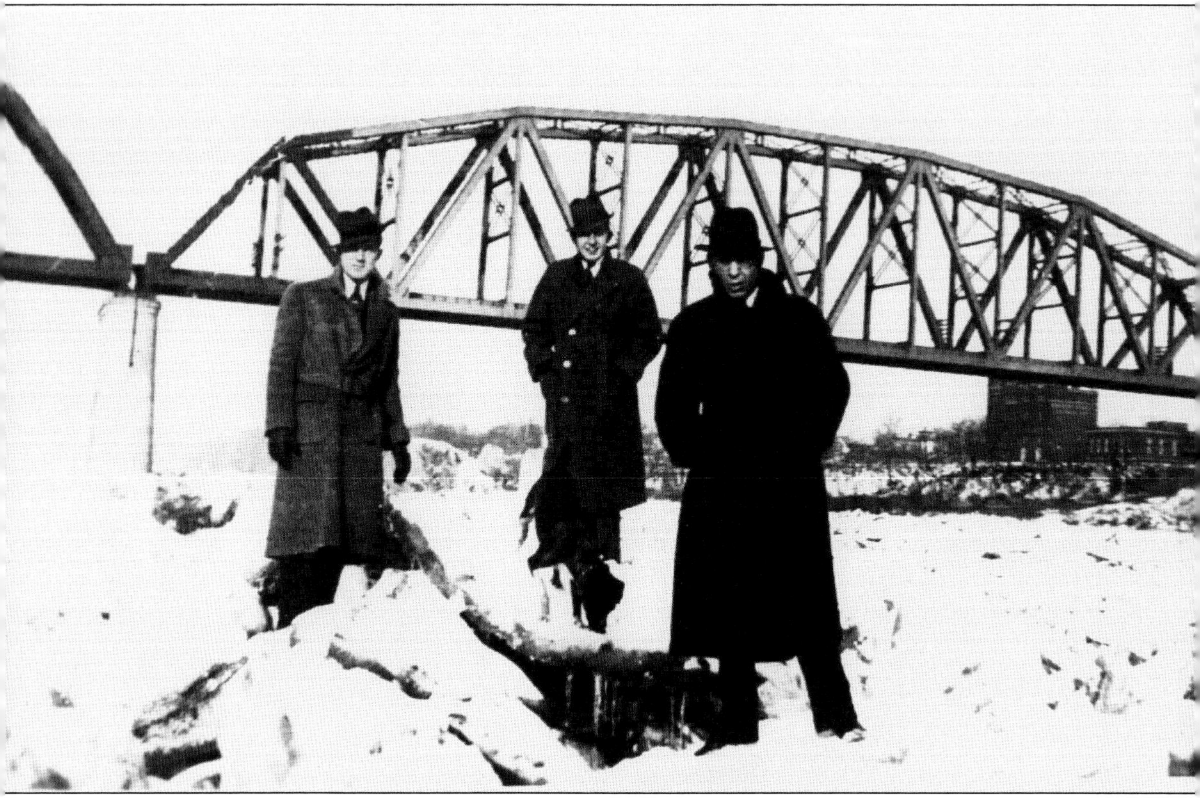

The Ohio River does not often freeze over, but when it does some local citizens dare to walk out on the ice. The *Gleaner* reported that on February 17, 1936, around 20 people "walked across the stream at Henderson." Pictured here atop ice floes in that 1936 freeze are Charles "Muggins" Sommers (left), father of the author; "Jockey" Roberts (center); and Eddie Funk (right). At far right, the Henderson Brewing Company towers at the corner of Fifth and Water Streets. (Courtesy of Donald Wathen.)

Eight

Strolling Around

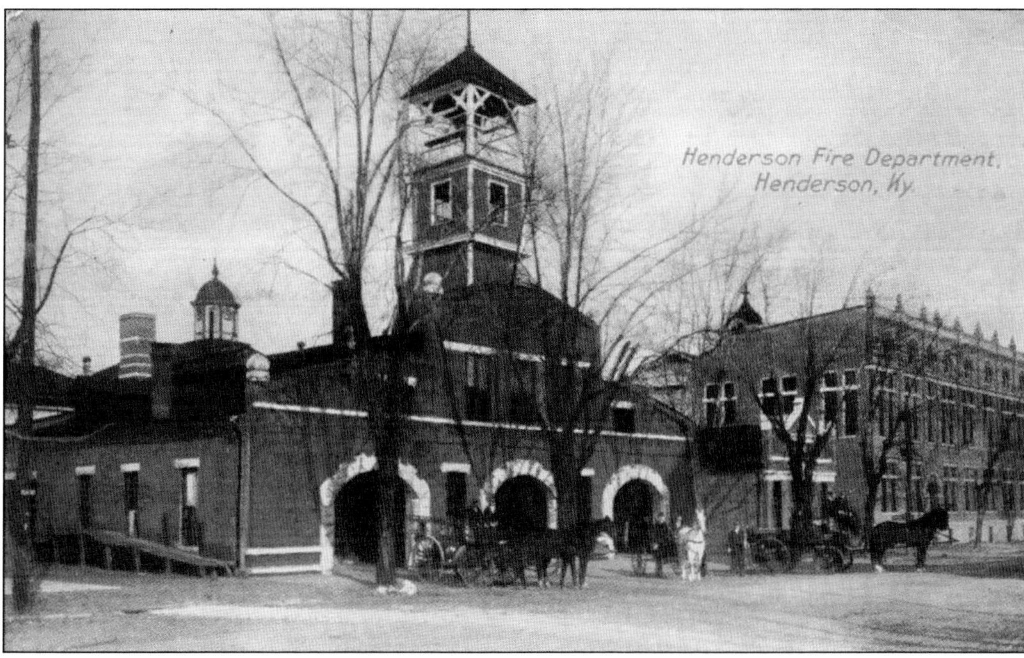

In 1895, construction for Henderson's first fire barn began. The building, located on the west side of Elm Street near the intersection of Center Street, was completed in 1896 at a cost of $4,858. Visible in this postcard is the fire tower, used to watch for smoke or fire; this tower was eventually replaced by a freestanding tower. At times, an elaborate system of bells, including the courthouse bell located just behind the fire station, was tolled to signal a fire and its location. The year 1895 was also historic for the firemen because it was then that they were first made regular, salaried employees.

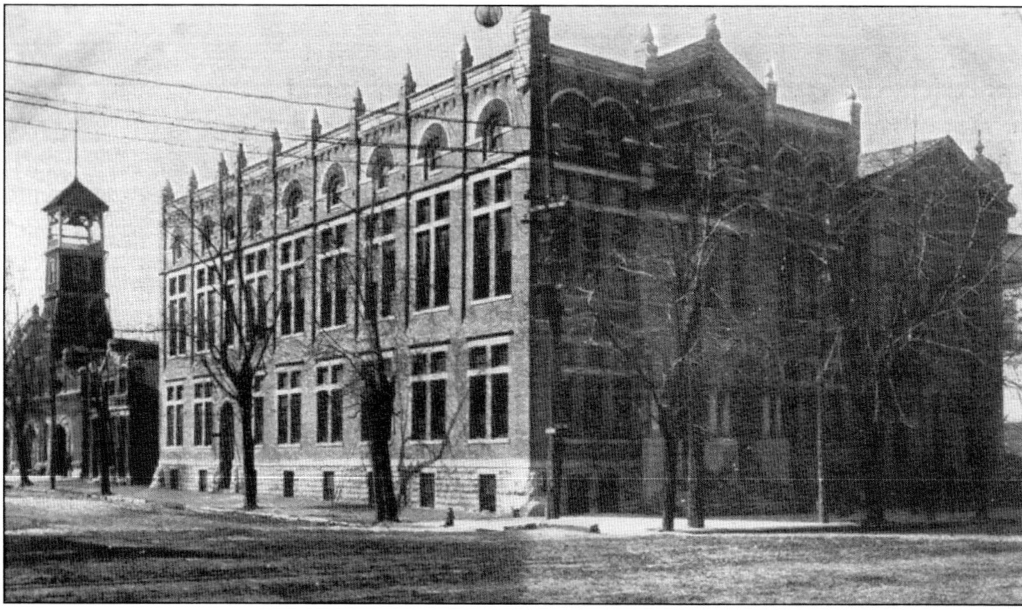

This scene at the southwest corner of Elm and First Streets depicts the three-story City Building with its double-arched entrance. The building was constructed in 1903 for $21,601, with additional expenses for the heating system, screens, and doors. After a 1968 earthquake, the building was deemed unsafe and was demolished on September 1, 1971. To the south (left) of the City Building was the fire department; to the west (right) was the police headquarters.

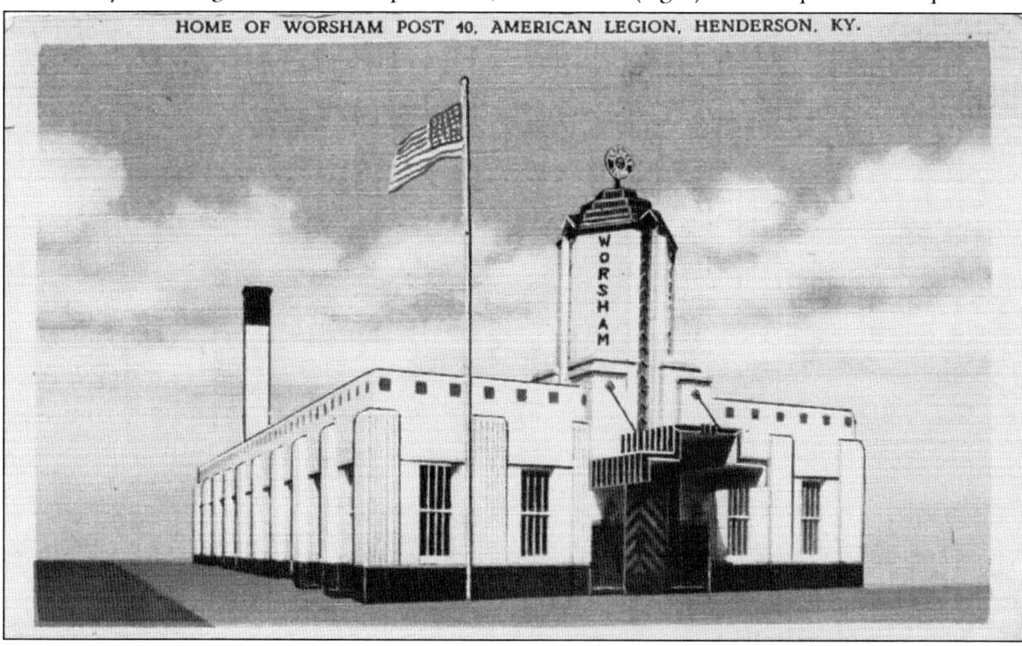

Worsham Hall, the art deco concrete structure designed by Henderson architect J. Alves Clore, was dedicated in 1936 as the home of American Legion Worsham Post No. 40. The structure was named for 31-year-old Lt. Archibald Dixon Worsham, the first Henderson County soldier to die in World War I. Worsham was killed in France and later received the Croix de Guerre. The building still stands at 215 North Elm Street.

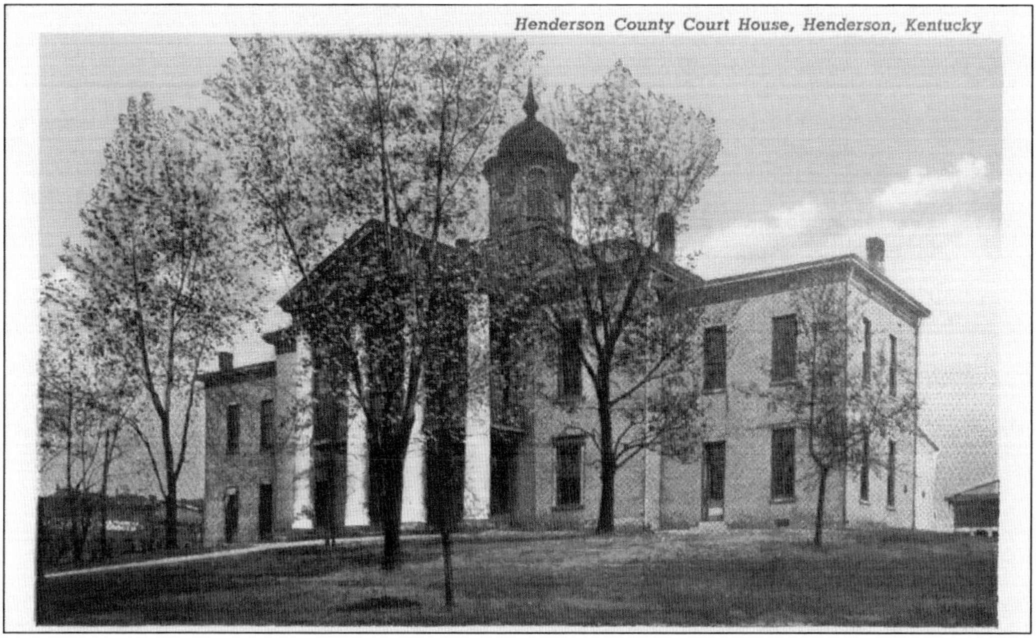

Henderson has been home to three courthouses, all erected on the same hill on the northwest corner of Transylvania (Central) Park. The courthouse seen here was the second. This stuccoed brick building, complete with slate roof, Doric columns, and octagonal cupola, was erected in 1843 at a cost of $9,400. The architect or builder was Littleberry Weaver. Later additions in 1874 and 1881 added the two-story wings.

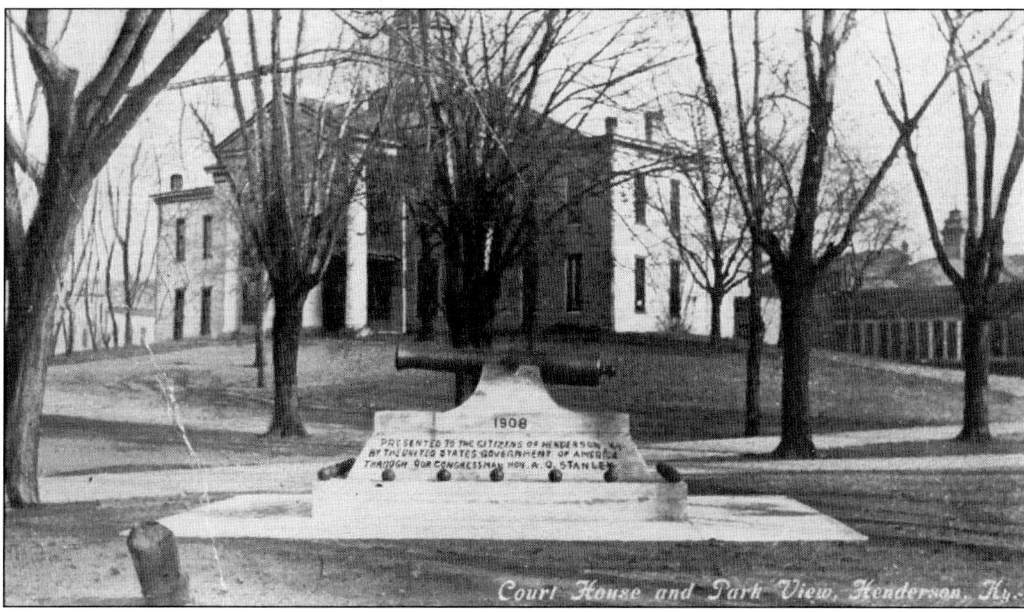

In 1908, a cannon, a relic of an unknown war, was placed on the Main Street side of Central Park in sight of the old courthouse. Donated through the efforts of Henderson resident A. O. Stanley (then a U.S. congressman and later a Kentucky governor and U.S. senator), the cannon was scrapped during World War II to aid the war effort. This courthouse was razed in 1963 and replaced by the present-day courthouse.

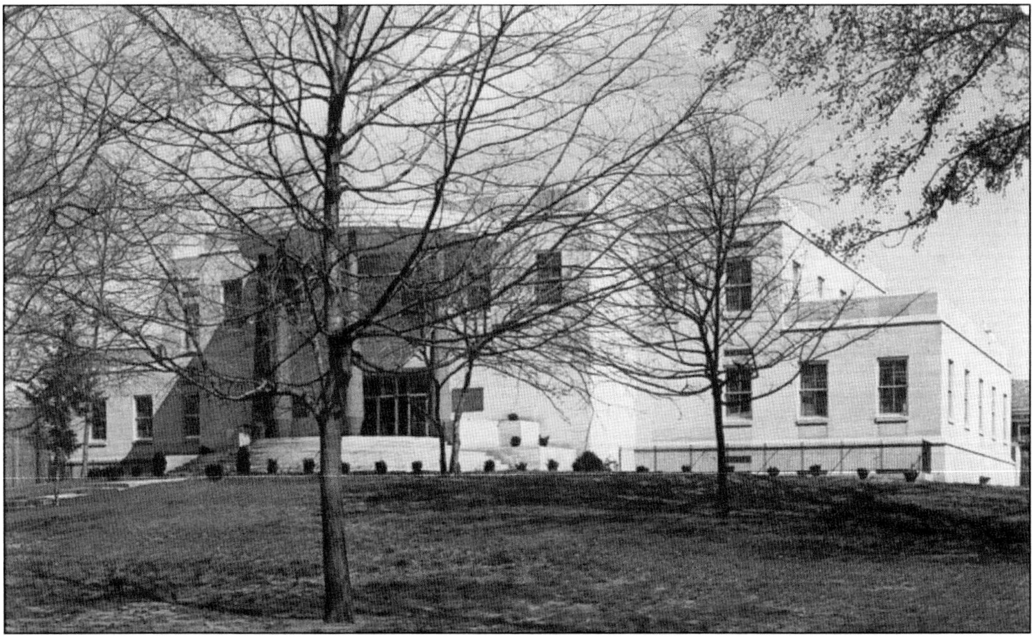

In the 1960s when a new courthouse was deemed necessary, concern arose about whether the courthouse hill was actually a Native American burial mound, as had been speculated for many years. A 1964 archaeological investigation determined that the hill was not man-made, and Glover Brick Contractors was awarded a $551,189 contract for the new courthouse. The architect was Tom M. Paine, and the designer was John Russell Baker. The courthouse was dedicated on May 15, 1965.

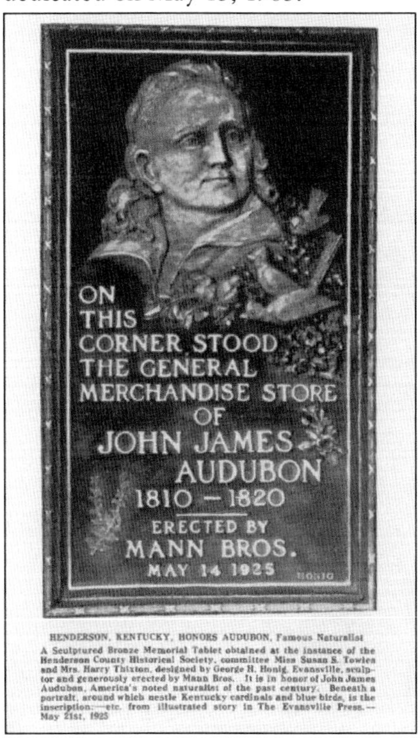

This plaque commemorates the general store that John James Audubon operated on the northeast corner of Second and Main Streets. Local leaders had long wished for a shrine to the ornithologist, and the back of this postcard invited bird lovers to assist Hendersonians in erecting "a National Audubon Memorial on the original spot of ground where most of the Audubon Bird Pictures were made."

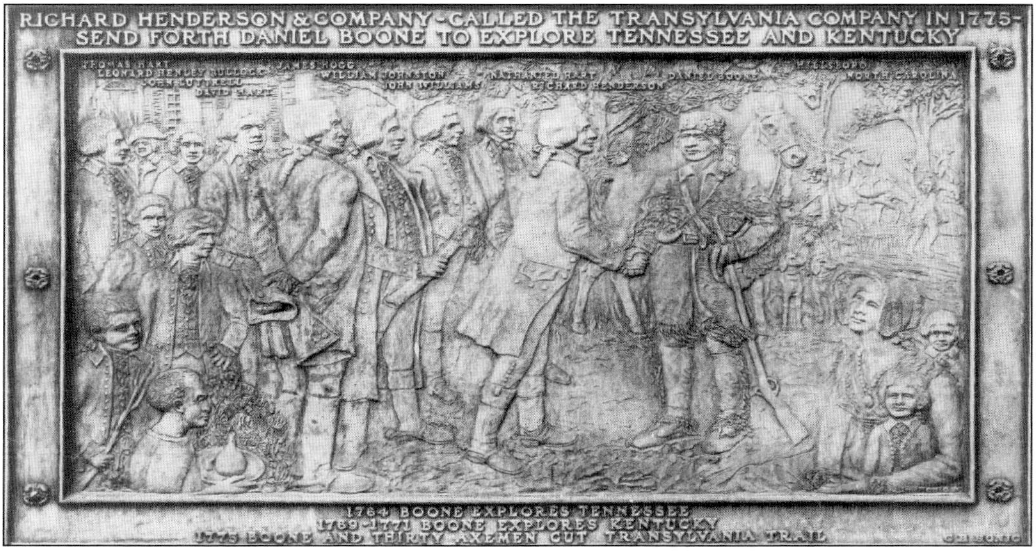

In 1929, six tablets commemorating the Transylvania Company were presented by Robert Bingham and were placed outside the existing courthouse. (Today two tablets flank the entrance to the courthouse; the other four are inside the main entry.) Chiefly the result of efforts by Susan Towles, the tablets were designed and sculpted by George H. Honig and were cast at the foundry of the Art Bronze and Aluminum Company. The tablets depict the explorations of Daniel Boone, the Treaty of Watauga, the address by Richard Henderson at Fort Boonesborough, the first Christian service in Kentucky, the petition that Transylvania be adopted as the 14th state, and the laying out of Henderson. (Both, courtesy of Henderson County Public Library.)

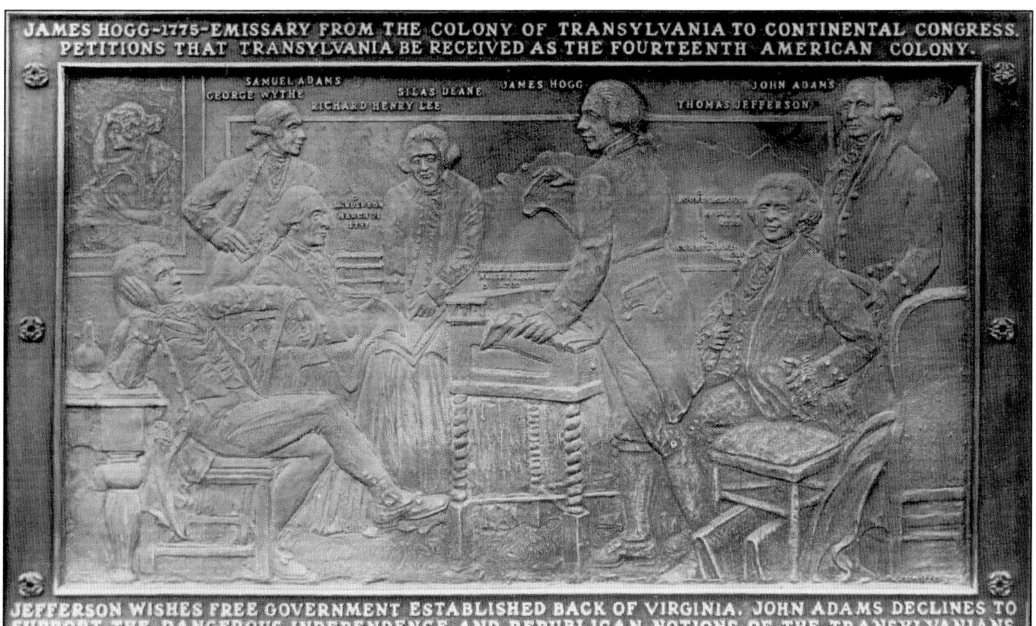

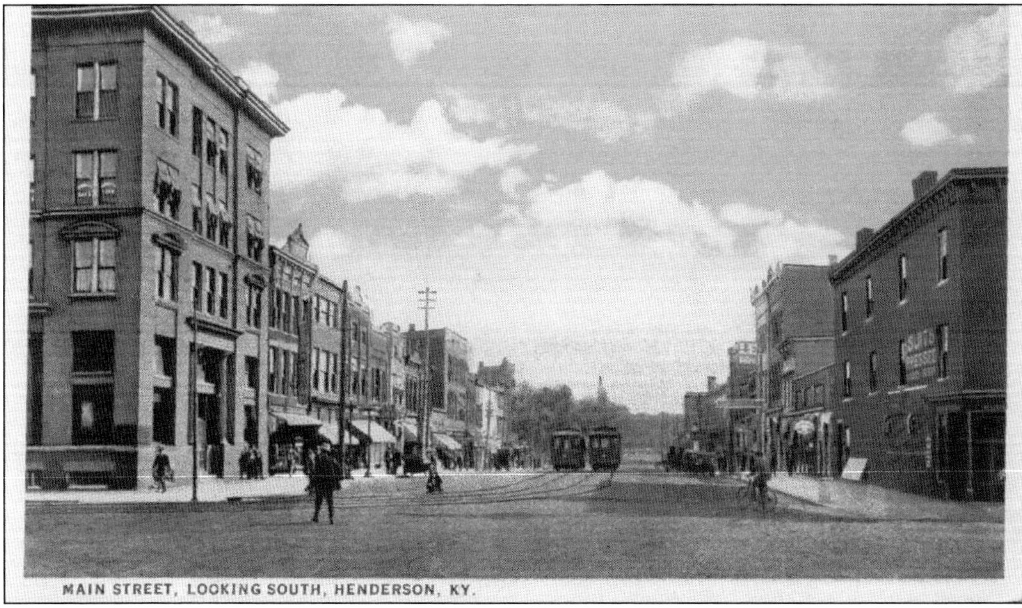

Taken looking south from the intersection of Main and Second Streets, this scene is one of the few showing the building that predated the Soaper Hotel on the southwest corner (right front). During the Civil War, this building was owned by James Rankin, who, in 1864, was attacked by Confederate guerillas demanding money from his safe. As Rankin was opening the safe, the guerrillas shot him; he later died of the wounds.

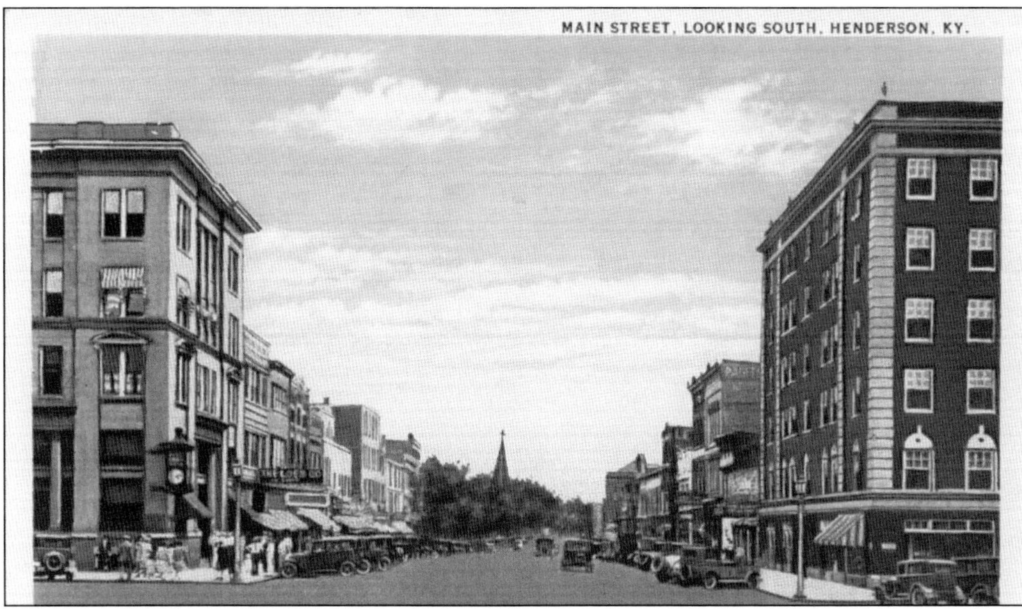

This postcard depicts the same intersection of Second and Main Streets. Changes include the clock at the Ohio Valley Bank (left), the Soaper Hotel (right), new streetlights, paved streets, and the modern mode of travel—automobiles. In 1923, members of the Automobile Club and the city government recommended that the top speed for "horseless carriages" would be 10 to 15 miles per hour in the business district and school zones, and 20 miles per hour in residential districts.

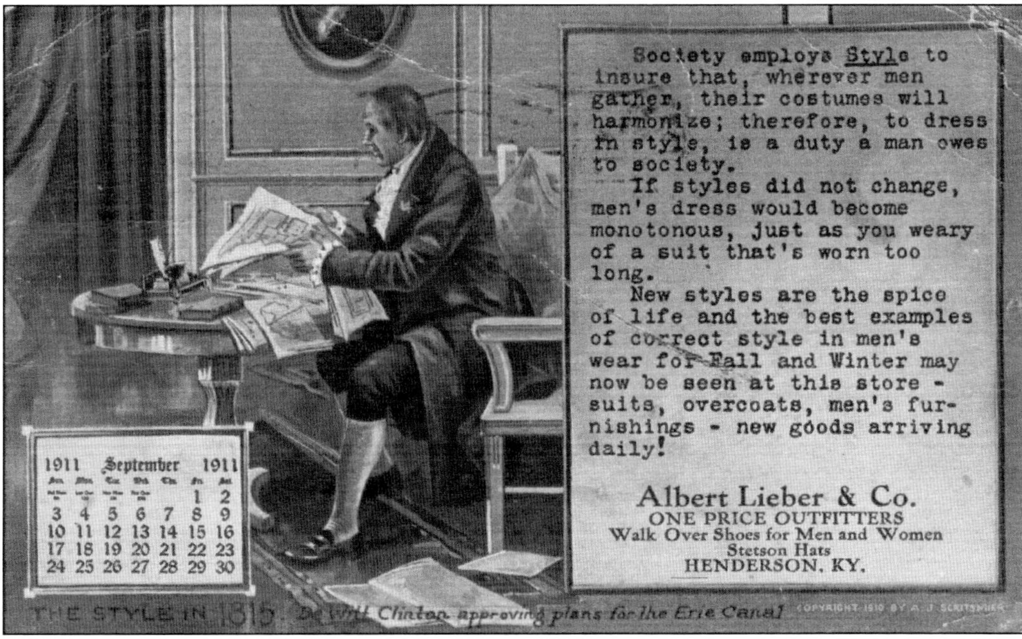

In 1911, the date of this postcard, the Albert Lieber and Company, which described itself as "One Price Clothiers and Men's Furnishers," was located at 136 North Main Street. When this postcard was mailed, Lieber's advertised the "Choice of any Boys' Knicker Serge, Cassimere or Cheviot $6.50, $7.50, or $8.50 Suit" for $5 and reminded customers to "Remember the Name—Remember the Place." (Courtesy of Pat Workins.)

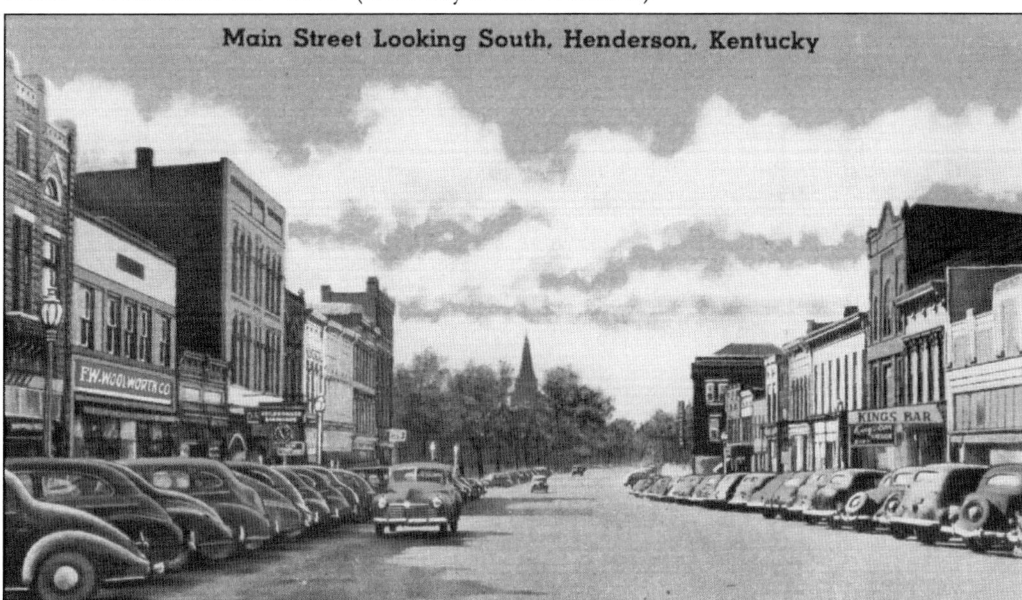

This postcard shows businesses in the mid-1900s on Main Street south of Second Street. Prominent are Woolworth's, King's Bar, and Heilbronner's Jewelers (with its sidewalk clock). The last building on the west (right) side was the site of the Nicholson Building that later became the Farm Bureau. In earlier days, that corner had housed the Hancock House, the Hord House, and the Barret House with its adjoining theater, both of which burned in 1896.

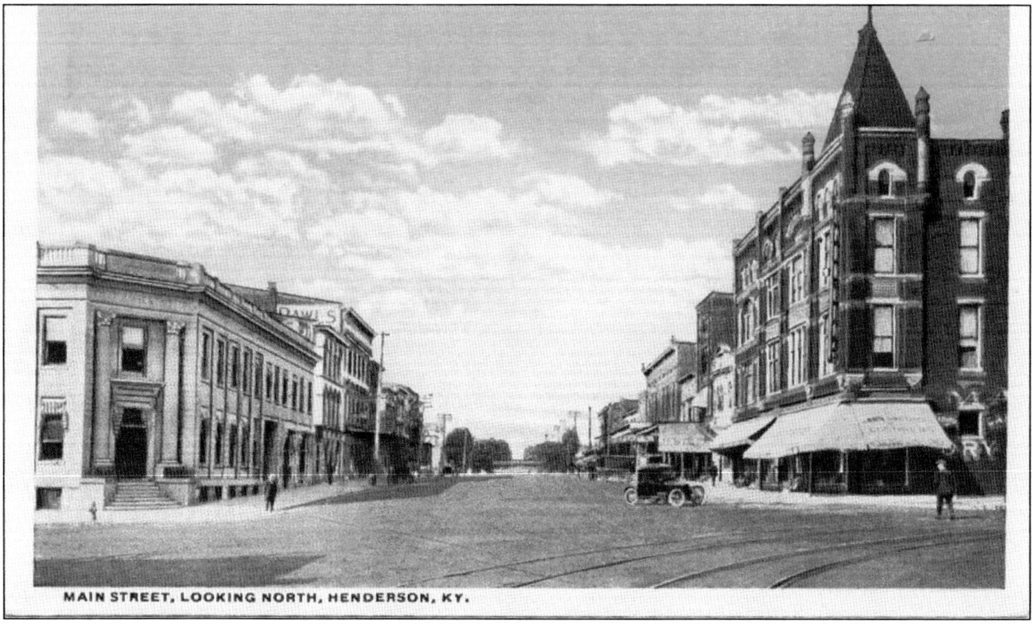

This scene looks north from Second and Main Streets. On the west (left) side of Main Street is the 1904 Bedford stone Union Bank and Trust that replaced the Moore and Oldham grocery. On the east is Mann Brothers, a Romanesque Revival–style building constructed about 1890 on the former site of John James Audubon's general store. Interestingly, this card features four modes of transportation: railroad (the bridge), trolleys (the tracks), automobiles, and horse and buggy.

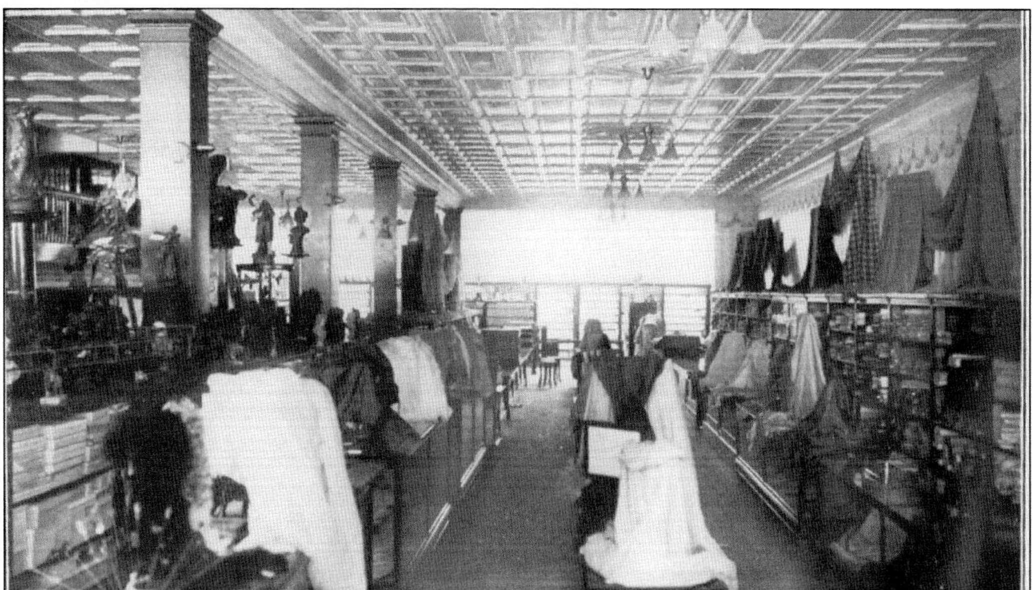

In 1913, the 90,000-square-foot Mann Brothers store boasted modern elevators and a "private telephone exchange" with 20 telephones throughout the store. Various departments, staffed with more than 60 "painstaking and efficient clerks," offered the latest in ladies, gentlemen's, and household "furnishings," as well as "dress goods," dry goods, and "wash goods."

Mann Brothers, which sold everything from carpets to clothing, sent this 1909 postcard to its customers inviting them to visit the store from October 25 through 30 for a "special demonstration" of American Lady and Lycra corsets.

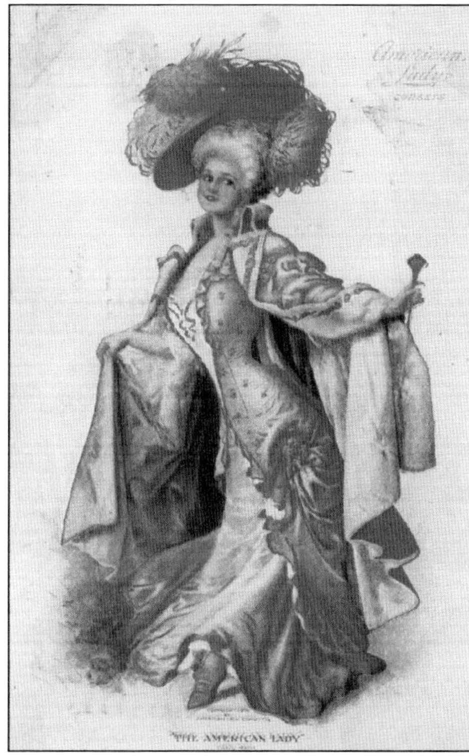

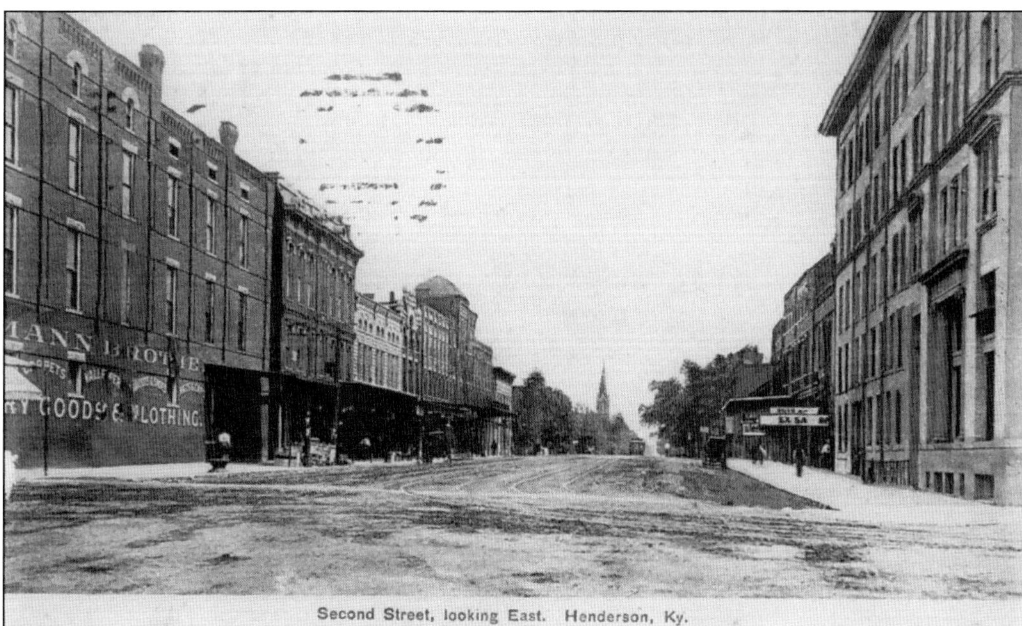

Pictured in the distance are a trolley, perhaps on its route to Union Station, and the steeple at the Holy Name Catholic Church. On the right, immediately behind the Ohio Valley Bank, is a saloon, probably owned by Louis Haag. In 1905, about the time this picture was taken, Henderson boasted 47 saloons. Mann Brothers, on the left, operated in that building until 1927; it is said to be the first company in the United States to offer installment buying.

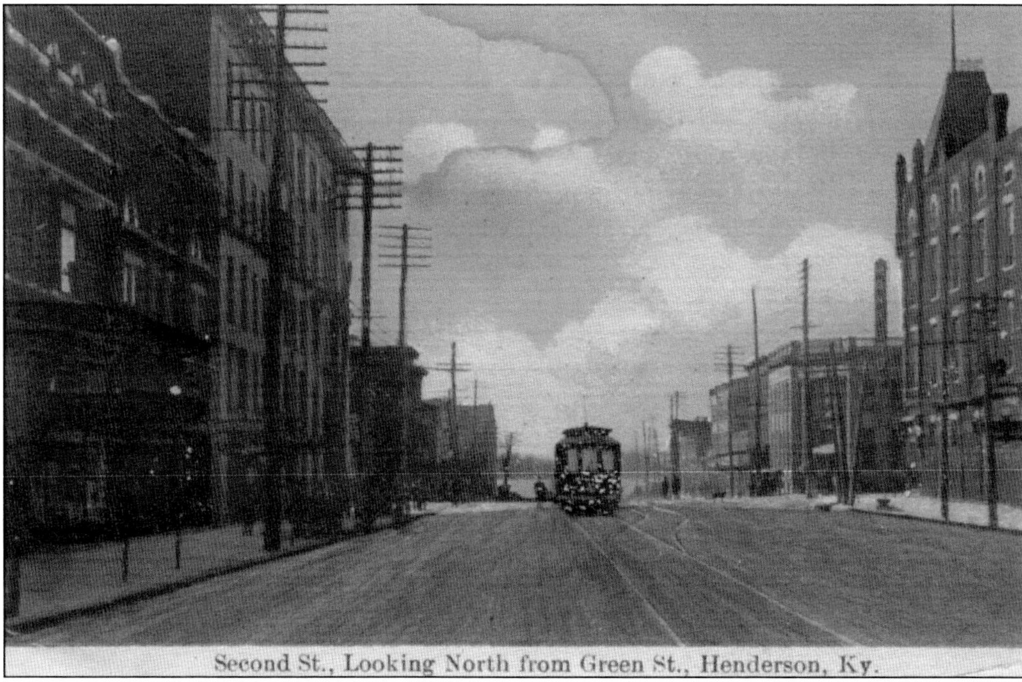

This image, taken sometime between 1904 and 1912, shows (contrary to its caption) Second Street looking west from Elm Street to the Ohio River. The streets are as yet unpaved, and numerous electrical wires dominate the skyline. (Courtesy of Pam Austin.)

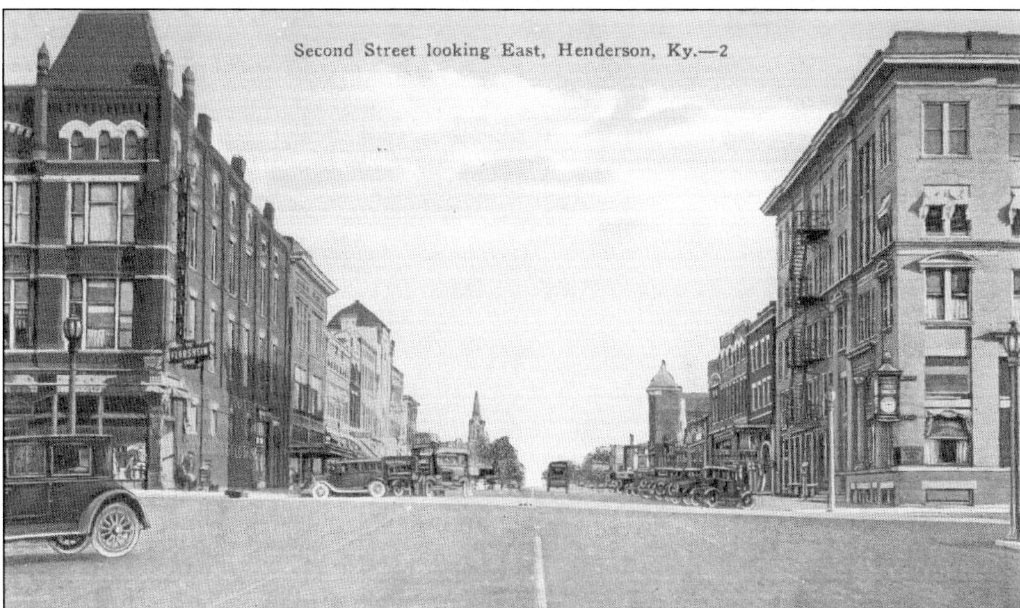

This postcard, probably from the late 1920s or early 1930s, gives a later view of the intersection of Second and Main Streets. Changes include the fire escape on the Ohio Valley Bank and the new streetlights, which were installed in the early 1920s. Trolley tracks have been removed. The shoe-shine operator who sits beside Mann Brothers is probably John Cloudy, who worked on that corner for many years. (Courtesy of Henderson County Public Library.)

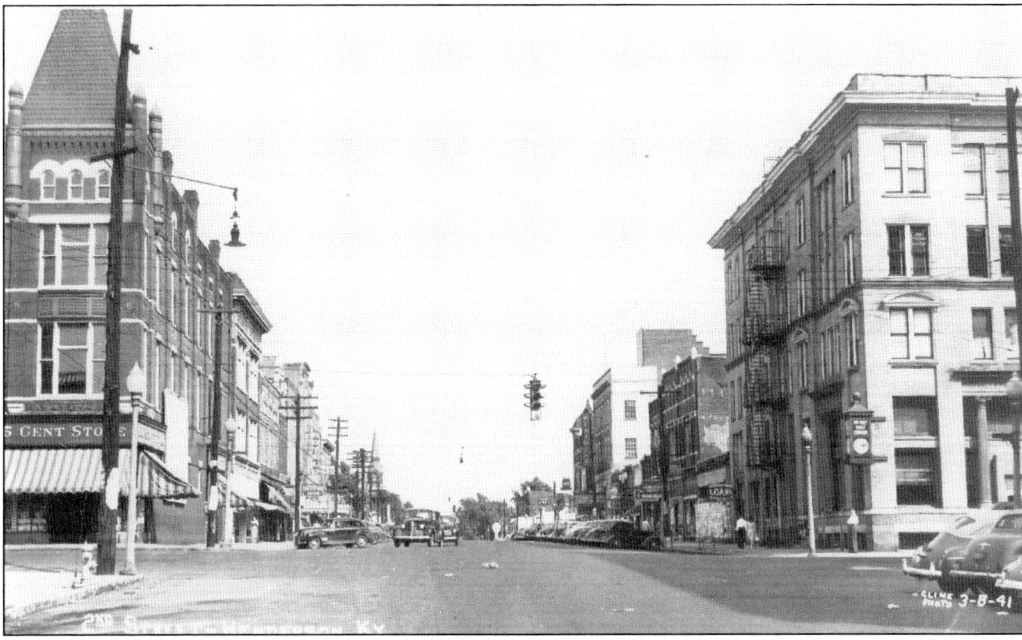

More changes are evident in this scene at the corner of Main and Second Streets. In 1927, the Mann Brothers building was leased to Newberry's, a dime store that remained in business until 1986 (the building was demolished in 1988). Traffic had increased so much that a stoplight had been installed. The Kentucky Theater is seen in the middle of the south (right) side of Second Street. (Courtesy of Henderson County Public Library.)

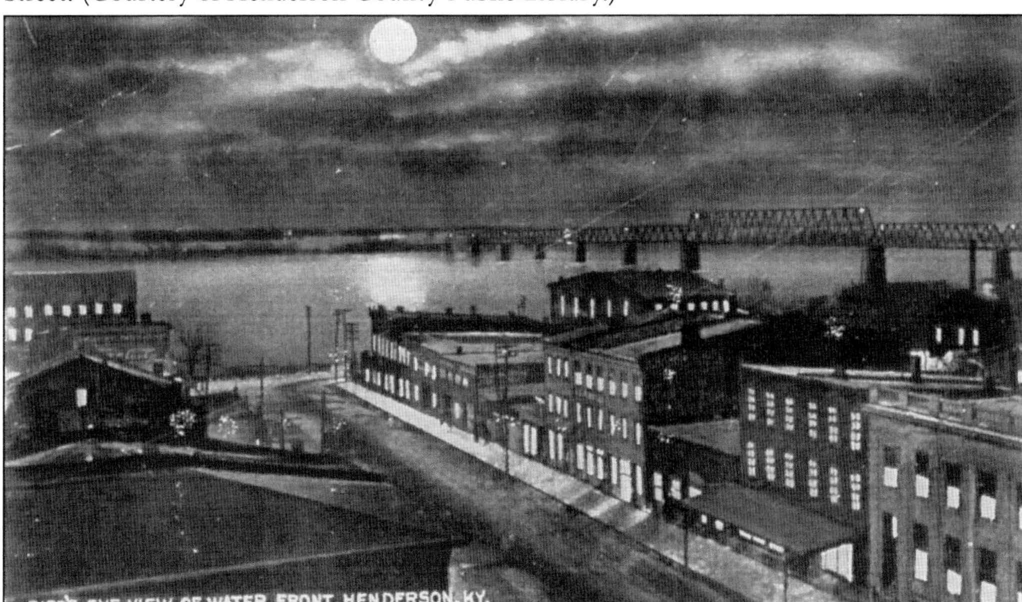

This postcard shows prosperous businesses on Second Street between Main and Water Streets sometime between 1904 and 1913, a time when several African American–owned businesses were located in the block. In the middle on the south (left) side was the Gaines Funeral Home. On the north side was the United Brotherhood of Friendship and the Sisters of the Mysterious Ten Hall and the Benevolent Aid Society Hall, sites of Emancipation Day celebrations each August 4.

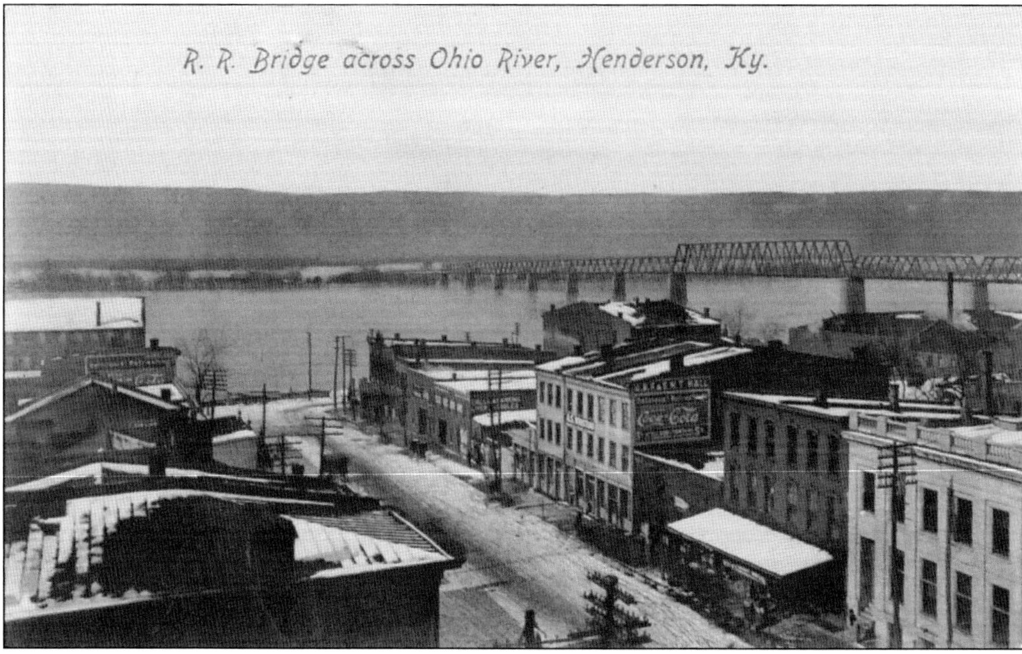

The picture in this panoramic double-view card, which originally folded out as a single view, looks north on Main Street and west on Second Street. It was taken sometime between 1904 and 1907 from atop a building at the intersection of Main and Second Streets. Sheds in front of various storefronts were in widespread use before Henderson Chamber of Commerce secretary Oscar Monrad vehemently urged their removal. The shed on the west (left) side of Main Street was used to shield customers of the P. A. Blackwell Implement Company from bad weather. The shed just north of it was in front of the early offices of the Henderson *Gleaner.*

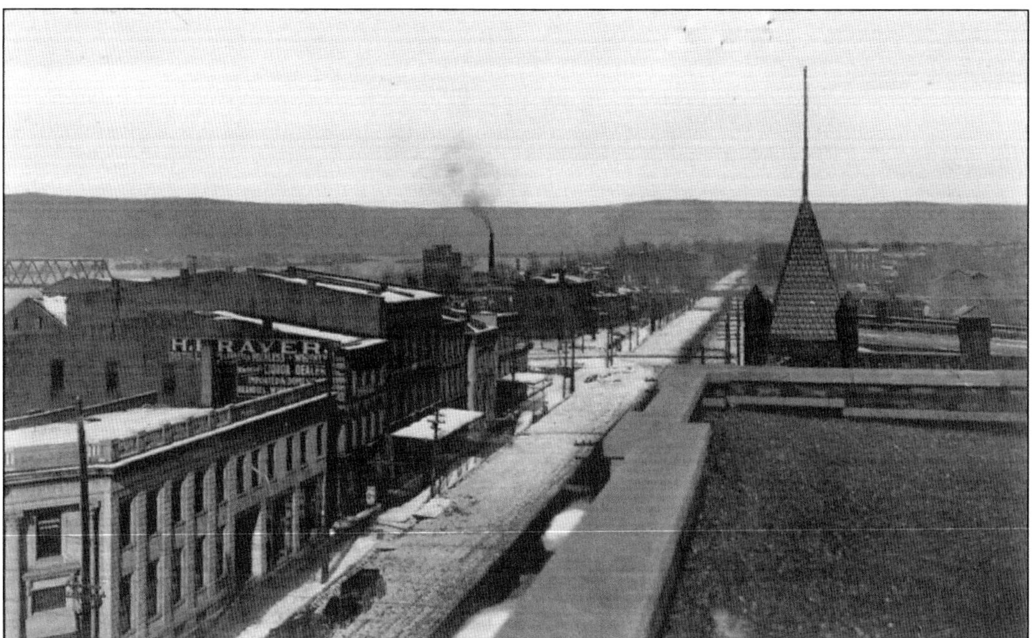

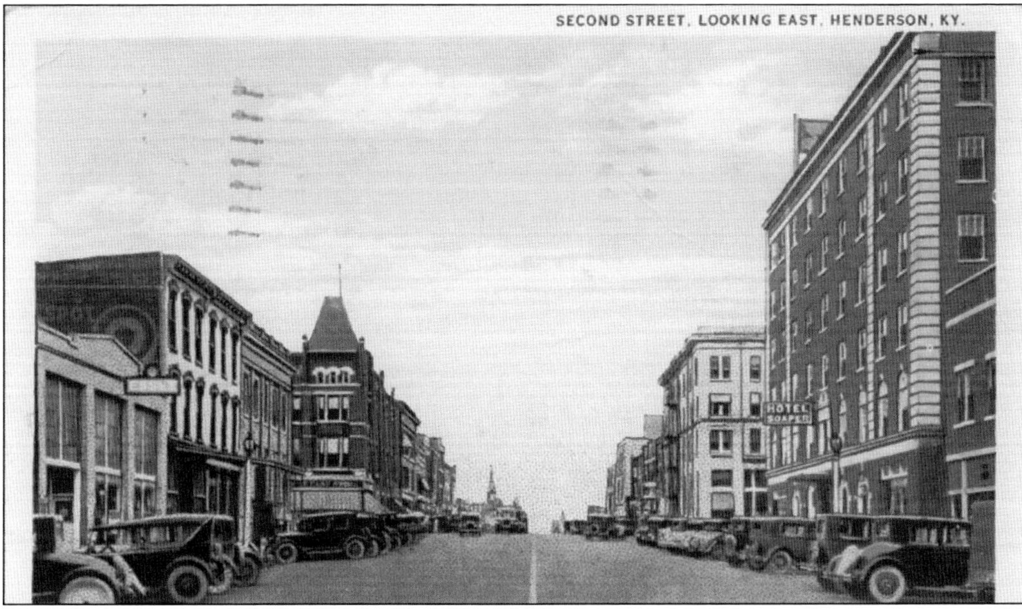

This postcard looks east on Second Street about a half block from the Ohio River. The second building on the left, located at 135 Second Street, housed Harry Fuchs's secondhand store. This building and others like it in downtown Henderson featured Mesker steel fronts. In the latter part of the 19th century, a number of businesses spiffed up their properties with prefabricated storefronts. Customers sent their specifications to the Evansville-based Mesker Steel Company, and the new storefronts were delivered by boat or rail.

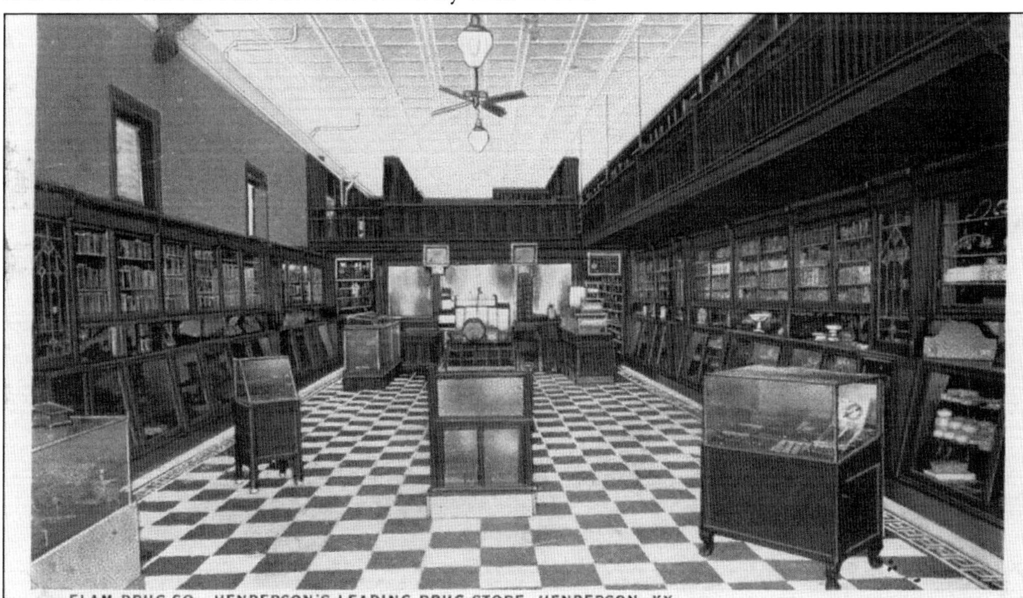

The Elam Drug Company was located on the southwest corner of Second and North Elm Streets. Formed in 1907 under a partnership between John T. Elam and E. C. Ward, Elam's was an "exclusive" drugstore, since it had no soda fountain or ice cream parlor. Elam's boasted such products as Wyeth's sage and sulphur hair tonic, Orrine for the "cure of liquor habit," and Bourbon hog cholera remedies.

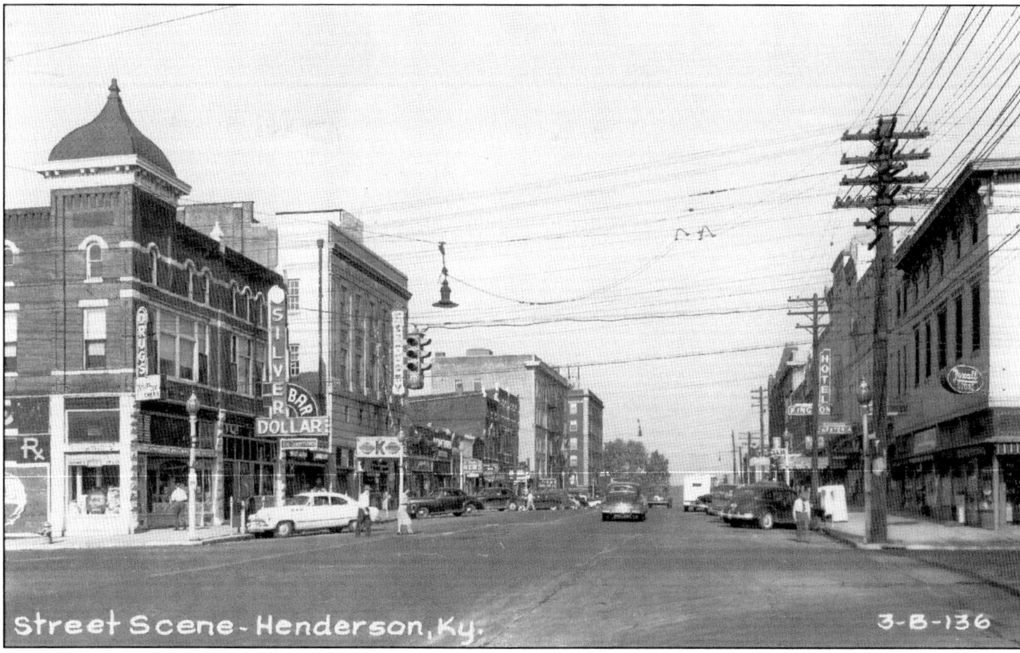

This mid-1900s postcard gives a picture of North Elm Street looking west at the intersection of Second Street. On the south (left) side, businesses of the time included Dunaway's Drugs, the Silver Dollar Bar, and the Kentucky Theater; Quinn's Rexall Drugs and the Kingdon Hotel are on the north (right) side. (Courtesy of Henderson County Public Library.)

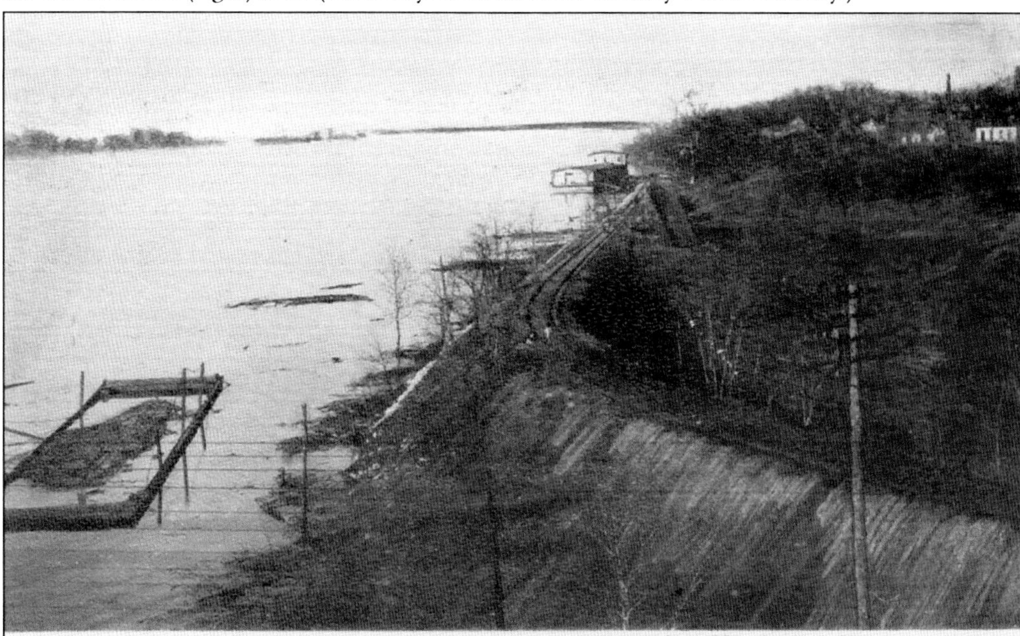

This postcard, postmarked 1912, is unusual because it looks upriver (north) from the original railroad bridge. The railroad tracks seen here delivered coal to the area's businesses and hauled cargo to and from a sawmill on Sixth Street and a brewery on Fifth Street. Notable also are the un-manicured terrain and the service wires on the high bluff.

Constructed in 1923, the Classical Revival–style Henderson National Bank at 208 North Main Street features brick masonry side walls and a dressed ashlar limestone facade with a flat front parapet. In the 1930s, the bank began operating under the name First National Bank. In 1993, it was acquired by Citizens Bank (later Civitas), and then it was acquired in 1999 by First Third Bancorp. In 2000, it reopened under its original name.

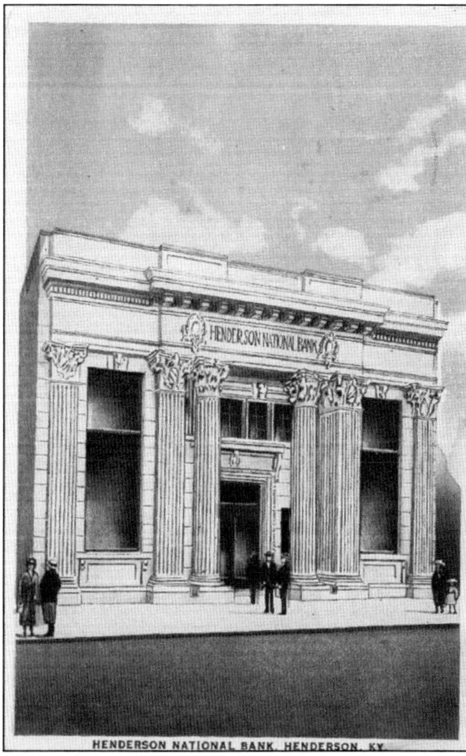

On January 15, 1932, Henderson National Bank experienced a run on its deposits and, as a result, closed its doors for a short time. After a federal comptroller took over the bank's assets, the institution reopened, changing its name to First National Bank. Less than two years later—in the midst of the Great Depression—its assets were close to a half million dollars.

FIRST NATIONAL BANK OF HENDERSON

Henderson, Kentucky

Condensed Statement

At the close of business October 25, 1933

RESOURCES			LIABILITIES	
Cash & Due from Banks,	$189,865.43		Capital Stock,	$100,000.00
U. S. Government Bonds, Federal Reserve Bank Stock, Other Bonds	78,667.55	$268,532.98	Surplus,	20,000.00
Safe Deposit Vault, Furniture and Fixtures		5,000.00	Undivided Profits,	352.03
Loans and Discounts:			Bills Payable, Rediscounts and Commitments,	NONE
Due in 30 days	79,771.33		Deposits,	320,791.93
Due in 60 days	56,663.50			
Due in 90 days	26,733.34			
Due after 90 days	1,847.05	$165,015.22		
Overdrafts,		NONE		
Other Assets,		2,595.76		
		$441,143.96		$441,143.96

OFFICERS

HENRY KRAVER, PRESIDENT

POPE WALKER, VICE PRESIDENT
ROBT. E. JOHNSTON, ASST. CASHIER

C. A KATTERJOHN CASHIER
G. W. CATON, ASST. CASHIER

DIRECTORS

FRANK H. DELKER
MARVIN D. EBLEN
R. A. HUGHES

HENRY KRAVER
ALEXANDER MAYER
F. J. PENTECOST

FRANK G. SCHMITT
POPE WALKER

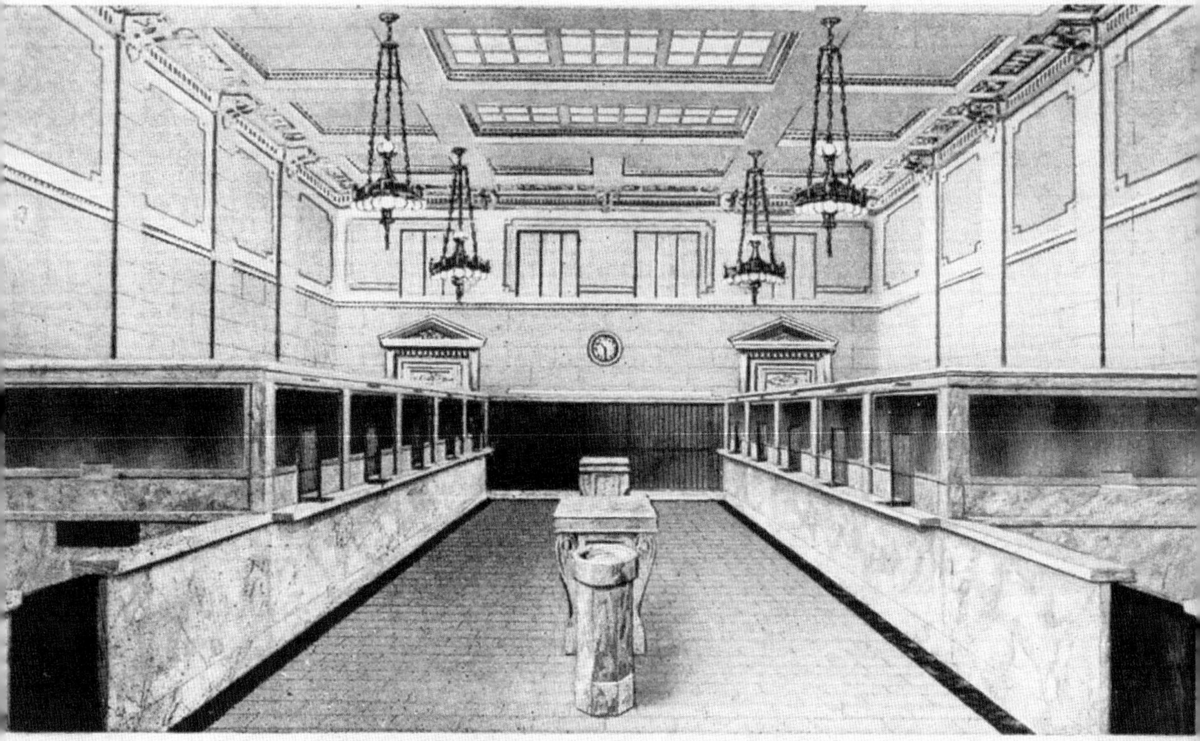

INTERIOR, HENDERSON NATIONAL BANK, HENDERSON, KY.

The original interior of the 1923 Henderson National Bank was a symmetrical, two-story central space with a coffered ceiling, acanthus leaf molding, four large central skylights, wall pilasters with corbelled brackets, tiled floors, impressive stone or marble teller cubicles, customers' writing desk, and water fountain.

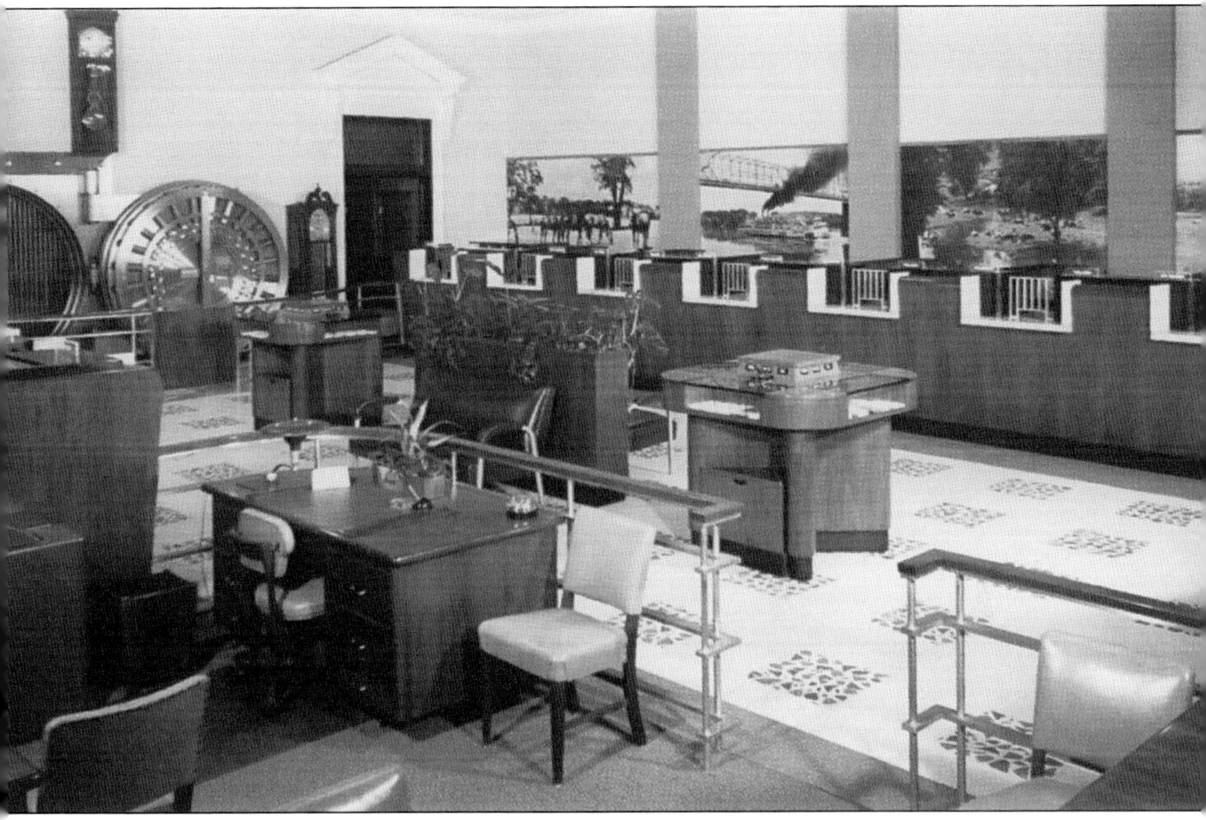

This renovation of the original interior lobby of the First National Bank (originally and currently the Henderson National Bank) showcases the bank's huge vault (left, rear), numerous teller stations, and large prints of various Kentucky scenes. The central space of the two-story interior retained its original coffered ceiling, acanthus leaf cove molding, central skylights, and wall pilasters with corbelled brackets. Wood replaced much of the original marble.

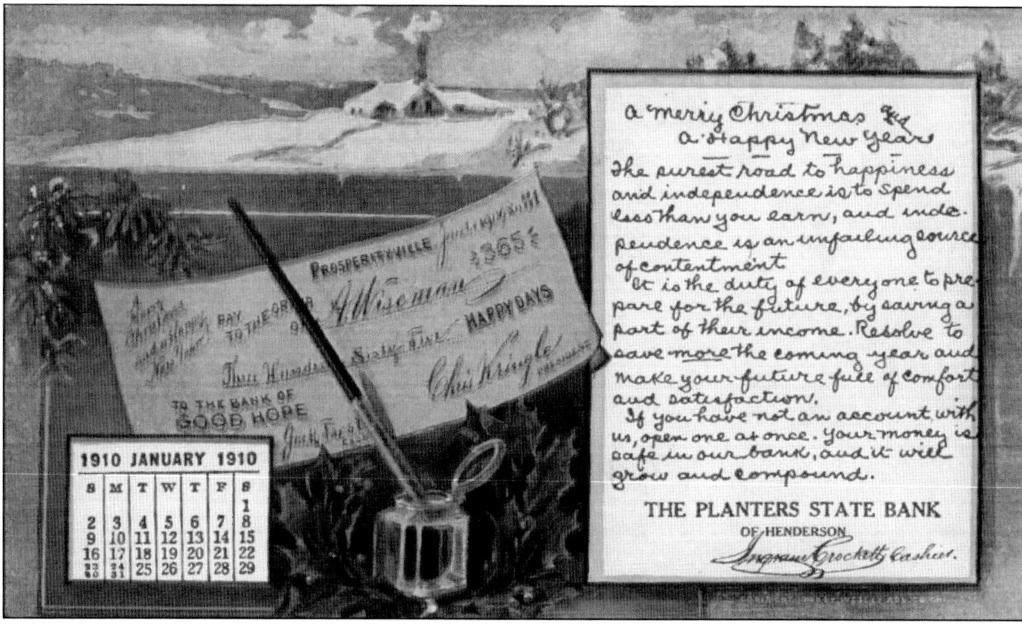

The Victorian Gothic Planter's State Bank at 130 North Main Street, with its original metal door (similar to those used in jails at the time) and its heavy stone facade and side piers, was originally the site of a grocery store. Gov. Lazarus Powell's son J. H. Powell sold the building in 1883 for $5,000, the year the bank was incorporated with officers Montgomery Merritt, president; John O'Byrne, vice president; David Banks, cashier; and A. Shelby Rudy, bookkeeper. Reflecting the bank's name, a number of its directors were prominent local farmers. In 1890, the bank changed its incorporation and name to the Planters' State Bank. In 1913, its directors included Montgomery Merritt, F. C. Klutey, Henry Kleymeyer, E. W. Winstead, John Mundo, Strachan Barret, James S. Alves, John O'Byrne, S. W. Norris, Joe Koewler, Ingram Crockett, and G. W. Ragan. Today the structure's original atrium has been restored.

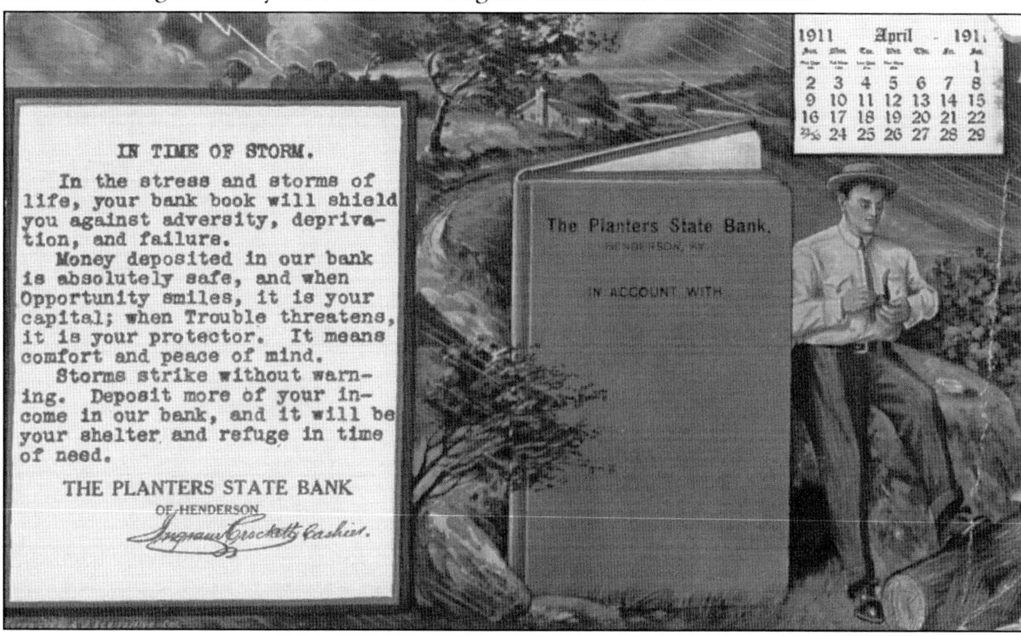

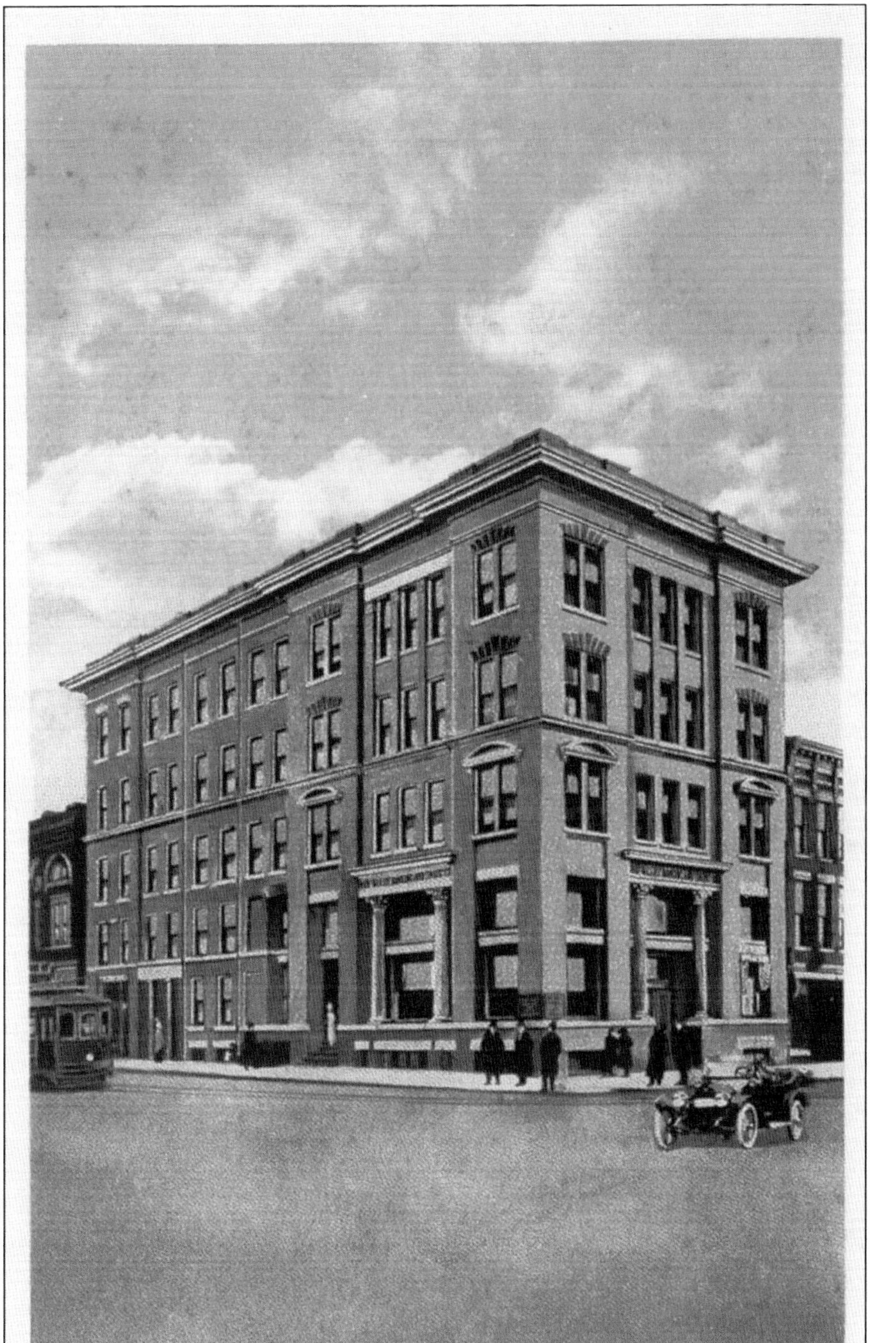

The five-story, yellow-brick Ohio Valley Financial Group (originally known as the Ohio Valley Banking and Trust Company), located on the southeast corner of North Main and Second Streets, was built in 1904 and was advertised as Henderson's first fireproof building. The landmark copper-and-stained-glass clock, not shown in this picture, was added about 1916. In 2007, the building's yellow brick was stained red.

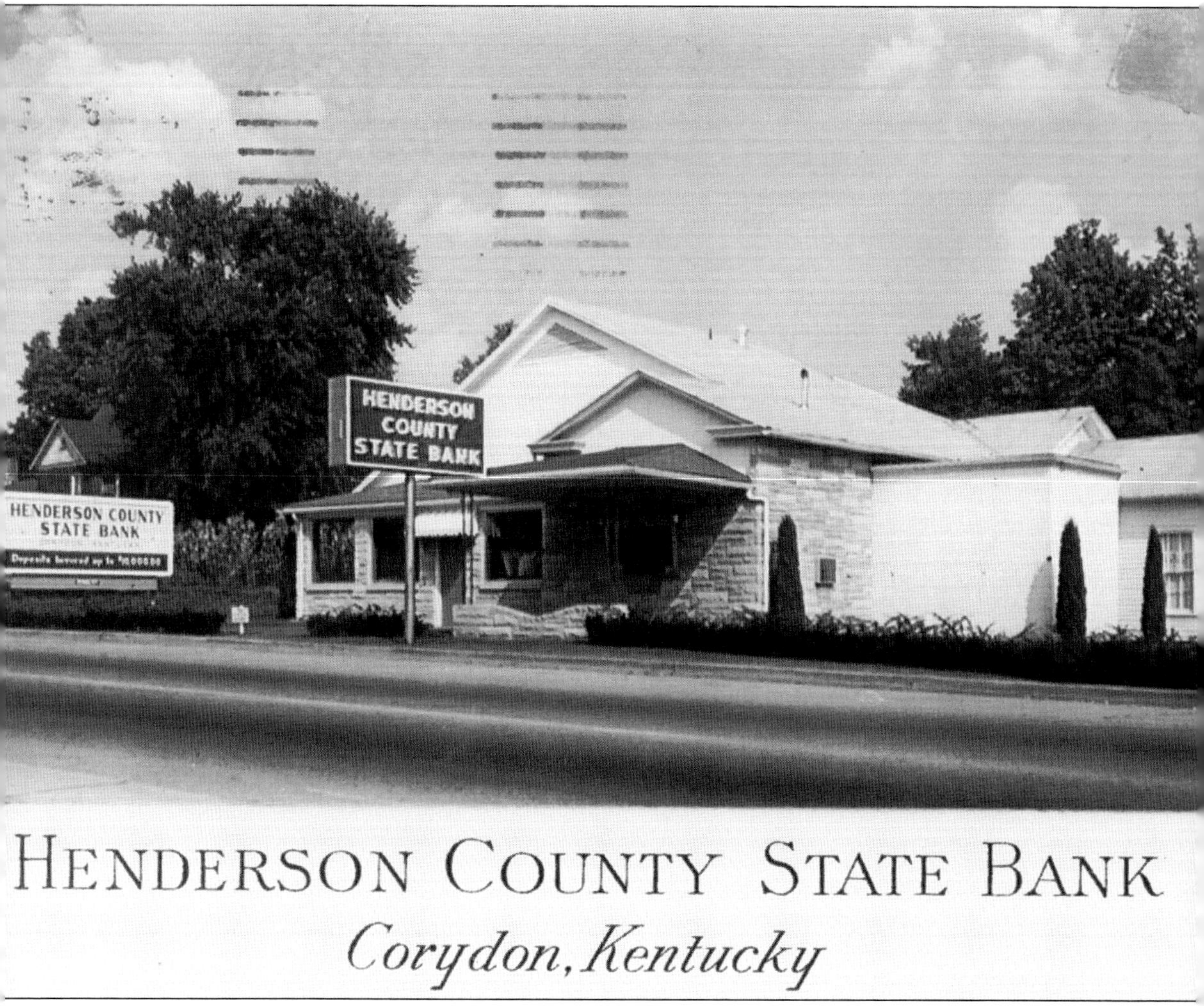

Located in Corydon, Henderson County State Bank opened in the mid-1950s. On the back of this postcard, which was mailed to one of the bank's box holders on Henderson County's Route 2, was printed, "I am almost two years old and the people have deposited nearly 1½ million dollars here."

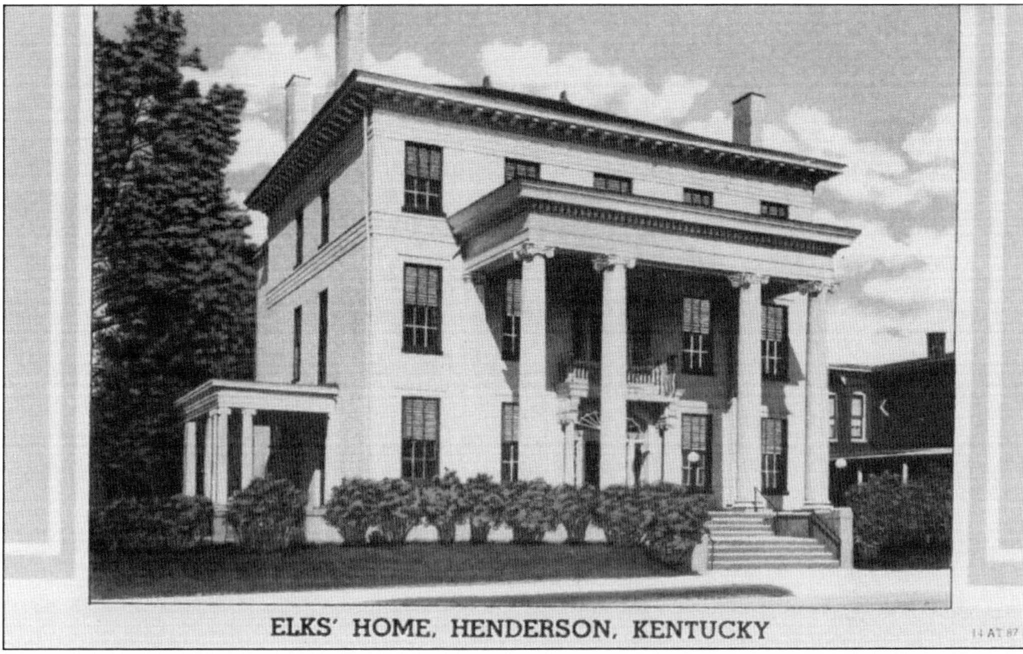

On the northwest corner of Third and North Main Streets sat a two-story house that George Atkinson had built prior to the Civil War. The local Benevolent Protective Order of Elks Lodge No. 206, which had begun in 1891, originally met in the Odd Fellows Hall on Second Street. In 1906, the group acquired the Atkinson home, spent around $40,000 renovating the building and adding a third story, and dedicated the property in 1909. During the influenza outbreak of 1918, this Elks Lodge was one of the sites used as a temporary hospital for local patients. The building was razed in 1974 after the Elks moved to new quarters on U.S. 60 East.

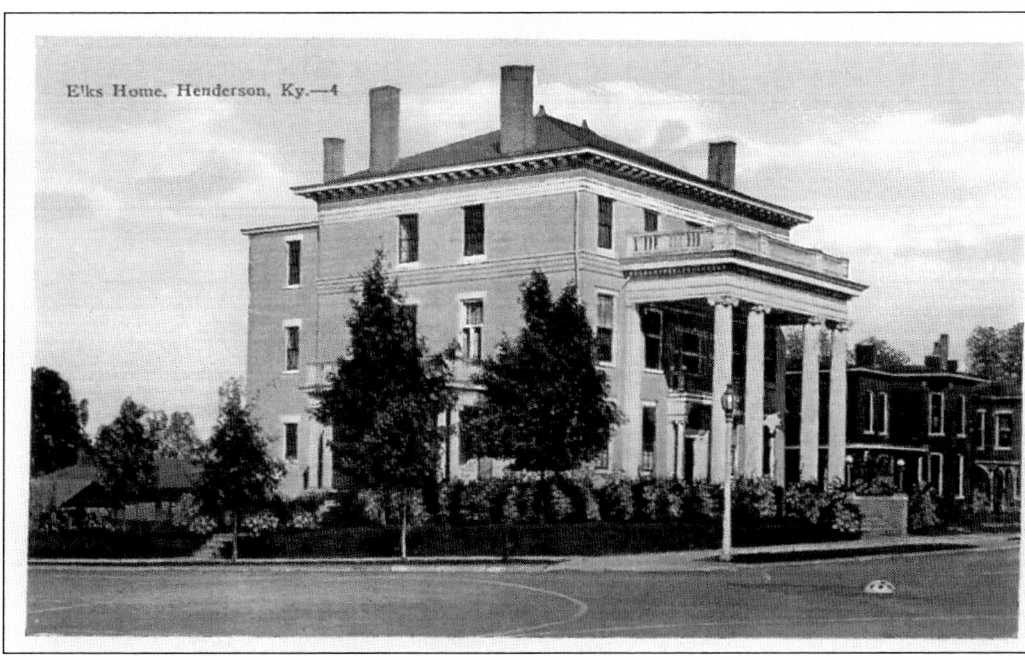

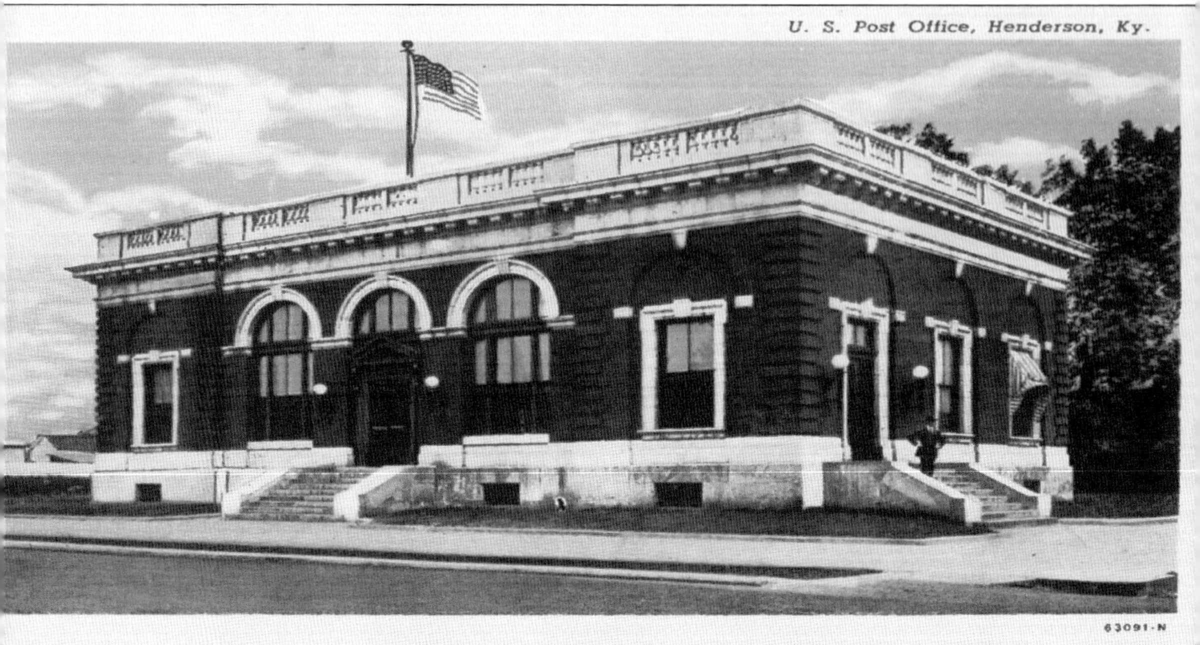

The post office shown in this postcard was completed in 1906, one hundred and five years after Henderson's first post office was established. This redbrick building, one of the most modern government buildings for its time, sat at the northeast corner of Third and North Main Streets on the former site of a tobacco stemmery and on the current site of Big Rivers. The cost for the lot, building, and construction of this post office was approximately $75,000.

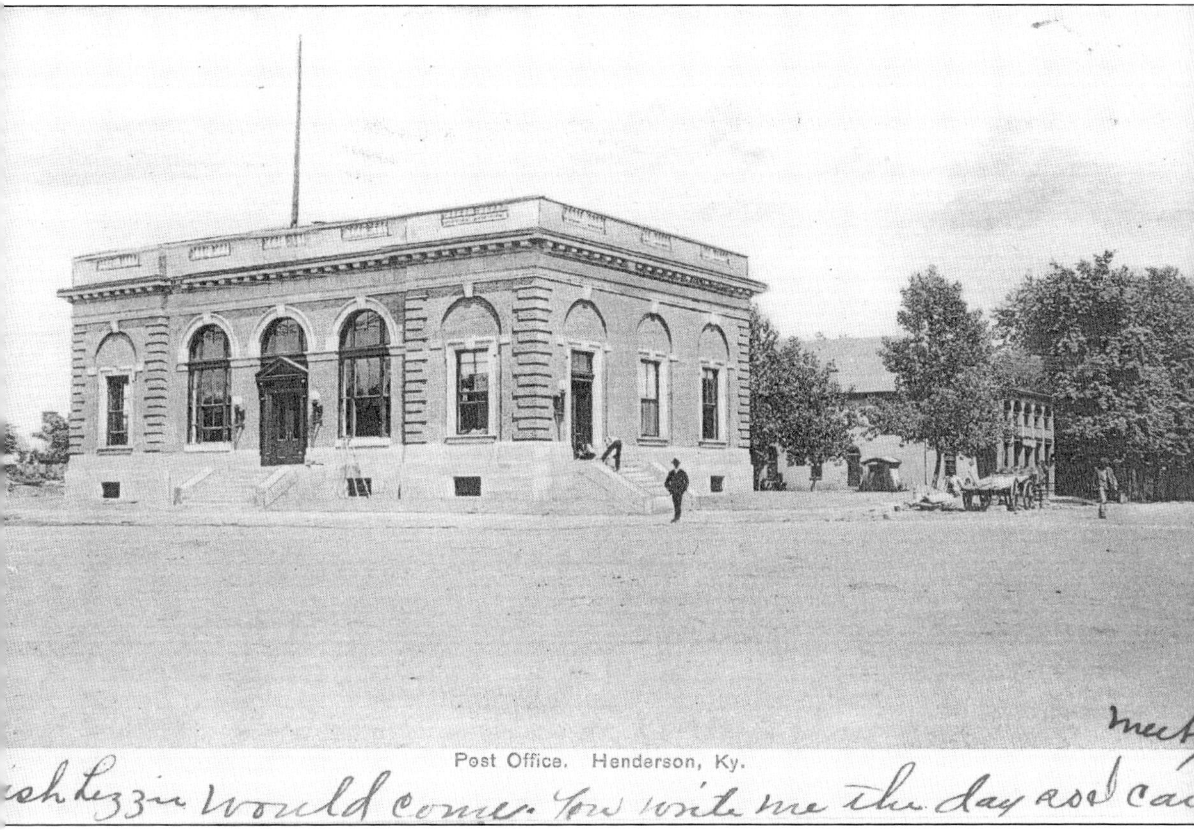

In 1913, seven postal carriers delivered mail four times each weekday in Henderson's business section and twice each weekday in the residential section. On this postcard, poles for electrical, telegraph, and telephone wires tower above the streets. Pictured to the rear of the post office is the Hotel Goodrum at 219 Third Street, with its wide front porches on both floors. This post office was used until 1965. (Courtesy of Henderson County Public Library.)

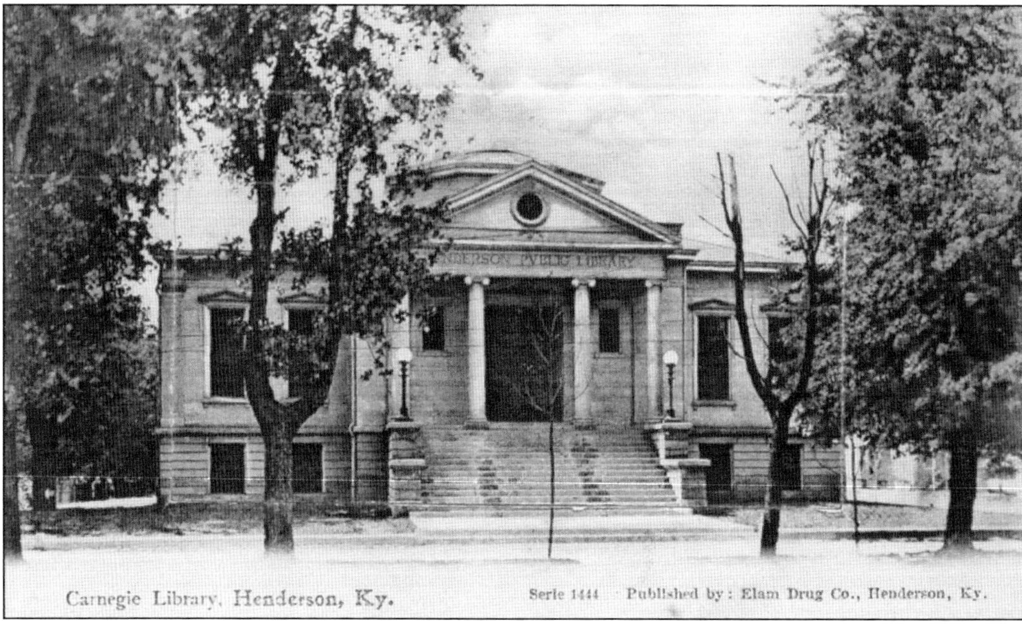

During a golf outing with philanthropist Andrew Carnegie, Henderson *Journal* publisher Edward Asher Jonas secured a $20,000 donation for the construction of a local library. Carnegie's two stipulations were that the city provide a site for the building and that it enact a tax to maintain and operate the facility. Jonas began raising money for a library site, and by 1902, he had secured sufficient funds to persuade the city to purchase a lot on the southwest corner of Main and Washington Streets. The white limestone, Italian Renaissance–style library opened in 1904 with 500 books. With its towering columns, classic Roman Ionic portico, and distinctive rotunda featuring an octagonal dome with a stained-glass skylight, it is the city's oldest public building still being used for its original purpose. The concrete curb outlining the property, visible in both postcards, has been removed.

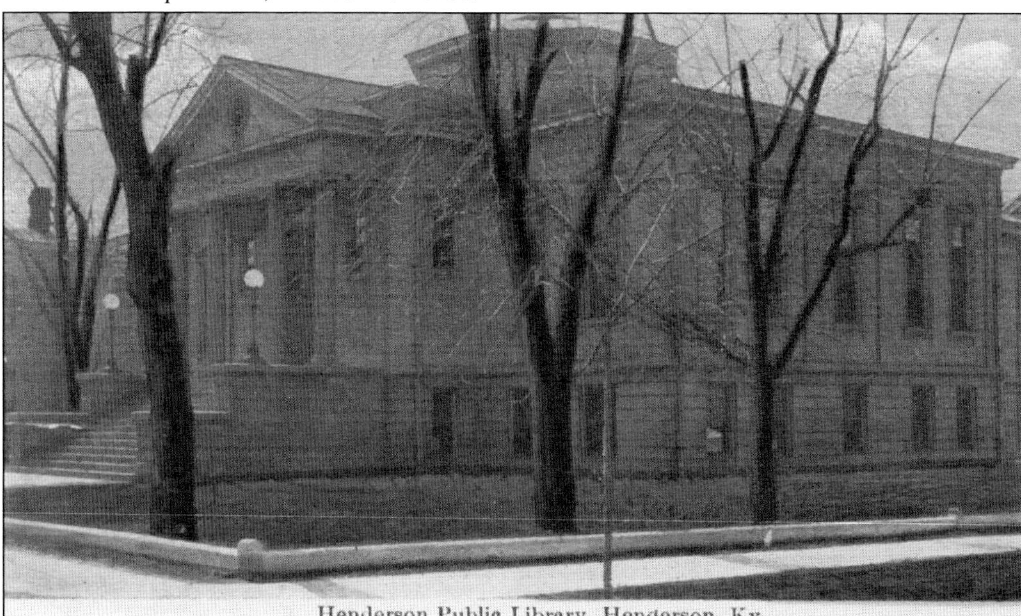

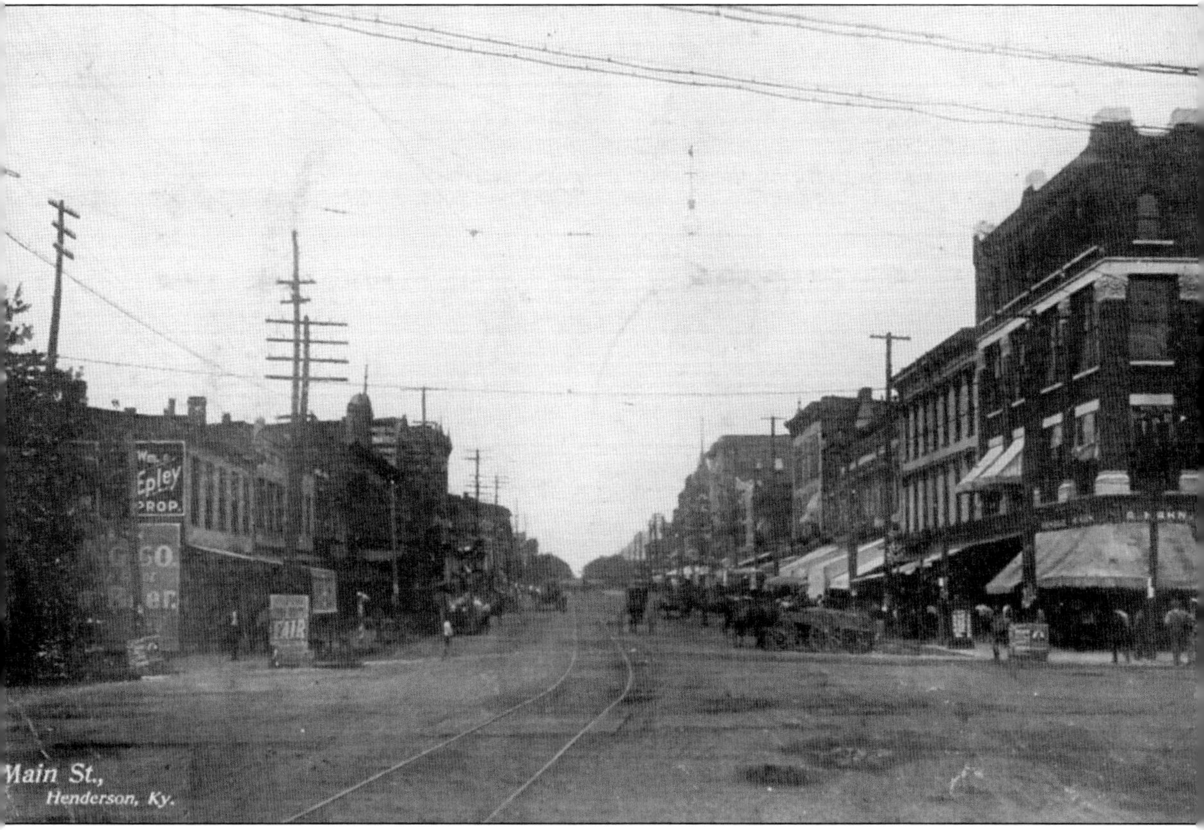

This postcard looks north on Main Street from First Street. The building on the left is the general store owned by Arnold Kahn, who operated this business until he sold it to Jake Simon in 1919. Simon also bought the building from a Mr. Riley; today Simon's descendants continue to operate a business on this corner. The single-car track on Main Street indicates that the trolley system was in its early days.

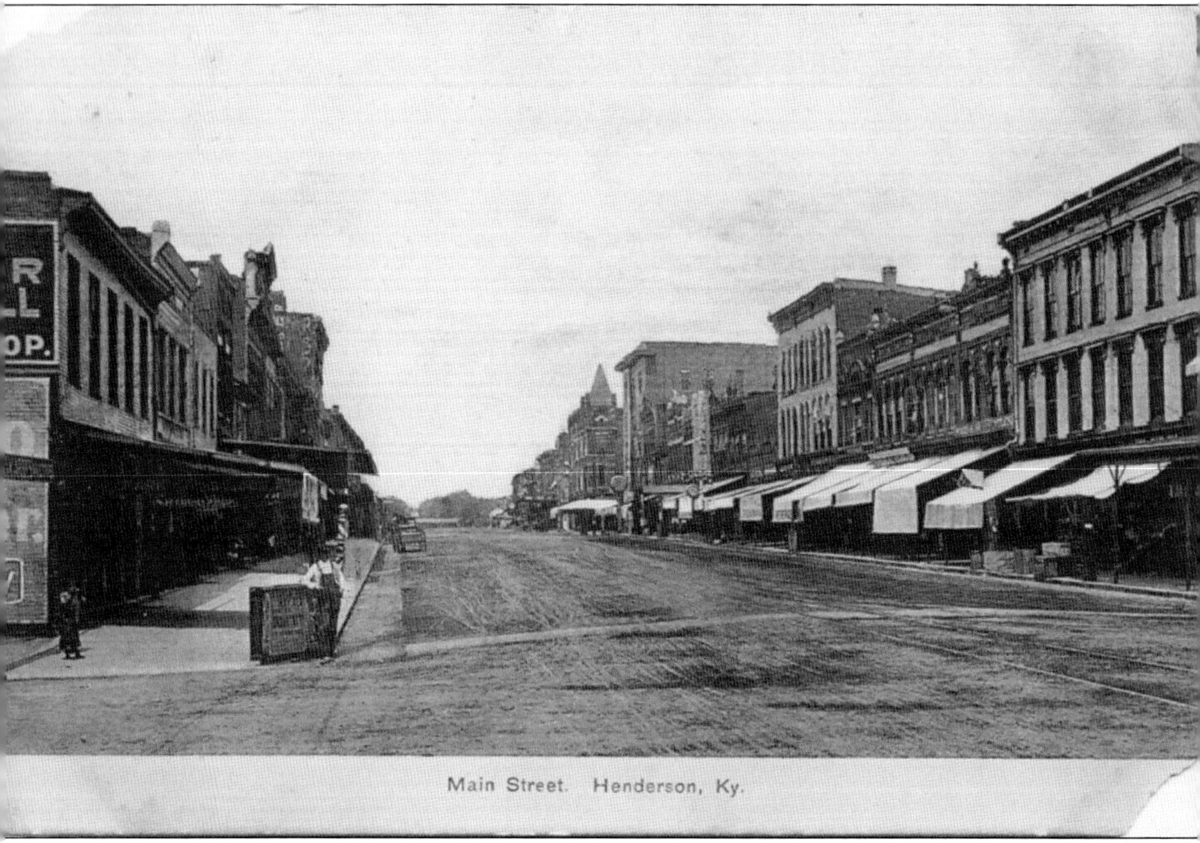

The picture on this card, taken before 1910, also looks north on Main Street from First Street. On the west (left) side of Main is a saloon, followed by a barbershop. The first building on the east (right) side is another saloon. Planks crossing the street, starting where the man on the left stands next to the sandwich board, aided pedestrians in the days before streets were paved.

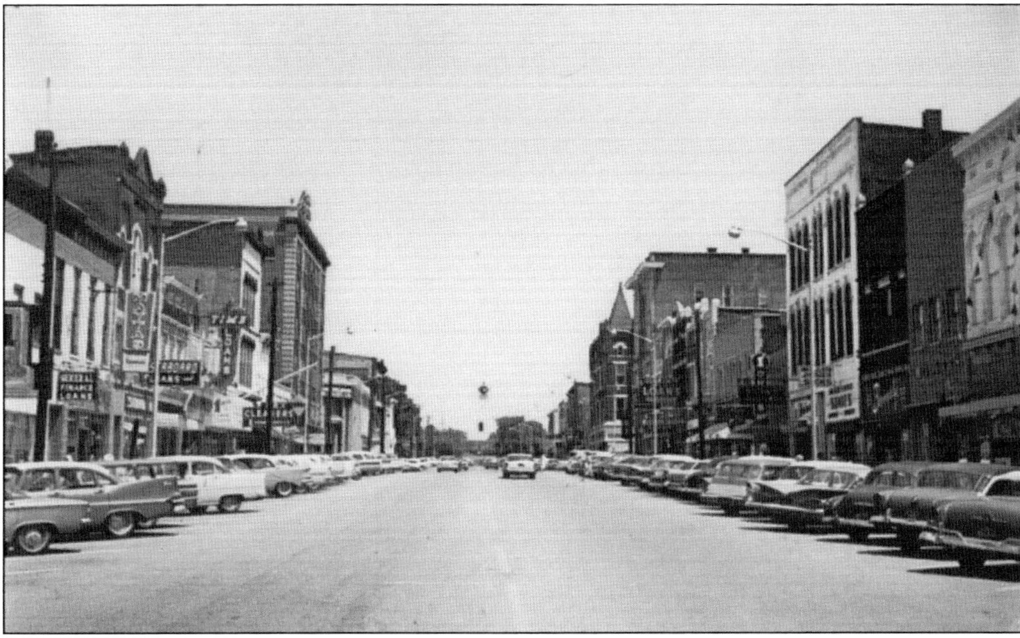

This Main Street scene, also depicting the area north from First Street, comes from the 1960s. The mercury streetlights and aluminum posts shown in this postcard were installed in 1954. Awnings remain on a few of the buildings, but air-conditioning had negated the need for them for most businesses. Three banks and at least four loan companies are visible in this postcard.

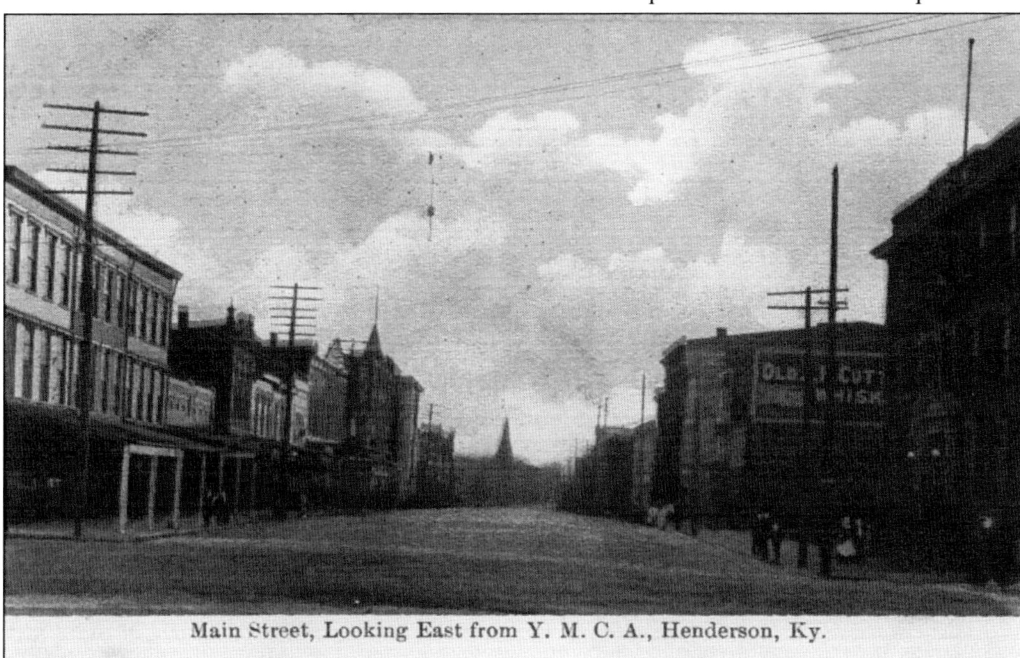

This Main Street scene looks south (contrary to the inscription on the card) from Third Street. On the west side (right) is the YMCA, which was new at the time of this picture. In the middle, four blocks away, is the steeple atop the Presbyterian church. Many of the buildings in the middle of the east (left) side of the street were demolished in the mid- or late 1900s.

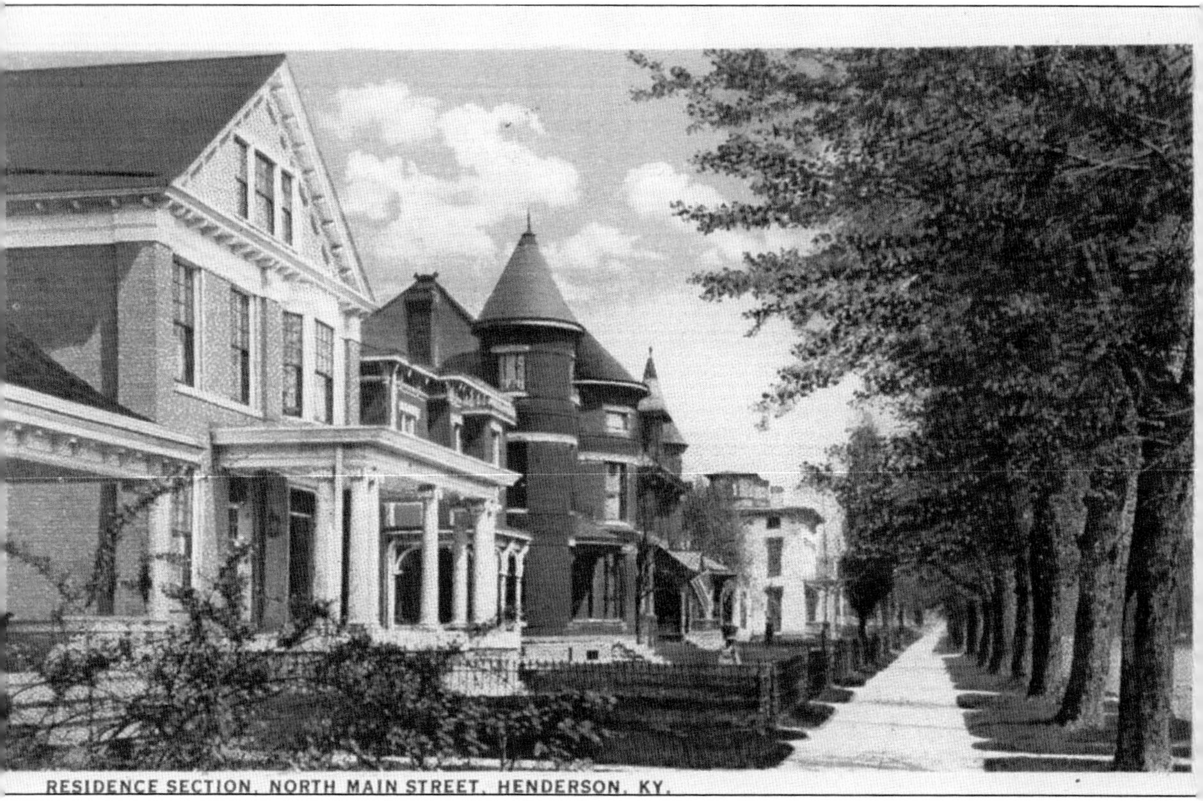

This card highlights the west side of North Main Street between Fifth and Sixth Streets. The first full house is the yellow-brick Jarvis-Sullivan home, a Victorian-style house built in the early 1900s by English tobacconist Arthur Jarvis and his wife, Minnie. Two houses north of that is the Chatequesque Blackwell–Vaughn home, built in the 1890s by Judge Paul Alexander Blackwell. The last house on the block burned in the mid-1900s.

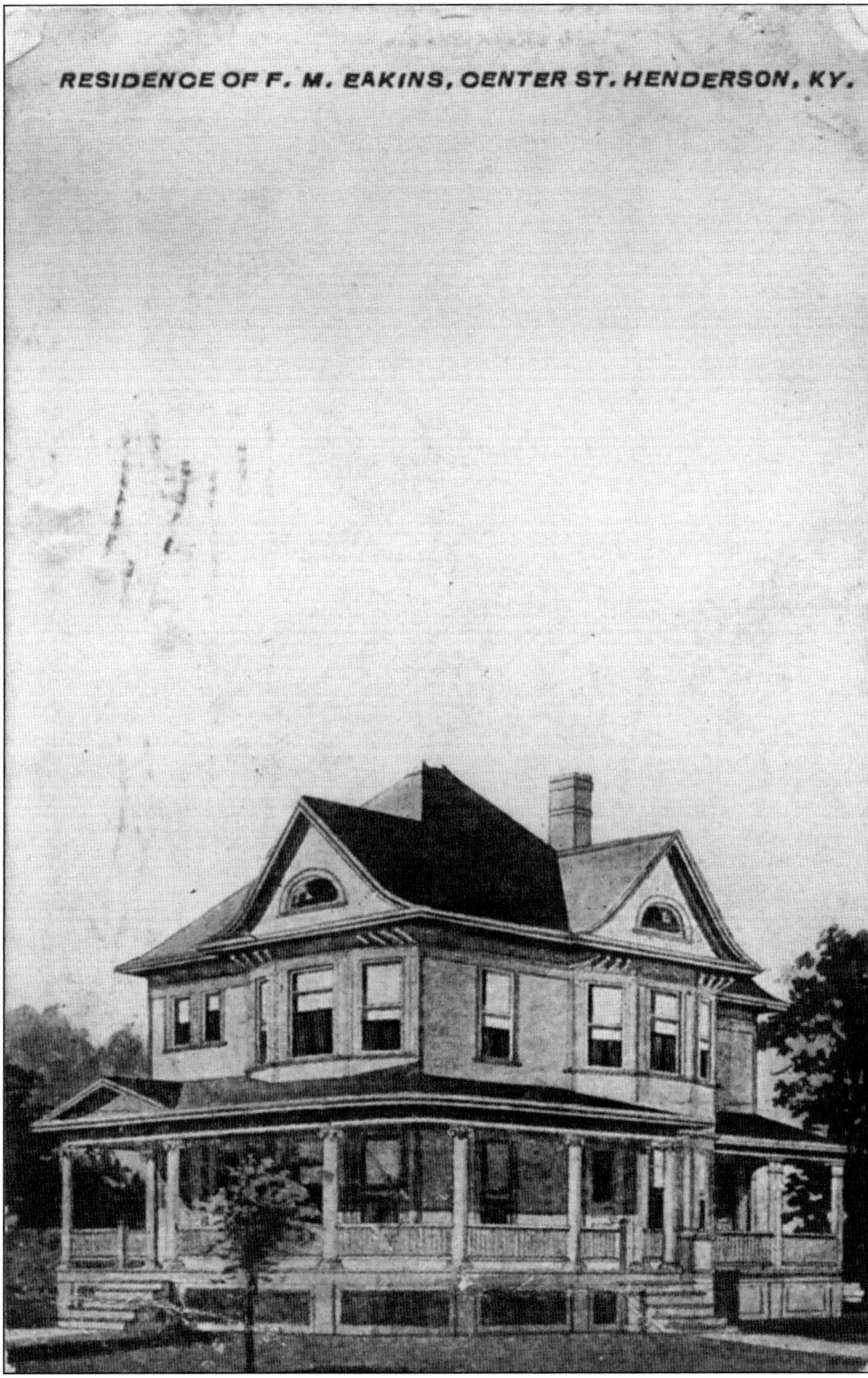

In 1909, local druggist F. M. Eakins lived in this Queen Anne–style house at 824 Center Street. Interestingly, the house pictured on the postcard is a mirror image of the actual house, which still stands. The postcard, addressed to Adam Myers of Robards, Kentucky, says, "Mr. Banks informed me he is paying off the J. D. Denton claims. He paid me; you had better look after it right away. F. M. Eakins."

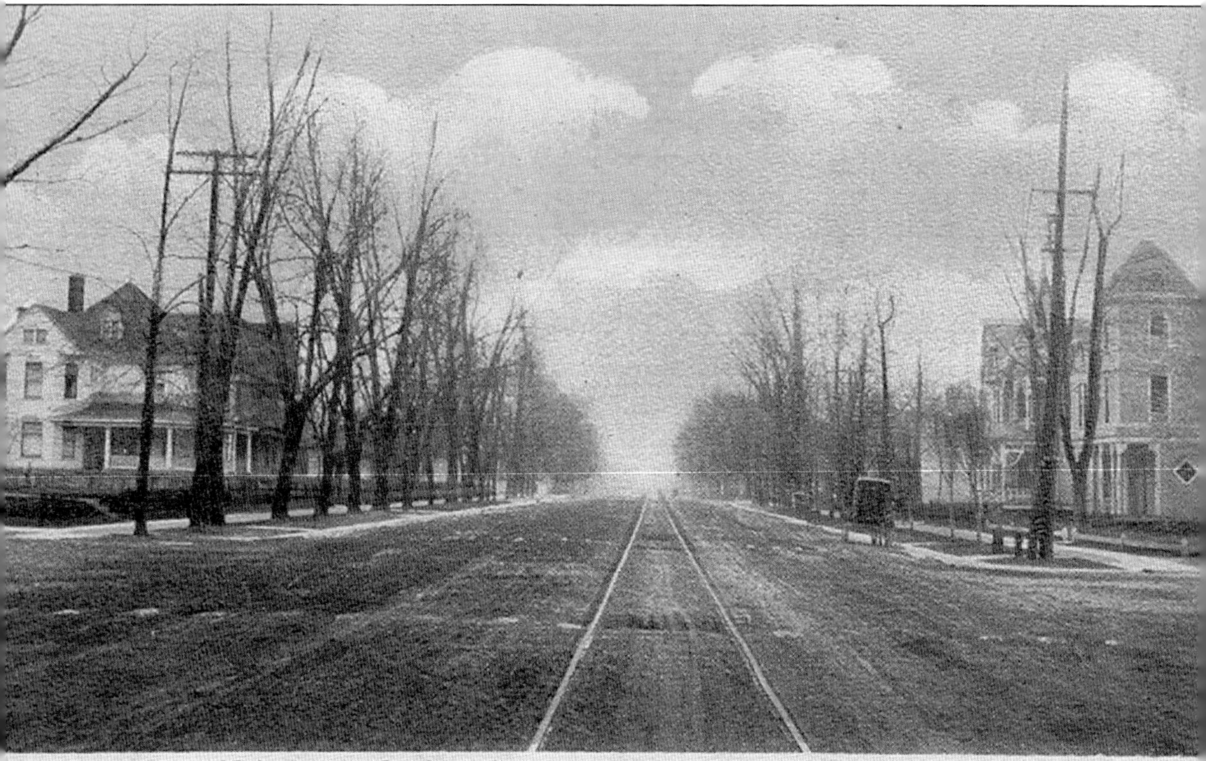

Main Street, Looking South from Powell St., Henderson, Ky.

This rare postcard shows South Main Street looking south from Powell Street. The first house on the west (right) side, the Victorian shingle that is now on the National Register of Historic Places, was built by the Swiss-born professor J. Maurice Bach and his wife, Henrietta. Professor Bach came to Henderson in 1883 and served as the organist for the First Presbyterian Church, music director for the Henderson Female Academy, and the leader of the local German Singing Society (a group of several hundred who met at the local Liederkranz Hall on the second floor of the building on the northeast corner of Second and Elm Streets). After his arrival in Henderson, Professor Bach met Henrietta Stolz, a local music teacher who had studied abroad. They were married in 1884 and built their home in 1891. During W. C. Handy's stay in Henderson, the future "Father of the Blues" worked at Liederkranz Hall and was also employed as the Bachs' gardener in this home.

Nine

A Mixed Bag

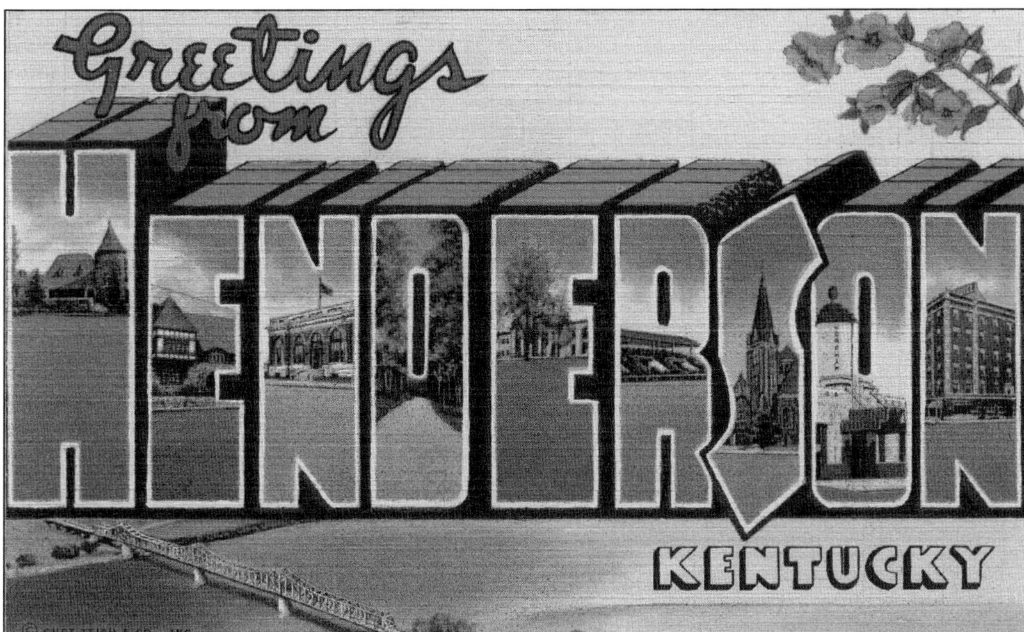

Large-lettered postcards, popular in the mid-20th century, used bright primary colors to illustrate a number of local scenes. Unlike previous large-lettered postcards, at this time actual photographic images began to appear in the backgrounds. The longer the place name, the more scenes it depicted. This postcard, postmarked 1942, highlights various Henderson scenes, including the Audubon Museum, the Audubon Tea House, the 1906 post office, a drive in Atkinson Park, the 1843 courthouse, Dade Park, the First Presbyterian Church, Worsham Hall, and the Soaper Hotel. Outside the lettering in the lower left background is the Audubon Memorial Bridge.

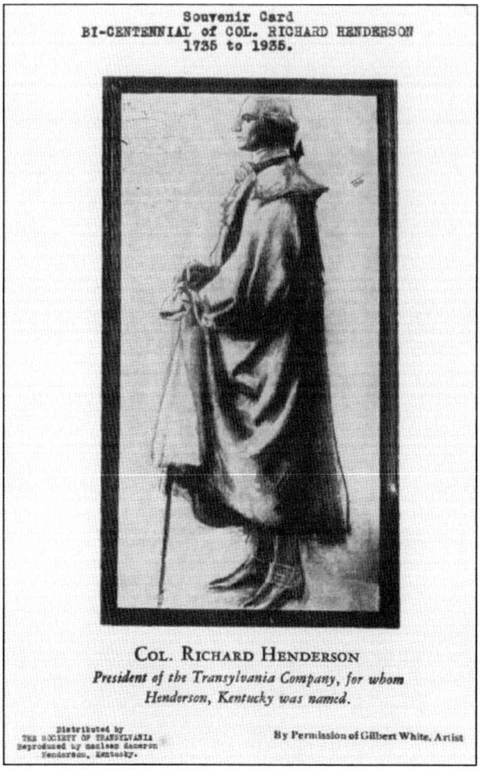

The namesake of both the city and county, Richard Henderson, organized the Transylvania Land Company and had visions of creating a new colony to be called Transylvania. His dreams were eventually dashed, and he died in 1785. Twelve years later, the remaining members of the Transylvania Land Company and their descendants came to this area and named their new town and county after the company's founder. (Courtesy of Martin Studio, Maclean Dameron Collection.)

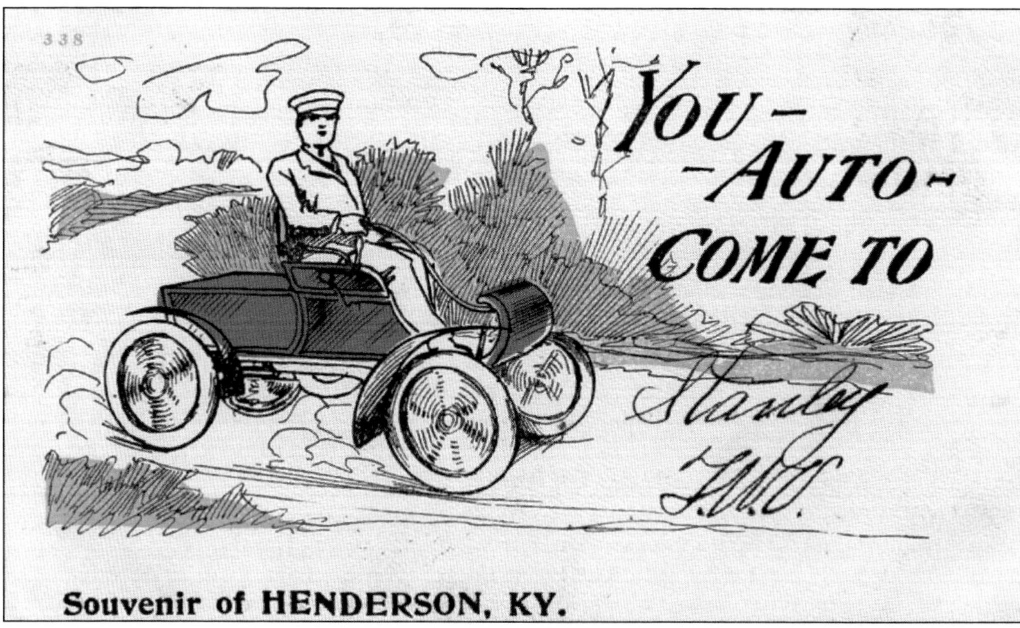

Postcards like this one were a generic variety designed to be sent as souvenirs from various locales. The new "horseless carriage" was a mark of affluence, and the implication was that the recipient could just jump in the automobile and go for a visit. This postcard, postmarked 1906, was mailed to Henderson's M. A. Kockritz with the unspecific address of "2nd between Elm and Green."

The Ancient Order of United Workmen (AOUW), founded in 1868, advertised itself as "the first major national life insurance order." This 1878 postcard advises Brother H. Kleymeyer of the deaths of three AOUW members and says that assessments amounting to $3.15 are due. Other local societies and lodges active at this time were the Odd Fellows, Masons, Knights of Pythias, Knights of Honor, United Brotherhood of Friendship, Sons and Daughters of Zion, and the Deutsche Order of Harugari.

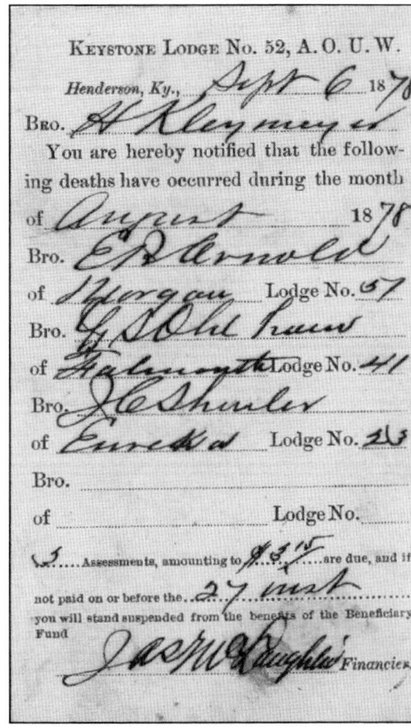

KEYSTONE LODGE No. 52, A. O. U. W.

Henderson, Ky., Sept 6 1878

BRO. H Kleymeyer

You are hereby notified that the following deaths have occurred during the month of August 1878

Bro. E A Arnold of Morgan Lodge No. 67

Bro. G S Uhlhorn of Falmouth Lodge No. 41

Bro. J C Shuler of Eureka Lodge No. 23

Bro.

of Lodge No.

3 Assessments, amounting to $3.15 are due, and if not paid on or before the 27 inst you will stand suspended from the benefits of the Beneficiary Fund

Jas McLaughlin Financier.

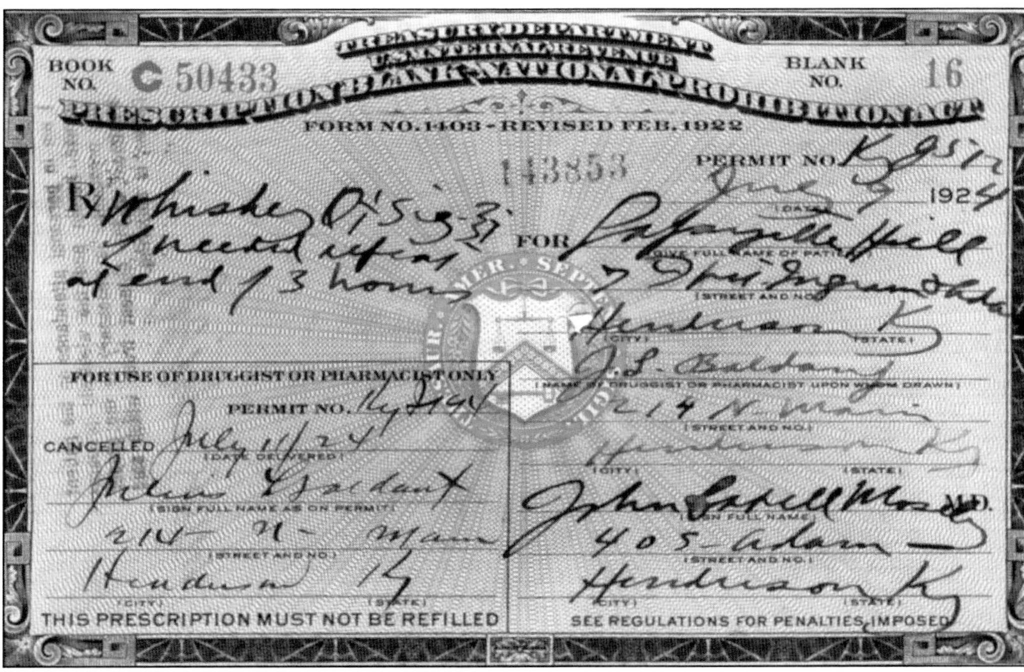

TREASURY DEPARTMENT
U.S. INTERNAL REVENUE
PRESCRIPTION BLANK—NATIONAL PROHIBITION ACT

BOOK NO. C 50433 — BLANK NO. 16

FORM NO. 1403 – REVISED FEB. 1922

143853 — PERMIT NO. Ky 9517

July 9 1924

℞ whiskey Pt 5-9-37 if needed at end of 3 hours

FOR Lafayette Hill (GIVE FULL NAME OF PATIENT)

(STREET AND NO.)

Henderson (CITY) Ky (STATE)

J. S. Baldauf (NAME OF DRUGGIST OR PHARMACIST UPON WHOM DRAWN)

214 N. Main (STREET AND NO.)

Henderson (CITY) Ky (STATE)

John Cardell Moseley M.D. (SIGN FULL NAME)

405 Adams (STREET AND NO.)

Henderson (CITY) Ky (STATE)

SEE REGULATIONS FOR PENALTIES IMPOSED

FOR USE OF DRUGGIST OR PHARMACIST ONLY

PERMIT NO. Ky 1941

CANCELLED July 11/24 (DATE DELIVERED)

Julius Baldauf (SIGN FULL NAME AS ON PERMIT)

214 N. Main (STREET AND NO.)

Henderson (CITY) Ky (STATE)

THIS PRESCRIPTION MUST NOT BE REFILLED

This 1924 prescription, issued during Prohibition, authorized patient Lafayette Hill to take whiskey every three hours if needed. Written by Dr. J. C. Moseley, the prescription was filled by Julius Baldauf of Baldauf's Pharmacy, located at 214 North Main Street. On the back is stamped, "I am in personal attendance on the patient named herein and the alcoholic preparation prescribed is necessary to the proper treatment of the ailment from which said patient is suffering."

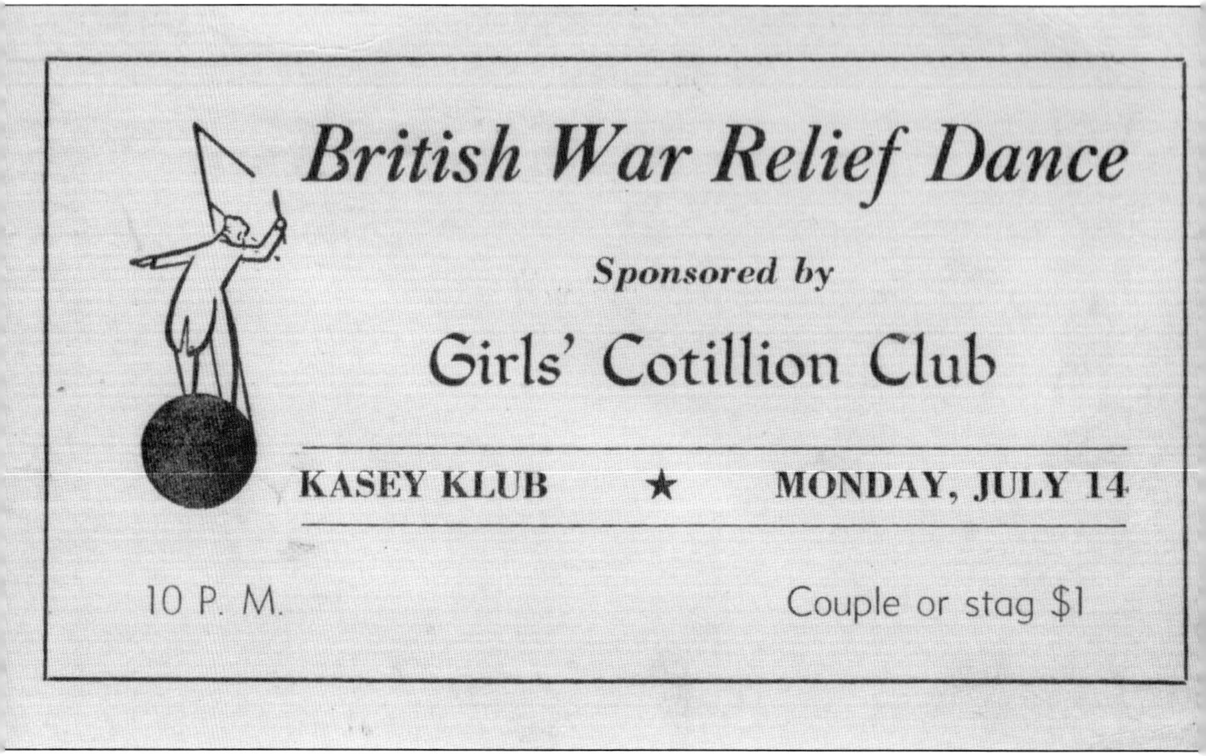

In July 1941, the Girls' Cotillion Club, a service and social organization that continues to this day, held a dance at the Kasey Klub on Henderson's south side. The $1 cost (per couple or stag) went to aid the British war relief. In less than six months, the United States would join in World War II. (Courtesy of Pam Austin.)

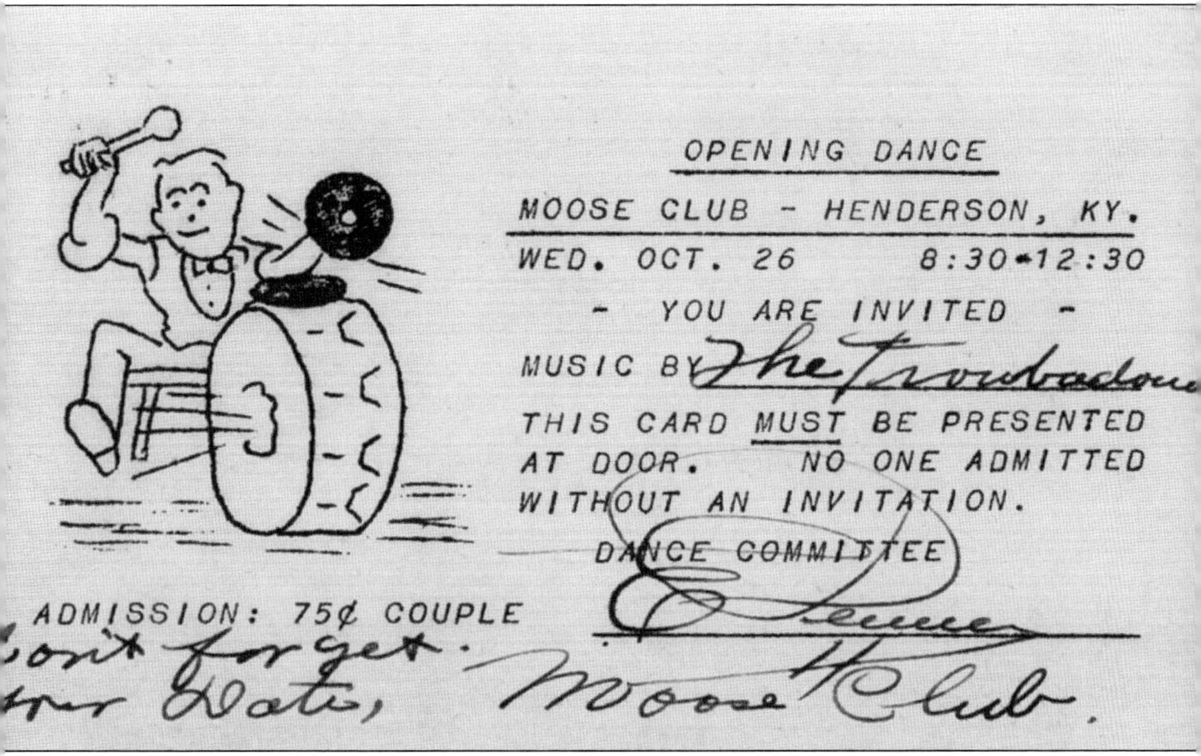

In 1932, the Loyal Order of the Moose sent this postcard to Mildred Pfluy on Jackson Avenue in Evansville, inviting her to an October dance to be held at the Moose Club, located at 338 Second Street. The invitation-only affair was the opening dance of the season. The cost was 75¢ per couple, and the music was provided by The Troubadours.